786· 2.

For Wycliffe College Library,
with best wishes,
David S. Grover, O.W.
13th December 1976.

THE PIANO

THE PIANO
Its Story from Zither to Grand

DAVID S. GROVER

ROBERT HALE · LONDON

ISBN 0 7091 5673 1

Robert Hale Limited
Clerkenwell House
45–47 Clerkenwell Green
London EC1

Printed in Great Britain by
Clarke, Doble and Brendon Ltd
Plymouth

Contents

Plates

7

Figures

FIGURES

Acknowledgements

My debt to my wife, Jenny, who has helped with checking and typing and patiently put up with a great deal, has been immense! I am grateful to Mr John Morley for checking the text and making numerous helpful suggestions, to Mr Stewart Broadwood for vetting the references to his illustrious forbears, Shudi and the Broadwoods, to Mr Frank Holland of The Musical Museum for checking the section on mechanical pianos, and to Miss Meriel Jefferson for reading the section on modern group teaching. To all of them my sincere thanks. Any inaccuracies are to be laid at my door and not theirs! I am indebted also to Mr John Hale and Mr G. Chesterfield for their continual courtesy and understanding.

Two-thirds of the photographs have not previously been published. I am indebted to so many friends for their kindness and help with illustrations. Mr C. F. Colt, Director of the Colt Clavier Collection in Kent, kindly provided me with Pls. 22, 25, 30, 34, 38, and 46 of instruments in his collection. He also generously lent me photographs for Pls. 26 and 27 of an instrument from the collections in the Division of Musical Instruments at the Smithsonian Institution, Washington, and reproduced by courtesy of the Smithsonian Institution, and material for Fig. 32. Forsyth Brothers Limited kindly provided me with Pl. 6 of a clavichord in the Forsyth Collection, Manchester, Habig-Kimball Ltd with Pl. 57, Mr Frank Holland of The Musical Museum with Pls. 47 and 53, Miss Meriel Jefferson and The Guildhall School of Music and Drama with Pl. 56, Mr Roy Mickleburgh with Pls. 24, 28, 36, 39–44, 49 and 51 mostly of instruments in his collection, Mr John Morley with Pls. 5, 8, 9, 12, 13, 14, 31, 37, 54 and 55, Schiedmayer & Soehne with Pl. 48 and Steinway & Sons with Pls. 45 and 58. Mr David Bannister of the Regent Gallery, Cheltenham took with Mr Roy Mickleburgh's kind permission Pls. 1–4, 33, 35 and 52 of instruments in the

ACKNOWLEDGEMENTS

Mickleburgh Collection, Bristol, also Pls. 17 and 18, and lent the Gillray cartoon (Pl. 29). Rud. Ibach Sohn kindly loaned the block for Pl. 49, and the *Stroud News & Journal* gave permission for me to reproduce Pl. 10 taken during the 1971 Stroud Festival. Plate 15 is reproduced by kind permission of the Royal College of Music, London, and Pls. 7, 11, 21 and 32 by permission of the Victoria and Albert Museum (Crown Copyright). Transparencies of the two instruments shown on the dust jacket were kindly loaned by the Piano Publicity Association. Fig. 4 is reproduced from the *Oxford Companion to Music* by permission of the Oxford University Press. Herrburger Brooks Ltd kindly allowed me to reproduce Fig. 17. Figs. 19 and 23 are reproduced by arrangement with the British Library Board. John Broadwood & Sons kindly allowed me to reproduce Fig. 33, and loaned me a print to reproduce Pl. 23. Universal Edition (London) Ltd allowed me to reproduce Fig. 34. To all of them I express my grateful appreciation.

Preface

I have presented in condensed form the principal factors shaping the story of the piano. I hope the result is an enjoyable narrative which will appeal to the musician, musical instrument expert and layman alike. I have linked the technical development with the wider social background and with changing styles of composition to show their interaction, critical both for the instrument maker and musician. I have not explored musical changes with any comprehensiveness, but I hope my references to perhaps still insufficiently known details prove stimulating.

I have inserted chapter V on selected technical characteristics of the modern piano before the chapters on the development of the piano, as I thought it would help to make the latter technical references, which have been kept as simple as is consistent with meaningful explanation, easier to understand. The diagrams which illustrate technical features should ensure that they maintain their interest for all readers. The method used to number the keys shown in the table 'The Extension of the Keyboard' (Fig. 35) is used also in the text. In the last hundred years fewer developments have taken place than in the previous hundred and consequently the stress is on progress to the middle of the last century. Comparatively little has been written about the period since, so I hope my chapters may help to fill a gap.

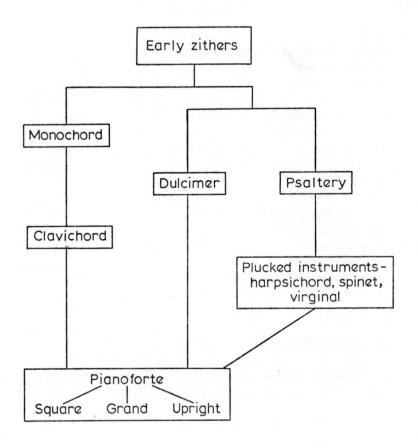

I

Primitive and Medieval Zithers

The story of the piano begins in the mists of pre-history when the first attempts were made with a string to produce a sound which proved pleasing, although it would not have been recognized as 'musical' in today's meaning of the word. The first stringed musical instrument may have been either the taut string of a huntsman's bow or a sinew stretched between the horns of an animal's skull or between two branches of a tree. As time passed man observed that by combining the component parts in varying ways contrasting sounds could be produced and the harp, lute, lyre and zither families of stringed instruments evolved. The forerunners of the piano belong to the last of these, the zither group.

A zither is an instrument with neither neck (Fig. 1) nor yoke

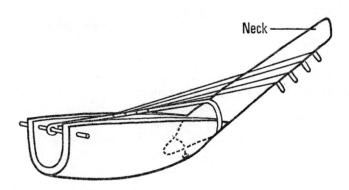

Fig. 1. Arched harp

(Pl. 1), but with strings which are struck or plucked, tensioned along the length of the body and stretched over bridges. Usually the instrument itself amplifies the sound, although a separate resonator may be added.

The simplest form of primitive zither is the ground zither

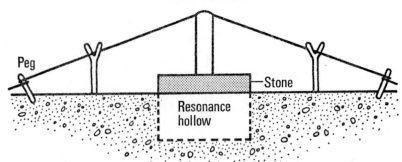

Fig. 2. Ground zither

(Fig. 2). The hollow made in the earth magnifies the sound produced by the string, which is struck with twigs. It was natural that primitive man should utilize the ground, which possessed religious and magical associations. While convenient, however, these instruments perished quickly!

The tube zither originated when man took a tube, commonly of bamboo, and cut a string from its body, which acted as the resonator.

First efforts had been to produce one sound, but gradually it was realized that different string sizes gave different tones and so several strings, often of varying lengths, were introduced (Pl. 2).

The bar zither is a variant of the tube zither. A stick forms the body of the instrument and a separate resonator, frequently a bottle-like gourd, is suspended underneath. Raised frets make possible the production one at a time of several notes from each string and assist the determination of the string portion which sounds. In their developed forms frets are a distinctive feature of the guitar and other instruments, the finger pressing the string at the fret to terminate the sounding length. Indeed frets frequently become the salvation of modern casual guitarists providing them, unlike violinists, with additional aids in deciding where the fingers should alight to give exactness of pitch. More advanced forms of the bar zither with two or three resonators often retained only two strings but sported a dozen or more frets, giving greater melodic range from the limited number of strings.

Eventually several tube zithers were bound together to form the raft zither (Pl. 2), which is held between the open palms and plucked by the forefingers in an upward movement.

16

Sometimes the thickness was varied to alter the tone and the discovery was made that a string could be made heavier and the pitch lower, if a second string was wrapped round the centre one. Early man had discovered the principle of modern covered bass strings!

The term 'idiochord' signifies that string and resonance body are formed from a single piece of material, both unsevered ends of the string returning to the tube from which the string length was cut. Hence the early tube zither is known also as an 'idiochord zither'. It became a 'heterochord' instrument when foreign material, perhaps hair, sinew, gut or plant fibre, was used for the strings.

The raft zither led to the trough zither, the several sections of the former being fused into a unified hollow body, its greater hollowness increasing the resonance to give a stronger tone. Exclusive to parts of Central and East Africa, the trough zither marks a step forward in the tensioning of the strings. A continuous string is used, each length passing tightly through a slot. Consequently the string does not slip, but maintains the original tension determined at the time the instrument was strung.

Found in its simplest form in Africa is the board zither. Its surface is flat or slightly rounded and the strings, which extend over its complete length, are raised on bridges. The board is so constructed that a resonator is either included or added afterwards. The board zither's more developed forms point towards the psaltery and dulcimer, predecessors of our stringed keyboard instruments.

The zither is believed to have originated in south-east Asia and to have spread from there to the Malagasy Republic (formerly Madagascar) and parts of Africa. As zithers were made of bamboo, raffia stalk and other perishable materials, early examples have not survived. Conversely specimens survive of primitive instruments made of bone, stone and other durable materials.

Zithers provide excellent examples of primitive instrumental types continuing in use in almost unaltered form among undeveloped peoples. The tube zither is still common in south-east Asia. To this day it continues as one of the most important instruments in the Malagasy Republic, and in Africa it is often encountered as a children's toy.

The first of the more advanced forms of zither appear to have evolved in the Far East, where in China they were known in 1100 B.C. Long and slim, unfretted and fretted, often with strings of silk, many variations existed.

One of the best-known is the koto, the national instrument of old Japan. 1·83 metres (6 feet) long it is usually played on the floor. Sitting near one end, the player wears three plectra on the thumb and two fingers of his right hand. His left hand damps the strings, presses them down behind the bridges to raise the pitch, and alters the position of the movable bridges.

Through the mediation of the Near East where the Qanun and Santir emerged, the zither, now a creditable instrument, reached Europe.

Qanun is the Arabic name for psaltery which, originating in Turkey, was known there in the tenth century A.D. It was the first type of trapezoidal zither formed when one side of the rectangle became shortened, following the shorter higher pitched strings (Fig. 3). In the tenth century the qanun is depicted with ten

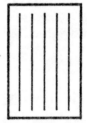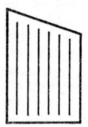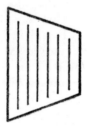

Fig. 3. Various psaltery shapes

strings, which compares with the thirteen of the koto, but by the fourteenth century the stringing had outpaced that of the Far Eastern zithers. A Persian treatise describes the qanun with sixty-four strings arranged in courses of three ('course' means a group of strings, usually tuned to the same pitch). Held vertically, the soundboard rested against the player's chest and the strings were plucked either with a quill or by the fingertips.

The qanun is first mentioned in Europe in eleventh-century Spain, and by the twelfth century it had been introduced to kingdoms which did not acknowledge Moorish influence. The Crusades also, led to the spread in Europe of many eastern ideas.

The plucked qanun assumed different shapes and names in the West, but was later simply called 'psaltery'.

The main difference between the psaltery and dulcimer lay in the method of playing, the latter being struck with small mallets.

The struck zither originated as the Persian santir and is known to have existed by the fifteenth century, although some authorities date it from the twelfth century. In contrast to the qanun, it was played in a horizontal position resting in the player's lap. Usually it had fourteen courses of four strings each.

The santir spread eastwards and by the eighteenth century reached China, where it is called yang ch'in or 'foreign zither'. Westwards it spread across North Africa and like the qanun penetrated Europe through the Moorish element in Spain. The zither's progress from the Far East to the Near East and finally to Western Europe bears witness to the Orient's cultural influence on Europe in the early Middle Ages.

References to the dulcimer (Pl. 3) in France, Switzerland, Germany and England are common in the fifteenth century, when it reached its greatest popularity.

The name 'dulcimer' derives from the Latin *dulce melos*, translated 'sweet sound'. The dulcimer had been known also by other names which, combined with the similarity in their outward shape, led to the obvious confusion between dulcimer and psaltery. The psaltery was favoured by the medieval clergy because of its biblical associations. It was popular also with the troubadours and wandering minstrels as an accompaniment to the voice.

Both the dulcimer and psaltery waned in popularity in the sixteenth century, the former yielding to the keyed clavichord and the latter to the plucked harpsichord. In 1536 Luscinius[1] wrote that the dulcimer 'Instrumentum ignobile est' !*

At the end of the seventeenth century Pantaleon Hebenstreit enlarged the dulcimer in size and tone volume, creating a new vogue for it. His pantaleon, so named by Louis XIV, had two soundboards and double-faced hammers replaced the usual mallets, resulting in novel expressive effects. Some seventy years later Dr Burney saw 'the ruins of the famous *Pantaleone*' in

* For this and following references see Bibliography and References p. 213.

Dresden and noted that 'it is more than nine feet long, and had, when in order, 186 strings of catgut . . . it must have been extremely difficult to the performer, but seems capable of great effects. The strings were now almost all broken. . . .'[2]

The dulcimer was accepted by society into the nineteenth century, when it was superseded by the piano. Its popularity as a folk instrument continues. In the Balkan countries, to which keyboard instruments have not penetrated to the same extent as in Western Europe, the modern zither remains in constant use, often in an accompanying role which further west the piano fills.

Throughout Eastern Europe it is known as 'cimbal' and in Hungary the dulcimer has reached its most developed form as the cimbalon (Pl. 4). Kodály includes a cimbalon part in his *Háry János* Suite.

In Austria and the Alps the shimmering tones of the zither are still heard. The zither introducing Harry Lime's theme in the film *The Third Man*, set in Vienna, became familiar round the world. Modern means of spreading ideas contrast with the centuries it sometimes took for an instrument to penetrate its neighbouring continent!

II

Pythagoras, the Monochord, Keyboard and Temperament

The ancient Greeks attempted methodical explanations of many natural phenomena, among them the relationship between musical notes of different pitch.

In *c.* 550 B.C. Pythagoras, the philosopher known to students of geometry through the theorem named after him, carried out the earliest recorded acoustical experiments. He demonstrated that intervals pleasing to the ear are produced when a string is divided into certain ratios. If the length is halved, the simplest relationship between two notes, the octave, is formed. By reducing the length to two-thirds, the pitch is raised by a perfect fifth, and three-quarters gives the perfect fourth.

Pythagoras formed such relationships between musical notes into an integral part of his philosophy. He believed that natural phenomena, possessing an inner preordained harmony, could be explained by numbers. Thereby he attempted to provide for the link between music and mathematics a justification which has proved useful solace and counter-argument for over-mathematical composers of the twentieth century, who argue that relationships between notes should be judged primarily by the intellect using numbers. Pythagoras applied his beliefs also to space and in seeking numerical proof of fundamental spatial relationships in the world, he laid the foundations of geometry. Next the Pythagorean school applied these ideas to astronomy, for the link between nature and number came to possess an almost mystic strength. The belief formed that the planets' orbits could be calculated by comparison with musical intervals, for were not regular patterns in nature themselves akin to the harmonies of music? The heavens soon were held to possess their own music, each planet producing a note dependent on its velocity, and the notes from the several planets, put together, were thought to form

21

a scale. Philosophy had provided an explanation for the 'music of the spheres', an idea which appealed to Gustav Holst when composing his suite *The Planets*. These notions elevated Pythagoras to a reverenced philosopher and gave to music a central position in Greek philosophy.

The remaining intervals of the scale, the major third, sixth, second and seventh were filled in gradually and in this way the basis was laid for the note series or scales, which were to be used universally in the West to provide music's tonal foundation. The gradual formation of a psychological need for a return to the tonic or key note at a composition's conclusion led to a limited number of accepted forms ('first movement' and 'rondo' forms, for instance) eventually fulfilling the requirements of the system known as tonality. Pythagoras' experiments marked the beginning of this gradual process, which culminated in the recognition of tonality as part of the innate order and in its establishment of a stranglehold broken only in the present century.

The precept demonstrated by the Greeks, 'the shorter the length, the higher the pitch', explains the shortening on one side of the psaltery and the characteristic curve along the treble side of a grand piano.

Pythagoras' aid in determining interval ratios was the monochord (fig. 4). A movable bridge is positioned at any one of a number of pre-determined points marked on the side of the resonance box.

Treatises on monochord string ratios began to appear in the tenth century and the writings of Boethius (c. A.D. 500) on the monochord were read widely by medieval musicians. The monochord remained primarily a tool for the measuring and demonstration of intervals. During the Middle Ages it developed into the multi-stringed instrument used in medieval singing schools to teach intervals and to provide choirs with the desired pitch level.

It also assisted theoreticians in investigating the laws of harmonics. Marin Mersenne, the French theorist, in his 1636 book *Harmonie Universelle*, the first extensive treatise on sound and music, analysed how a string produces related higher pitched sounds at the same time vibrating at its fundamental pitch. Vibrating simultaneously in smaller segments (by forming 'nodes' or points of no motion) the octave, twelfth, fifteenth and higher

Fig 4. Monochord with movable bridges. Medieval

intervals can be heard. These are 'overtones' or 'upper harmonics' important in building the richness of harmony.

Galileo Galilei, the astronomer, and Mersenne, who were both alive in the first part of the seventeenth century, discovered independently the relationship between the frequency of vibration and the length, diameter, tension and density of the string. For instance, if either the string's thickness or its length is doubled, the frequency or pitch is halved. If the lowest string in a piano was of the same thickness as the string of the highest note (4186 Hertz (cycles per second)), it would need to be over 6·40 metres (21 feet) long to give the required pitch (27·5 Hertz)!

The monochord survived longest as an aid to the organ tuner, who might tune his monochord to a trumpet and then the organ to the monochord. In Paris monochords were still being made as tuners' tools as late as the 1820s.

Although there is a record of a third-century B.C. Alexandrian water organ using crude keyed-levers, the keyboard was of no importance until the Middle Ages. Early keys were heavy levers, struck by a clenched fist protected in a leather glove. The small portative pipe organ, which became increasingly common and which required an easy method of controlling the air flow to the pipes, was the chosen instrument for the keyboard's initial development. Also widely found was the hurdy-gurdy, utilizing a simple slide system which, however, had little influence on the keyboard's progress.

At this stage only today's 'natural' keys identified by the first seven letters of the alphabet, A to G repeated in every octave, were provided, their music giving a simple melodic line. When the interval of an augmented fourth, F to B, was judged unpleasant to the ear, a new key, B flat, was inserted between notes A and B, which were cut away for the purpose (Fig. 5). By the fifteenth

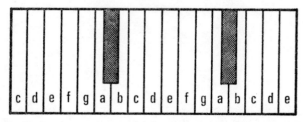

Fig. 5. Early sixteenth-century keyboard, showing added B flat

century the keyboard had become fully chromatic, the five raised sharp and flat notes in each octave forming an upper row. The oldest surviving example of this chromatic keyboard is found on the organ of Halberstadt Cathedral and dates from 1361.

As the keyboard developed so did a system of recording relative pitch. The staff originated as a single line around which the neums (Fig. 6), the first notes, used in plainsong, gave the approximate

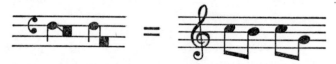

Fig. 6. Early neums on a four-line stave

melodic and rhythmic shape. A staff of four lines became usual for plainsong. In the seventeenth century the five-line staff (≡≡≡≡) became conventional for every other branch of music, and today's exactitude of recording pitch was arrived at.

When B flat was introduced, the flat sign originated as a round B (b) attached to the lower B. The upper natural B was given **a** square B (♭) sign, later modified to our natural sign (♮). The sharp sign originated as a 'cancelled b' with a stroke through it.

During the early centuries of the keyboard's existence, the letters A to G were often marked on the appropriate keys in order to differentiate between otherwise identical keys. The introduction of raised sharps and flats, and familiarity with the keyboard made this practice superfluous.

The increase in the number of notes led to the slow disintegration of the old modal system, which had been built around different combinations of the diatonic 'natural' keys. Its place was taken by the familiar major and minor scales, better suited to harmony. Formerly eight modes had been available, but now there were only two—major and minor, each available in twelve keys.

The prevailing system of tuning, however, made the distance between the semitones unequal and a passage played in one key sounded discordant in another as the new key appeared to be out of tune. Adventurous movement from key to key was therefore impossible. Consequently the keyboard music of Purcell, Couperin, Handel and others is set in comparatively few keys and has only limited modulations.

To understand why the adoption in one or another form of temperament became essential involves mathematics. Temperament is a compromise necessitating an adjustment in pitch to overcome discrepancies inherent in the physical order. The intervals revealed by Pythagoras' experiments and recognized by the ear to be most pure or 'perfect', were adequate for simple harmonics based on a handful of common chords supporting the melodies of the modal system. When the modes were discredited, however, and the modern system of keys with modulation from one key to another arrived, the problems caused by pure intervals grew acute.

Mean-tone temperament, a system constructed in the sixteenth century around the accuracy of the major thirds, had provided temporary respite until the pressures created by the desire for *distant* modulation, which exposed the shortcomings of the mean-tone method, proved irresistible. Equal temperament, however, a device which divides each octave into twelve equal semitones and in so doing slightly adjusts each semitone from its natural position, was to provide a lasting solution.

25

More detailed explanations of both mean-tone and equal temperaments are given below, but the reader who shudders at the prospect of arithmetic may omit this section and turn now to page 29.

A glance at a seven-octave piano keyboard shows that top a (a''''), seven octaves above lowest a (A''), is also twelve fifths above A'' (see p. 210). Pythagoras showed the frequency ratio of an octave to its fundamental as $2:1$, and of a fifth to its fundamental as $3:2$. To cover seven octaves commencing from A'', one would expect $(2/1)^7$ to yield the correct answer and likewise to arrive at a'''' through twelve fifths, $(3/2)^{12}$ to be the required formula. $(2/1)^7$ produces 128 and $(3/2)^{12}$ throws up 129·75. This difference in frequency is known as 'Pythagoras' comma' ('comma' is the Greek word for a very small interval, just as a comma in a sentence is a small interval or pause), and although less than a quarter of a semitone, this comma is the stumbling-block necessitating the compromises which have to be made by tempering. The twelfth fifth starting from any A would be G double sharp. If its pitch differs from A then on a keyboard instrument an additional key would be necessary. Repeat this process for the other notes and the absurdity of such a suggestion, both for the instrument maker and for the performer, is obvious. This problem is especially acute for those concerned with keyboard instruments, for the designer and in his turn the tuner determine the frequencies.

The same dilemma, which did not occur to Pythagoras because he did not think in terms of a compass as large as seven octaves (Greek melodies were confined to a compass of an octave) and therefore did not attempt to reconcile intervals to each other over a range so large, is demonstrable in numerous ways. One will suffice. The frequency ratio of Pythagoras' third is 81/64 times the frequency of the fundamental. The fraction taken for the tempered major third, however, is 5/4. $81/64 \div 5/4 = 81/80$, a difference often called 'Didymus' comma'.

The solution to this quandary most frequently encountered prior to the adoption of equal temperament was mean-tone temperament, a system developed in the sixteenth century by Schlick, Zarlino and most importantly Salinas, a blind professor at the University of Salamanca. The mean-tone system was founded on the accuracy of the major thirds, entailing compromise with

26

some other intervals. Taking C′ as the fundamental, the fourth fifth reaches e which, however, failed to form an exact major third with c immediately below it. Mean-tone temperament solved this dilemma by flattening e so that a correct major third was formed, but this involved a slight flattening of the four fifths which had been passed through. Intervals in some six major (C, G, D, A, F, and B flat) and three minor (A, D and G) keys were consonant and pleasant, but outside these keys unpleasant roughness resulted, explained by the accumulating error arising from the considerable flattening of the fifths. The next key using sharps in the signature, E major, entails the use of E flat instead of D sharp, but the difference between them approaches half a semitone. E flat major necessitates substitution of G sharp for A flat with the same difficulty. Remote key signatures containing these notes became impracticable. The interval between g sharp″ (the eighth fifth reached from C′) and e flat‴ became nearly one third of a semitone greater than a perfect fifth, the falseness of the interval establishing such a diabolical roughness or howl that it became known as the 'wolf fifth' or 'quinte-de-loup'. False thirds, for example b to e flat, established further wolves in more distant keys.

A simple explanation of modulation helps an understanding of changing key signatures and of progress through fifths. To modulate to the nearest related key with one additional sharp, the tonic of the new key is the dominant (or fifth) of the old (for example C major to G, then G to D). To introduce a further flat the progression is a fifth downwards (which is the same as a fourth upwards). For instance C major to F introduces one flat, F to B flat the second. By the time the progression has reached F sharp major, which contains the same notes as G flat major, a major scale has been commenced on each of the twelve semitones contained in the octave.

Modulation passes through a pivot chord (the second chord in Fig. 7), which belongs to both the original and the new key. It is followed by the dominant of the fresh key which introduces the new sharp or flat and then moves to the new tonic, forming a perfect cadence (V:I) and imparting a sense of belonging in the unfamiliar key. Key colour and the listener's awareness of it change as additional sharps or flats are introduced. The romantic composers exploited ordered modulation, understanding the

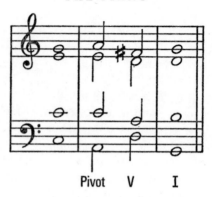

Pivot   V   I

Fig. 7. Modulation

psychological benefits bestowed by the sense of stability and belonging which is imparted when a movement concludes in the tonic key from which it started, after visiting different keys.

On the other hand modulation in mean-tone temperament to distantly related keys not tempered to accommodate it generated daunting problems. So long as composers were satisfied with key signatures restricting the numbers of sharps and flats and so long as they did not seek the variety obtainable through rapid modulation, all was well with mean-tone temperament and no unacceptable roughness was encountered. Within its limitations it served musicians satisfactorily because it retained more true intervals than the equally tempered scale, preserving a smoothness and harmoniousness which the latter sacrificed. For this reason it retained many followers even in the present century. Pipe organs continued to be tuned to mean-tone temperament (in England until the mid-nineteenth century) long after its supremacy in the tuning of other keyboard instruments was in dispute, and often it is claimed that this longevity explains the limited choice of key signature and restricted modulation contained in Bach's organ music compared with his clavichord and harpsichord music.

Attempts were made to overcome the problems of mean-tone by dividing selected keys into a front half and back half and providing two pipes for G sharp and A flat for example, or for D sharp and E flat, but the impracticability of providing cumbersome extra pipes or strings tuned to different pitches to quieten all the 'wolves', ruled out acceptability beyond the experimental stage of any such solution.

The answer adopted ultimately was equal temperament. Tempering equally divides each octave into twelve equal semitones so that only the octave is correct and all other intervals, slightly adjusted or tempered from their natural position, are theoretically very slightly out of tune, although so insignificantly as to be inaudible to the average ear. As twelve fifths produced a pitch higher than seven octaves each fifth is flattened fractionally to a ratio below $3/2$,* so that a progression through twelve fifths arrives at the same frequency as a progress through seven octaves. The problem of Pythagoras' comma, the source of all the trouble, is resolved effectively.

This solution produces a new figure, the semitone multiplier. All semitones are now an equal distance apart so that the frequency of each note can be multiplied by the semitone multiplier to give the frequency of the next semitone above. The ratio is usually given for practical purposes as $1 \cdot 05946$, which is the twelfth root of two $(\sqrt[12]{2})$, twelve semitones forming the octave with an octave having twice the frequency of the octave below it, but $\sqrt[12]{2}$ is $1 \cdot 05946, 30943, 59295, 2646$! Thus a′440 Hertz $1 \cdot 05946 = 466 \cdot 15$ Hertz $=$ b flat′. It is possible also to work out ratios for each note of the octave so that, for example, to calculate a major third from a′440, $440 \times 1 \cdot 25993 = 554 \cdot 36$ Hertz $=$ c sharp″.

There had been some knowledge of equal temperament for centuries before it was widely adopted. It is said, although with what validity is uncertain, that the Chinese were aware of the problems posed by temperament a thousand years before Christ. In the later Middle Ages the Spaniards are believed to have utilized equal temperament when fastening the frets to their guitars and in Italy Zarlino in the following century showed that equal tempering could be applied to the lute. Several of John Bull's virginal works show modulation so extensive as to suggest use of adjustments akin to equal temperament. Mersenne explained the system and by the end of the seventeenth century

* The perfect fifth $= 3/2 = 1 \cdot 5$ frequency ratio. Equally tempered it equals $\sqrt[12]{128} = 1 \cdot 49831$. (cf. mean-tone temperament, where it equals $\sqrt[4]{5} = 1 \cdot 49535$). Hence it is slightly flat.

there were isolated examples of organs tuned to principles approaching equal temperament and of organ compositions making use of modulation so wide-ranging as to exceed the possibilities of mean-tone temperament.

When extensive modulation was demanded, it became inevitable that the greater harmonic vocabulary offered by equal temperament would lead ultimately to its universal acceptance, because while intervals except the octave were theoretically slightly out of tune, it was not noticed by the average ear and so easy modulation to distant keys could become a matter of course, enhancing composers' inventiveness. It is probable that German pianos were tuned to equal temperament before English ones, for Broadwood adopted equal temperament tuning only in 1846 and the English piano makers followed in the 1850s. Pianos tuned to mean-tone temperament must have made difficult satisfactory performance of advanced Beethoven, Chopin and Liszt.

Expert opinion about the role J. S. Bach played in the spread of equal temperament tuning has changed in recent decades. For laymen who find difficulty in understanding why the interpretation of past events changes from generation to generation of historians, Bach and the adoption of equal temperament provides a fruitful example. Frequently research establishes new facts which lead to rejection of former clear-cut opinions and to change of emphasis in the interpretation of new and old facts alike; too frequently interpretation is coloured by a subjective outlook.

It used to be claimed that J. S. Bach was the first great propagandist of equal temperament tuning, his contribution to the debate *Das Wohltemperierte Klavier* (*The Well-Tempered Clavier*), preludes and fugues set in all twelve major and all twelve minor keys and designed specifically for equal temperament to show the range of key signatures available through the new system. Thus they were intended to demonstrate its undoubted superiority over mean-tone temperament and just intonation (a lesser-known system in which it was only possible to play in tune in one key). Contemporary musicologists, however, have moderated their opinions and approach the problem with greater circumspection as appreciation of fresh considerations has grown. They point out that as the '*Bebung*' and similar variations in finger touch alter the tension and therefore pitch of the clavichord's strings, fine differences in tuning resulting from tempering can be lost. Renewed interest in the instruments of the past has restored an appreciation of the importance of Bach's attachment to the clavichord. The organ, harpsichord and clavichord were the three keyboard instruments he was accustomed to compose for, and it is recognized that a number of preludes and fugues in *The Well-Tempered Clavier* were intended by their composer to be played on the clavichord at least as much as the harpsichord. In addition it is argued now that *Das Wohltemperierte Klavier* should not be translated as *Equally Tempered Clavier* because '*Wohl*' means 'well' and 'well tempered' is not necessarily the same as 'equally tempered'. It is realized that viewed more critically there is little clear-cut indication that Bach tempered equally his tuning and so no decisive evidence that the 'Forty-Eight' were intended for an instrument tuned to equal temperament.

Nonetheless it is probable that Bach, aware of the shortcomings of mean-tone temperament, favoured equal temperament or something approaching it. He may have tuned his instruments in a manner that approached equal temperament, but variations in the tonal colour of different keys almost certainly existed. It is possible therefore that each of the 'Forty-Eight' sounded 'well' in its appropriate key and suited its distinctive colouring, which it is unlikely that Bach eliminated entirely when tuning.

Musicians who establish the note's pitch at the instant they play the note do not suffer from the predetermination which restricts keyboard players. When singers and string players perform in conjunction with a keyboard instrument, automatically they adopt equal temperament, but when there is no pressure on them to conform the frequencies of the notes they produce often wander away from equal temperament.

The tuner's task is connected with problems of equal temperament and with introducing the correct amount of distortion or 'beat' between intervals so that adjacent semitones are separated by identical distances.

The tuner's first task is to 'set the scale' in the middle of the compass—usually the thirteen notes within the octave a to a' are chosen. The most popular note sequences used establish the correctly tempered intervals between fifths and fourths checking with thirds and sixths, which are 'rougher', as they become available. Fifths are tuned a shade narrow or flat to be correctly tempered and because a fifth above c′ (g′) is the same note as a fourth downwards from c″, a fifth and a fourth forming an octave, fourths are tuned slightly wide or sharp. The tuner listens for the beats formed between nearly adjacent overtones of the interval he forms. In tuning the interval of a fifth, the second overtone of the lower note is in theory identical to the first overtone of the upper note or fifth. In practice, however, due to equal tempering there will be a beat between them. The second overtone of a220 Hertz = 660 Hertz. The equally tempered e′ above has a frequency of 329·63 Hertz and the second overtone is therefore 659·26 Hertz. The difference between 660 Hertz and 659·26 Hertz is ·74 Hertz, or to use former terminology 'cycles per second', which will be heard as ·74 beats per second or one beat every 1⅓ seconds. The beat arises from the compressions and rarefactions of air particles passing in and out of phase. When either the compressions from both notes or the rarefactions from both notes coincide, they reinforce each other giving a moment of maximum volume; if the compression coincides with the rarefaction from the second source, when they are equally intense they cancel out and there is a momentary silence. The gradual change from maximum to minimum coincidence causes the beat.

Having set the scale, the tuner proceeds in octaves (untempered of course!) upwards to the highest treble notes and downwards to the lowest notes in the bass. Various practices, however, destroying theoretical precision have grown up. Some prefer to stretch or sharpen slightly the octaves in the treble from about c‴ and the piano's topmost notes are sometimes tuned up to a quarter of a semitone sharp, the intention being to introduce greater brilliance as the sharp harmonics formed by lower notes then incline to coincide with the high notes and so reinforce them. Some tuners tune the bass octaves too narrow, a result partly of excessively high overtone content and poor presence of fundamental tone.

Thus the theoretical divisions of equal temperament are moderated in practice and in addition it is absurd to expect tuners to count beat rates, for example 9·4 beats in 10 seconds, systematically. Consequently the tuner's ear relies on 'impressions' of beat rates. These factors account for dissimilarities in the work of different tuners, whose skill is vital to the resultant tone quality of the piano, for the merest suggestion of a beat in the

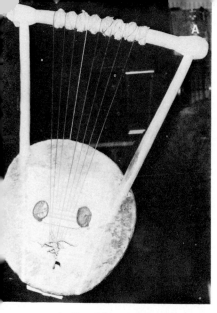

1. Bowl lyre of the Luo type. Modern. Kenyan. Key: A, yoke

2. *(left)* Tube zither with several strings. Modern. Made in the Philippines. *(right)* Raft zither. Modern. West African

3. Dulcimer. Mid-nineteenth century. Eastern European

4. Cimbalon. 1890–1900. By Schunda of Budapest

5. Detail of clavichord, showing mechanism. *c.* 1976. By John Morley of London. Key : A, damping cloth ; B, tangent

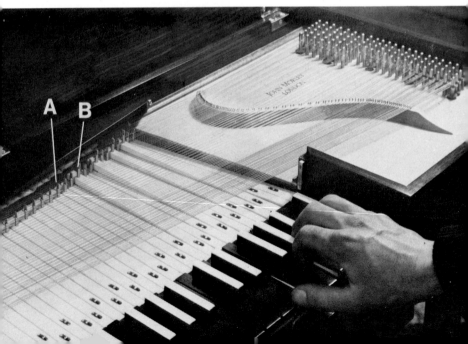

6. Clavichord. *c.* 1750. Unsigned, but by a member of the Hass family of Hamburg. Unfretted. Casework mahogany. Inside of lid lacquered with red chinoiserie

7. Octave spinet. *c.* 1600. Italian

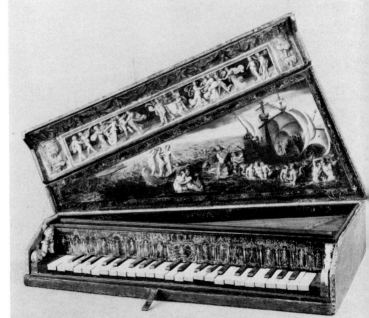

8. Pentagonal spinet. Late seventeenth century. Italian

9. Spinet. *c*. 1680. By Stephanus Keene of London

10. Spinet with period figures. *c*. 1740. Probably by the younger Thomas Hitchcock of London. The male figure holds a Neapolitan mandoline

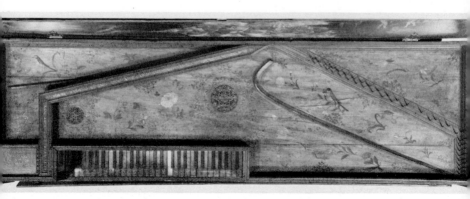

11. Virginal. 1655. By John Loosemore of Exeter

12. *(above)* Harpsichord. Late seventeenth century. Flemish. Rebuilt
in Paris in late eighteenth century

13. *(above right)* Harpsichord. 1763. By Kirkman of London

14. *(below right)* Harpsichord. *c.* 1976. By John Morley of London.
Incorporates 16 foot on separate soundboard. Key: A, 16-foot
bridge; B, 8-foot bridge; C, 4-foot bridge; D, jacks for 16-foot,
lower manual; E, jacks for 8-foot, lower manual; F, jacks for 4-foot,
lower manual; G, jacks for 8-foot, upper manual; H, jacks for 8-foot
lute, upper manual; I, 'harp' or 'buff' stop on 8-foot, lower manual;
J, 4-foot bridge; K, 8-foot and 16-foot bridge

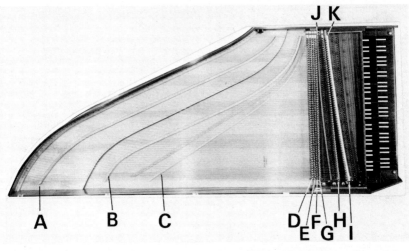

A   B   C   D E F G H I   J K

15. Upright harpsichord (clavicytherium). Second half of fifteenth
century. North Italian. Earliest
surviving example of an upright
harpsichord

three strings of a trichord may impart a dead quality to the tone. Their work is significant also in the survival of individual key character (e.g. lively C major, sombre G flat major) which in theory should be eliminated by equal temperament.

Such factors explain why the introduction of electronic tuners is not so straightforward as the uninitiated might think. Resultant tunings may be too dry, lacking the extra colour which minute divergence gives, unless those who use them are trained to exercise their judgement in the same way as skilled tuners. 'Setting the tuning pin' is a further ability demanded of the tuner. The pitch is raised slightly above the required level and then brought back to the correct frequency. At the same time any 'twist' in the steel tuning pin, caused by its being turned when under severe strain, is removed and it is 'set', so that heavy blows from the hammers will not easily cause it to jump and the fine tuning to be lost. A tuning using electronic aids is no faster than tuning by ear and considerable skills are required still. The problems encountered and the physical strain imposed on piano and tuner alike by high string tensions demonstrate that the 'do-it-yourself' approach is impracticable, even with electronic assistance.

III

The Clavichord to 1820

The art of music progressed until it became impracticable to move the monochord's bridge for the different notes required in musical performance. At an unknown date in the twelfth century or the two centuries following, a series of monochords was fitted with the simple key action of the organ, giving birth to the clavichord (*clavis* = key, *chorde* = string).

The early history of the new instrument is uncertain, although it appears to have been associated with minstrels. Old habits died hard and confusion resulted as the early clavichord frequently was called 'monochord', although it had acquired an identity of its own. In the fifteenth century literary references and paintings depicting the clavichord became more common.

The action is very simple. The small metal blade called the tangent (Pl. 5) has a dual function—to strike the string setting it in motion, at the same time determining the speaking length in similar fashion to a monochord bridge. The length of cloth (Pl. 5) silences the string after the key is released and prevents the non-speaking length on the 'wrong' side of the tangent from vibrating. Unlike the harpsichord, the clavichord has no 'stops' and the absence of quills is an additional factor making maintenance comparatively easy.

The light casework was too weak to carry any considerable strain. Consequently the strings, on the early instruments of brass, steel or iron, were thin and strung at low tension. This characteristic, the small soundboard and the short distance covered by the light tangent account for the soft tone, which may be drowned by the buzz of conversation. The clavichord was reputed to be popular in nunneries as it did not disturb those close to it, and the sixteenth-century Benedictine rule permitted its construction and use in cloisters.

The clavichord was suited ideally for simple harmonies and therefore for teaching. It also became a practice instrument for

34

organists, for which purpose as early as about 1460 two clavichords had been mounted on top of one another and a pedal board fitted.

Until the early eighteenth century all clavichords were 'fretted' or *'gebunden'*, each string being struck by the tangents of several keys, although if the keys in question were depressed simultaneously, only the higher pitched note provided by a particular string would sound because its tangent would be nearest the soundboard bridge. An individual string for every note was unnecessary as notes a semitone or tone apart rarely were played together. Fretting was adequate for the predominantly melodic music of the time.

Each note in the bass octave usually had its own string. A typical arrangement was for two or three keys to share a string in the middle section, and two, three, or four keys per string in the treble.

The early clavichords had some twenty notes. In the fifteenth century the number of strings increased and for the first time different sizes of string were employed. Extra sonority was obtained from the stringing, which was now often bichord (i.e. one tangent struck *two* strings tuned to identical pitch). By the early sixteenth century a typical compass provided two to two and a half octaves. In the seventeenth century the usual compass was four octaves fully chromatic with an upper row of notes, and with a short octave in the bass.

The 'short octave', inherited from the primitive organ, was a device employed on many early clavichords and harpsichords. To save space the distribution of notes to keys was rearranged in the lowest octave, so that no keys were provided for unnecessary chromatic notes. The most common arrangement was the 'C short octave' (Fig. 8). Some contemporary compositions show the left hand apparently playing a tenth, c to e, which is in reality an octave.

The title page of sixteenth-century compositions often proclaimed that they were intended 'for organ, clavichord or harpsichord', the three frequently being in domestic use. J. J. Froberger's music composed in the seventeenth century seems to have been the earliest to specify the clavichord to the exclusion of alternative instruments. By the late eighteenth century sacred music was reserved for the organ, now confined to church use, while the

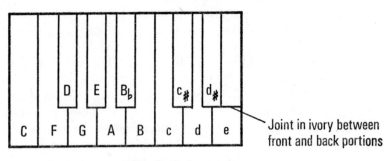

Fig. 8. C short octave

clavichord and harpsichord family shared the secular repertoire.

In Tudor England the virginals and spinet largely superseded the clavichord, which had never won widespread popularity, those clavichords which were in use being imported. In Italy, on the other hand, the small clavichord remained popular. In France the clavichord never acquired any influence and in the Low Countries it was largely supplanted by the harpsichord. The latter's greater dynamic range, however, was not decisive with the German burghers, who made the clavichord peculiarly their own.

Northern Germany witnessed a clavichord revival, becoming from 1650 the centre of clavichord making and playing. Its cheapness appealed to a population which, ravaged by the Thirty Years War, lacked prosperity and political stability. The sixteenth- and seventeenth-century German clavichord was unpretentious, a small one costing only one-third to one-quarter the price of a harpsichord. Andreas Werckmeister, however, who in the closing decades of the seventeenth century perfected the 'equal temperament' tuning system, wrote that 'such are not worth troubling about, for they are only suitable to be used as firewood for cooking fish'.[3]

Due to its economy in space and price, the fretted instrument remained in frequent use until the clavichord itself went out of fashion. In the early eighteenth century, however, the first unfretted or 'bundfrei' clavichords with a separate string, or pair of strings, for each note were made, this arrangement soon becoming popular in the larger clavichords being developed in Germany (Pl. 6).

Their usual compass was five octaves, occasionally extending to six. Their expressive capabilities were improved and a separate row of octave strings, one for each bass note as the bass lacked brilliance, was often added.

Superb examples of decorated casework were made. Usually a separate stand was provided and towards the end of the eighteenth century screw-in legs became normal.

The clavichord's delicate expressiveness was suited especially to music of a sentimental melancholy nature, which was the rage in contemporary northern Germany. Its ethereal tone was aided by the instrument's most characteristic effect, the *'Bebung'*. A slight variation of finger pressure on the key alters the tension of the string and therefore varies the pitch, producing a vibrato. Contemporary musicians asserted that it took fifteen years to master the instrument and in particular this refinement of touch sensitivity, which is unique to the clavichord.

The clavichord repertoire consisted of short pieces, often written in two parts only, this simplicity of outline being acceptable only on the clavichord. Therefore when the instrument was forgotten, so was its music.

C. P. E. Bach's compositions mark the final blossoming of the clavichord. Dr Burney, indefatigable traveller, who in 1772 visited Hamburg and was treated by Bach to a conducted tour of its churches and their organs, gives an account of the great clavichordist's playing :

> . . . he conducted me upstairs, into a large and elegant music room, furnished with pictures, drawings and prints of more than a hundred and fifty eminent musicians : among whom, there are many Englishmen, and original portraits, in oil, of his father and grandfather. After I had looked at these, M. Bach was so obliging as to sit down to his *Silbermann clavichord*, and favourite instrument, upon which he played three or four of his choicest and most difficult compositions, with the delicacy, precision, and spirit, for which he is so justly celebrated among his countrymen. In the pathetic and slow movements, whenever he had a long note to express, he absolutely contrived to produce, from his instrument, a cry of sorrow and complaint, such as can only be effected upon the clavichord, and perhaps by himself.[4]

The clavichord, simple, cheap and easily portable, was developed in Germany into the square piano, possessing a greater dynamic range and also capable of nuance, which had been the greatest advantage of the clavichord over the harpsichord. The clavichord lingered on into the early years of the nineteenth century, but by 1820 interest in the instrument and its construction was virtually extinct throughout Europe with the exception of Scandinavia, where it continued to enjoy a limited and discriminating appeal. Nineteenth-century Scandinavian clavichords were often of gigantic dimensions and sweetness of tone was sacrificed for percussive volume which almost rivalled the earlier square piano. Interest in the clavichord revived gradually during the present century.

IV

The Harpsichord Group of Plucked Instruments to 1820

Probably in the thirteenth or fourteenth centuries the first experiments were made at plucking the strings of a psaltery with a keyed action, giving rise to a further family of instruments.

Compared with the harpsichord (Fig. 9), the main member of the plucked group, the virginal (Fig. 10) and spinet (Fig. 11), the shape of a recumbent harp, are small and simple normally possessing only one string per key.

The harpsichord, virginal and spinet share, however, their method of plucking the string (Fig. 12). The plectrum sets the string in vibration by lifting it vertically until it slips off the plectrum. During the jack's descent, the string's pressure on the plectrum causes the tongue to pivot enabling the plectrum to pass the string without plucking it. A hog's bristle spring then returns the tongue to its original position.

When more than one set of jacks is provided, they fit into movable slides (Fig. 13) which can be activated by a hand stop or knee lever, moving the jacks either to the correct position to make contact with the strings or sufficiently far away to avoid sounding. Harpsichords are fitted with a number of these registers or jack racks, which usually correspond to the number of strings per key, two, three or occasionally four.

Many early harpsichord makers were primarily organ builders and organ terminology for pipe lengths was applied therefore to string lengths. The term '8 foot', which to the organ builder signifies a pipe eight feet long, denotes normal pitch (Pl. 14). To halve the length doubles the pitch. Therefore a 4-foot register denotes a set of strings tuned an octave higher and a 16-foot set sounds an octave lower than the 8 foot. By providing both 4 and 16-foot registers a seven-octave compass can be obtained from a five-octave keyboard. A 16-foot set of strings does not make the

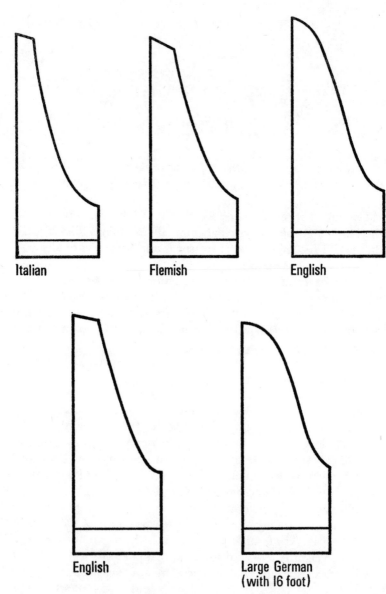

Fig. 9. Typical harpsichord shapes

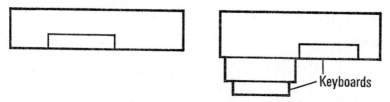

Fig. 10. Virginal and double virginal shapes

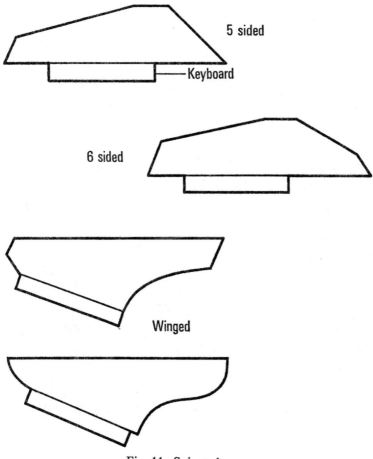

Fig. 11. Spinet shapes

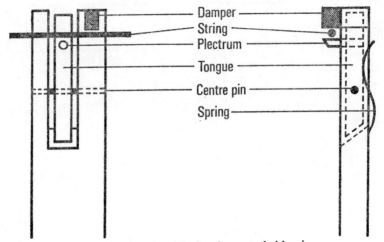

Damper
String
Plectrum
Tongue
Centre pin
Spring

Fig. 12. Harpsichord jack—front and side views

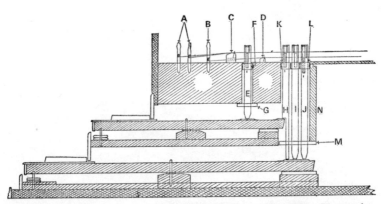

Fig. 13. A two-manual harpsichord layout—side view. Key: A:
8-foot tuning pins; B: 4-foot tuning pins; C: 8-foot bridge; D: 4-
foot bridge; E: jack for lute stop; F: slide for lute stop; G: guide
for lute stop; H: 8-foot jack, both manuals; I: 8-foot jack, lower
manual; J: 4-foot jack, lower manual; K: 8-foot slide, both
manuals; L: 4-foot slide, lower manual; M: guide for both 8-foot
and the 4-foot jacks; N: head rail

instrument twice as long as thicker wire is employed to give the required mass.

Part of the harpsichord maker's craft lies in solving successfully the problem of providing different combinations of registers to give optimum variety of tonal colour and volume, at the same time maintaining an essential balance.

The harpsichord family flourished between 1500 and 1800, a number of national schools coming to the fore during the three hundred years of its supremacy.

The plucked keyboard instruments originated in Italy, where in the Renaissance period keyboard music was more advanced than elsewhere in Europe and was sufficiently developed to demand refined instruments. The casework of plucked instruments amplifies sound and the simple, exceedingly light case of the Italian instruments, usually of cypress wood, contributes to their short precise tone. When not being played, the instrument was placed usually in a separate protective casing, which was either painted or decorated with leather or fabric. The most frequent layout for an Italian harpsichord was one keyboard with two sets of strings at unison 8-foot pitch.

The five or six-sided spinet (Pl. 8) was the most popular form of smaller instrument. Italy also produced a large number of octave spinets (Pl. 7), their single set of 4-foot strings explaining their name and small size.

The clavicytherium (Pl. 15), an attempt at standing the harpsichord on end to save space, originated in Italy. Its mechanism was complicated, an extra lever and spring being inserted to assist the tongue's return. The vertical harpsichord was never built in any quantity, although it was revived in the eighteenth century to enjoy limited popularity.

The Italian designs and musical concepts strongly influenced the subsequent Flemish school, of which the Ruckers family, working in Antwerp in the later sixteenth and the first half of the seventeenth centuries, was the most famous representative. Family expertise and continuity in chosen crafts were characteristics of the period, the Breughel and Cranach families, for instance, each producing a line of noted painters. Ruckers instruments were prized highly for beauty of sound, and many of the instruments attributed to the family either are by lesser makers or have been altered extensively in later years to accommodate the developing musical requirements of the seventeenth and eighteenth centuries. Many virginals and harpsichords bore the Ruckers name and the family made harpsichords with both one and two keyboards. The single manual invariably incorporated a 4-foot stop with occasionally one 8-foot or more often two 8-foot stops. Hans Ruckers was the first builder to make the 4-foot a regular feature of the harpsichord, thereby reducing the popularity of the octave spinet. The double manual also had an 8-foot and a 4-foot stop, but four rows of jacks were provided, enabling each stop to be played from both keyboards. The Ruckers were the first builders to make the double manual instrument well known. In their original form double manual instruments were predominantly transposing harpsichords possessing a lower manual which produced a note a fourth lower than the key (e.g. key f''' sounded c''' below), while the upper-manual keys produced notes of the usual pitch. This device helped to align the instrument with the range of the singer's voice and was appreciated in Flanders, if not in England.

The Jean Ruckers harpsichord supplied to King Charles I for £30 with a Rubens depiction of Cupid and Psyche on the inside of the lid (the price without the painting would have been £15), aroused official displeasure as the transposing keyboard was unwelcome. State Secretary Windebank complained that 'it wantes 6 or 7 Keyes, so that it is utterly unserviceable. If either he could alter it, or wolde change it for another that may have more Keyes, it were well : but as it is, our musick is marr'd'.[5]

In the later seventeenth century the transposing arrangement was discontinued when Jean Couchet, Jean Ruckers' nephew, introduced an arrangement of an 8-foot stop on the upper keyboard and a second 8-foot and a 4-foot on the lower keyboard with a coupler between the manuals. Vividly contrasting effects between keyboards now could be obtained for the first time.

The disposition of two 8-foot and one 4-foot was soon adopted by many leading makers, providing the framework for the harpsichord compositions of the great eighteenth-century period.

Van Dyck, Breughel and other artists painted lids of the often elaborately finished Antwerp harpsichords. Unlike the Italian instruments the soundboards were decorated in tempora with fruit, flowers, birds and insects, surrounded by blue scrolls. The soundhole or rosette, inlet into the soundboard's surface, was a device taken over from the lute, guitar and similar instruments where the vibrating air was enclosed within the instrument's body, its escape provided for by the sound-hole. The sound-hole on harpsichords of box construction helped to equalize air pressure otherwise trapped between the inside of the box and the underneath of the soundboard. Later, however, after the outer box was dispensed with, it had a largely ornamental role and frequently was decorated as a rose or elaborate geometric pattern. Thin veneer or embossed parchment was employed and on some Flemish instruments cast lead later covered with bronze paint. Flemish craftsmen regularly incorporated their initials in the tracery together with a symbol, as a means of identifying the instrument's maker. Hans Ruckers designed a seated angel playing her harp. Later Kirkman chose as his trademark King David playing the harp. Shudi on the other hand relinquished the rosette, for by the eighteenth century it was no longer regarded as a necessary convention, but his firm fitted a series of holes in the head rail (Fig. 13) about 25 millimetres (1 inch) in diameter.

The Flemish instruments were placed on a separate stand, the musician often standing to play the keys which were at a higher level than they are today.

More chromatic notes were now needed and as a step towards full chromaticism, a variation on the short octave enjoyed a brief popularity from around 1660 to 1725. The two lowermost sharps were split in the middle, the back halves providing the missing F sharp and G sharp.

Boxwood, bone, which is less prone than ivory to turn yellow, pear, cedar and other materials were used to cover the keys. Usually the raised keys were a light colour, perhaps ivory-topped, on the most precious instruments inlaid with tortoise-shell or mother-of-pearl designs, and the lower natural keys were covered with ebony or a dark-coloured wood. The intention may have been to display to greater advantage the white hands of the performer by contrasting them with the dark keys.

The Ruckers instruments were sent all over Europe, their influence being felt particularly strongly by the English and French makers. This high esteem for the Ruckers harpsichords with their bright general-purpose tone meant, paradoxically, that it was judged worthwhile virtually to rebuild them, updating them to the requirements of a later period. So enthusiastically was this task taken up that only one substantially unaltered example survived and is now preserved in Edinburgh University.

The French makers devoted much energy in the first half of the eighteenth century to the conversion of the Flemish instruments, a process known as '*ravalement*', to fit them for the music of Couperin, Rameau and the prescribed formalities of the Louis' court. Their keyboards were extended to five octaves with corresponding lengthening and widening of the soundboard and case (Pl. 12).

Clearly the harpsichord maker's craft was prized highly and the attainment of the Ruckers' tonal excellence was considered a rare achievement. The large eighteenth-century French harpsichords made by the Blanchet family and by Pascal Taskin are virtual copies of the rebuilt Flemish ones.

While the French makers were concentrating on rebuilding the finest products of the Flemish school, German instrument-making came into its own. Hieronymus Hass of Hamburg produced some of the finest and largest harpsichords of all time. A three-manual example made in 1740 measured 2·70 metres (9 feet 3 inches) in length and was fitted with 2-foot and 16-foot registers. The Hass workshop was one of the few to use a 16-foot, for which a second soundboard was provided, and the only one known to use a 2-foot register.

Significant keyboard-instrument making began in England in the seventeenth century with the Haward family probably the major English harpsichord-making family of the century. The earliest surviving English instruments show strong Italian influence, but as Flemish imports gradually supplanted the Italian during the course of the seventeenth-century English harpsichords and virginals turned away from the Italian style to imitate the Flemish. Italian influence was visible still, however, as English makers began to develop a style of their own from Italian and Flemish influences. A dark oak case and the division of the casework sides into panels became characteristics of the indigenous English style.

Rectangular virginals (Pl. 11) were particularly popular in England, where Henry VIII and Queen Elizabeth were accomplished performers. Contemporaries found difficulty in distinguishing between the early spinets and virginals, and in Tudor and Stuart England the term 'virginal' or 'pair of virginals' was used

to describe all plucked keyboard instruments. The diarist Samuel
Pepys described the Great Fire in 1666 :

> River full of lighters and boats taking in goods, . . . and only I
> observed that hardly one lighter or boat in three that had the
> goods of a house in, but there was a pair of Virginalls in it.[6]

In the Elizabethan period English music enjoyed its greatest
flowering and the virginal compositions of William Byrd, Orlando
Gibbons, John Bull and others rank with the compositions of all
time for the plucked instruments.

Towards the end of the seventeenth century the spinet (Pl. 9),
arriving from France on the crest of Charles II's wave, supplanted
the virginal, to enjoy a century's use as a convenient domestic
instrument. Well-known spinet makers included Charles Haward,
Stephen Keene and John Player. The Hitchcocks became the
best-known family specializing in spinets to the almost complete
exclusion of other instruments (Pl. 10). For the casework they
used walnut, which had supplanted the earlier oak and which
was mounted with elaborate strap hinges of brass. The fashion for
walnut furniture coincided with the period of the spinet's greatest
popularity.

In about 1700 the English makers still were producing few
harpsichords when compared with the number of spinets made.
At the turn of the century they adopted the second manual and
the English harpsichord matured in the succeeding half-century
into the large full harpsichords of Burkat Shudi and Jacob
Kirkman, both immigrants. They served their apprenticeships
under Hermann Tabel, who brought with him to England the
traditions of his native Flanders. On Tabel's death in 1738,
Kirkman married his widow barely a month after the funeral!

Shudi and Kirkman developed the larger harpsichord (Pl. 13)
with one or two five octave keyboards (Shudi and his partner
John Broadwood occasionally extended the compass to five and a
half octaves), with two 8-foot sets of strings and almost always
one 4-foot. The restrained mahogany or walnut veneer used for
the casework was laid usually on oak and gave an impression of
massive solidity.

English harpsichords of the mid-eighteenth century made use
of an 8-foot 'lute' stop (Pl. 14), which plucked an existing set of
strings nearer the bridge at the keyboard end, providing a thin

47

brittle tone. Rarely found except in England was the 'harp' stop (Pl. 14), which muted the string and produced a short dry note by bringing small felt or buff leather pads into contact with each string of an 8-foot set.

Shudi developed the 'machine'. A pedal attached to one leg of the instrument, it brought into play combinations of pre-set registers so that without removing his hands from the keyboards to operate the hand knobs, the player could produce dramatic changes in tone colour.

The 'Venetian Swell', patented by Shudi in 1769, was an attempt to give to the harpsichord the ability of gradually getting louder and softer. The Venetian blind suggests the principle. An inner lid composed of a set of shutters placed above the strings was operated by a foot pedal, which opened the shutters to allow the sound to escape, thereby altering the volume and tonal colour. Shudi's competitor, Kirkman, retaliated with the introduction of his 'nag's head', a hinged section of the casework lid which could be opened and closed at the discretion of the player, producing a comparable effect for his instruments. These swell devices enjoyed considerable popularity and their principle is familiar also to organists.

Shudi, his son, Shudi the Younger, and John Broadwood made nearly twelve hundred harpsichords in sixty-five years of activity from 1729. Although fewer than the number made by Kirkman, Shudi's instruments became so famous that Handel, Frederick the Great and the Empress Maria Teresa numbered among their owners. The larger harpsichords of Kirkman and Shudi represented the apogee of English harpsichord construction, admitting no rivals for sheer magnificence of tone with full sonorous basses. At their best in stately imposing passages, these instruments were least successful when constraint and clarity were called for.

The effects which Shudi did so much to develop were required because musical taste was changing, and the harpsichord was suffering from a want of expressive capabilities, which the advancing piano offered.

In 1768 in a further defensive step in the war with the piano Pascal Taskin, working in Paris, reintroduced plectra (Fig. 12) of buff leather, which had been little used for over a century. In the intervening period crows' and ravens' quills were used regularly and whalebone, shell, brass and even vultures' quills had been tried. Quills gave a brighter shriller tone than the sweet pure sound of the leather, hardened in olive oil.

Regulation and voicing of the fragile plectra requires much skill and time, and is critical in determining tone colour and smoothness of touch. Players used to requill and tune their own instruments, which often contained a drawer for their tools.

Like the clavichord, the harpsichord was long popular as an organist's practice instrument. In the seventeenth century public performances of secular music became more frequent and the harpsichord acquired a new role as a 'continuo' instrument, providing the underlying harmony. Monteverdi's *Orfeo* performed in 1607 was one of the earliest works in a new Italian art form, the opera. Two *'gravicembali'* were included in Monteverdi's orchestra, accompanying the recitative from a figured bass. Figured bass is a musical shorthand, the figures indicating the chords to be added.

In time the harpsichord was placed at the front of the instrumental ensemble. Its greater carrying power compared with the spinet, virginal and clavichord, and its ability in an orchestral context to blend and thicken the sound texture, suited it ideally for continuo duties, although for a considerable time the organ, enlarged lute and viols provided competition. As the continuo player came to devote more time to directing, playing only intermittently, a second accompanying harpsichord often was provided (Fig. 14).

For trio sonatas, orchestral suites and concerti grossi, among the

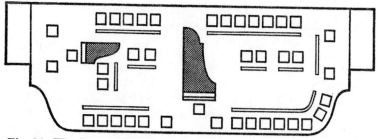

Fig. 14. The Dresden Orchestra in 1753 showing second harpsichord. The Capellmeister's harpsichord is placed centrally, and the accompanist's harpsichord faces it at a right angle. The players at the front have their backs to the audience, as all the players face inwards towards the Capellmeister

most popular instrumental forms, the harpsichord was able to provide the continuo, a role it kept until the arrival of the modern symphonic form whose first great masters were Haydn and Mozart. As a boy of twelve Beethoven provided the continuo in the opera band of the Elector of Cologne.

The plucked instruments provide a bright lucid tone making them ideal for portraying the clear-cut lines of contrapuntal music (the different voices in a fugue, for example), which prevailed into the eighteenth century. The harpsichord developed a valuable repertoire as a solo instrument. Domenico Scarlatti was perhaps the instrument's most outstanding virtuoso of all time, although his contemporaries would not have recognized the word in today's accepted sense. He composed for a one-manual harpsichord, often crossing hands at lightning speed in his one movement sonatas which, with the fugues and dance suites of Bach and Handel, provide typical harpsichord music.

Because the tone was short-lived (Mersenne had suggested that it could be enlarged by allowing wind blowing through the windows to strike the strings!), ornaments became the hallmark of the plucked string in an attempt to prolong its brief sonority. Although adding little to the harmonic sense, these embellishments were the main contribution of the harpsichord to musical style. Trills, mordents and turns abounded, and C. P. E. Bach was eloquent in their praise :

Consider their many uses : They connect and enliven tones and impart stresses and accent; . . . Expression is heightened by them; let a piece be sad, joyful, or otherwise, and they will lend a fitting assistance. . . . Without them the best melody is empty and ineffective, the clearest content clouded.[7]

Despite the increasing use of pedals, 'terrace dynamics', so-called because hand knobs meant that the registration could be altered only at the end of a section, remained a characteristic of the harpsichord style and, like the echo effect obtained when a passage was repeated softly, now palled. The limited range of timbres and degrees of volume were insufficient weapons in the hands of composers who sought the gradations in between as a means of greater musical expression. These qualities the piano offered.

In the last years of the eighteenth century the piano made rapid strides towards acceptance at the expense of the harpsichord. Kirkman and the Shudi partnership, whose fortunes now lay in the hands of John Broadwood, were wise enough to pioneer the new art of piano making. Kirkman made his last harpsichord at the turn of the century and Broadwood made only pianos after 1793. During the cold winter of 1816 the harpsichords confiscated from the nobility during the French Revolution, and which had been stored in the Paris Conservatoire, were used as firewood. The harpsichord and spinet were vanquished.

V

Aspects of the Mature Piano

Grand pianos are made today in various lengths from 1·37 metres (4 feet 6 inches) to the 2·90 metres (9 feet 6 inches) of the largest regularly made concert model. Two English makers, Danemann and Welmar, produce full length concert grands. The usual compass consists of seven-and-a-quarter-octaves, although since the turn of the century Bösendorfer has produced an eight-octave concert model providing in the bass an extra nine notes which are used occasionally in original compositions. Arnold Bax's Second Piano Sonata includes in its final chord G one tone below the usual lowest A (A''); at the more usual seven-and-a-quarter-octave keyboard pianists play G' a minor seventh above A''. The highest eighty-eighth note c'''' has been turned to account by Rachmaninoff and Dohnányi.

Most modern upright pianos offer a seven or seven-and-a-quarter-octave keyboard (Pl. 20), contemporary English manufacturers producing a larger proportion of seven-octave pianos than makers in other lands, most of whom make only seven-and-a-quarter octave models as many insist on the three additional top notes, although they are played seldom and their tone frequently lacks sparkle. The seven-and-a-quarter-octave compass is referred to often in Germany as seven-and-a-third-octaves as, if the highest a'''' of the seven-octave compass is counted, the extra third of an octave provides four notes and the octave comprises twelve notes. In addition a few six-octave uprights are built as limited space is occasionally a paramount factor.

The majority of piano owners have space sufficient only to house an upright piano, although technical and musical factors establish the primacy of the grand over the upright. The heavier hammers, greater string mass and larger soundboard area of the bigger grands create superior tone volume better projected by their horizontal form, the grand becoming automatic first choice for public work. Good upright tone, however, is satisfactory in

52

the average room. Because the strings of the grand piano are horizontal the hammer, striking from underneath the string, falls back from it influenced by gravity. Consequently the hammer is less reliant on the artificial devices of springs and tapes found on the vertical piano where gravitational forces alone are insufficient to return it to its position of rest. As a result the touch of the grand has greater 'springiness' and its repetition (the speed with which the note can be repeated) is usually superior to the upright. The grand action is more responsive therefore to the performer and this finesse places him in a better position to create and control effects of tone nuance. In ideal surroundings the tonal balance between bass, tenor and treble sections of the grand is superior, although if a large grand is played in a room too small, the bass may swamp the other registers and generate excessive overtone noise. The average pianist, however, finds that the upright is adequate to his requirements.

The heart of every piano is the strung back (Pl. 16). The strings' minute vibrations are transmitted to the soundboard which acts

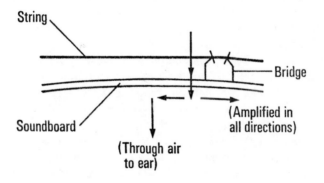

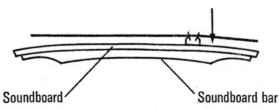

Fig. 15. *(above)* Transfer of vibration from a string. *(below)* down-bearing stress of a string on the soundboard

as an amplifier (Fig. 15). The strings and soundboard are attached to the iron frame which, sometimes assisted by the wooden parts, is the main stress-bearing component. A typical upright has 214 strings each strung at up to 84 kilogrammes (185 pounds) tension, exerting stresses on the iron frame of some 18,300 kilogrammes (18 tons). 183 metres (200 yards) of over forty different varieties of wire may be used.

The strings exert a down-bearing stress of up to 1015 kilogrammes (1 ton) on the soundboard (Fig. 15). To counteract this pressure, bars, made of the same pine or spruce resonance wood as the soundboard, are spaced across its back (Pl. 17). The soundboard is usually between 7 millimetres and 10 millimetres ($\frac{5}{16} - \frac{7}{16}$ inch) thick, the higher measurement normally in the board's treble section where greater stiffness is required—the thicker the board, the stiffer it becomes. Some makers have dispensed with this taper, the board becoming the same thickness throughout, and find the tone to be equally good. The soundboard is curved, producing a crown in the centre of some 5 millimetres ($\frac{1}{5}$ inch) when new, making it into a highly elastic spring. The crown increases the board's vibrational capacity and aids its resistance to the pressure of the strings.

The best resonance wood is strong, highly elastic and light, and so responsive to the most minute blow. Ideally the annual rings should be an even 1–2 millimetres ($\frac{1}{16}$ inch) apart—the sign of slow growth. The grain should be straight and free of knots and gum pockets. The wood should be cut 'on the quarter' (i.e. in the direction of the centre, Fig. 16), reducing dimensional changes in sympathy with humidity variations and also minimizing the risk of splitting. A cool climate assists slow growth and so resonance wood is grown often at 1,000–1,250 metres (3,000–4,000 feet) or higher. Absence of sunlight discourages rapid growth as does planting close together, which also encourages straight grain and discourages branches, which after removal leave knots. Mountain wind and snow by 'stretching' the trees encourage elasticity, another desirable characteristic. Trees between seventy and one hundred years old are believed to provide the strength and elasticity characteristic of the best resonance wood. They should be felled in winter and the best lower trunks selected for soundboard wood—an old method of selection, now no longer in common use, was to peel the bark to 1 metre (3 feet) above the

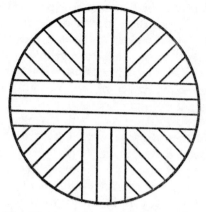

Fig. 16. A method of quarter sawing

ground on the south side of the trunk and to strike the exposed spot with a chopper. A pure bright tone denoted quality, a deep dull one was a sign of poor resonance. Another method of selection was to listen for a high lasting singing tone as the trunks slid down a wooden chute. It used to be thought that to split, rather than cut, the trunk 'on the quarter' produced a better tone as the fibres would remain uninjured. A crude method of measuring elasticity was to drop a hammer on the board and to measure the distance of its rebound.

All the boards for one soundboard should come from the same trunk, although various theories were entertained about the best choice for certain areas of the board—frequently it was thought that boards with the closest annual rings should be allocated to the treble area and those with the widest rings to the bass. Sometimes allocation to bass or treble was carried out in the piano factory by 'tapping'.

In the twentieth century, however, it is uneconomic for the average producer to select trees with such care. The highest grades of commercially-cut timber are purchased by the piano trade, but often boards with as few as five growth rings per inch (indicating that the tree took five years to produce an inch of growth) compared with the ideal of fourteen to twenty, have to be accepted—not to do so would be to invite phenomenal waste and resonance wood is costly to obtain.

The early piano makers used Bavarian and Alpine pine. When

suitable material from these sources became exhausted during the last century, pine from the Carpathian mountains of Rumania became popular (violin makers to this day often refer to the Carpathian material as 'Swiss pine'). Now genuine Rumanian pine is scarce. The West German piano industry normally uses Bavarian pine (confusingly often spoken of in this country as 'Rumanian') offering a near-white appearance, and many English makers use Alaskan or Canadian sitka spruce, both having a pinkish tint.

An extremely critical native climate has led several American makers to introduce laminated, often three-ply, soundboards, which with the grain running in opposite directions, are unlikely to split. Considerations of cost have induced some to present outer layers of spruce with a core of a cheaper mahogany—with inevitably poorer tonal properties.

Experiments have been carried out with non-wooden materials. Glass has the conclusive disadvantage of breaking easily! Light metals transmit soundwaves rapidly, but have higher densities than the best pine. Iron transmits soundwaves fastest of all the metals at 5,110 metres (16,800 feet) per second, but is too heavy. Nylon, perspex and other plastics transmit at lower speeds than pine, for the best pine and spruce possess most of the desirable characteristics. Soundwaves travel along the grain of the pine soundboard at some 16,640 kilometres per hour (10,400 miles per hour), or fourteen times the speed of sound through air, known as the sound barrier. The waves travel at only a quarter of this speed across the grain. A function of the bars is to help speed the vibrations in this direction, so increasing the evenness of the board's vibrations.

The purpose of linking the strings, which by themselves determine the pitch of the note, to the soundboard is not often appreciated. Wire with its small diameter covers only a small area. When in vibration one side of the string produces a condensation, or squeezing together of the air, at the same time as the other allows the formation of a rarefaction, or reduction of air pressure. The small diameter permits the air to slip round behind the string, making the audibility of the string's vibration negligible. So the string alone does not move enough air to create a truly audible soundwave. Therefore the piano maker transfers the strings' vibrations via the bridge to the soundboard, which covers a much larger area thereby setting in motion a greater volume of air, producing sound more audible to the human ear. Sound-waves are created from 76 millimetres (3 inches) to 12·20 metres (40 feet) in length.

The relationship between the thickness and length of the strings is a factor determining tonal quality. A long thin string at high tension has a high overtone content and so produces a brighter more penetrating tone. The upright of some 1·04 metres (41 inches) and upwards produces a purer tone in the bass than the miniature upright, as in the latter the soundboard area is too small for the long wave-lengths of the low frequencies. In addition the bass strings are too short and too thick, and therefore too stiff, causing the string to vibrate in uneven segments, forming fewer overtones and those largely unpleasant inharmonic ones. Tonal quality is affected by additional factors, often difficult to control and even to identify, in the soundboard. A thick sound-board under great tension produces a hard, sharp tone; if it is less tensed the overtones do not form so readily and a softer tone results. The more effective the soundboard, the more rapidly it uses up the string's energy and so the volume is louder, but the duration shorter. If on the other hand the dissipation of energy is slower, the tone sounds for longer, but its power is less. The relationships between strings and soundboard and their various properties are delicate. The soundboard is rightly called the heart of the piano. It has been described also as a mass of nerves, responsive to the most minute shocks.

The strung back and the hammers are the main determinants of tone. The hammers are thick in the bass in order to be of sufficient weight to set in motion a thick heavy string. In the treble they are light and pointed, as otherwise the short-lived vibrations of the short and very stiff treble strings would be smothered and deadened.

Tone colour is influenced by toning, the process of pricking the hammer felts with a needle to bring the felt to its required density—hard in the treble, tapering to a softer texture in the bass. In its untoned state felt graduates from hard to soft with insufficient accuracy and produces an uneven tone, many notes sounding brighter or duller than their neighbours. If the felt is toned with a needle sufficiently, it becomes softer and less tight-packed. Consequently it rebounds more slowly from the string and stays in contact with it longer (about 1/250 second). The longer the hammer remains in contact with the string, the less chance the string stands of breaking into smaller vibrating segments which form the higher overtones, adding to the harshness and brightness of the tone. The most exacting standards lead to as many as eight hours spent on toning in the piano factory.

Frequent use leads to the hammer's impact on the string compressing and hardening the felt. The striking surface is flattened by the string cutting into it, increasing the area of contact and deadening the tone, which becomes gradually harsher. Some toning may become necessary to restore the felt to its original softer state.

The intermediary between the finger on the key and the hammer is the system of levers known as the action (Pl. 18, Fig. 17). A mechanical relationship of 1:5 exists between the distance

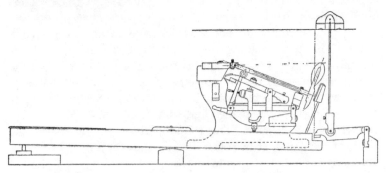

Fig. 17. Schwander modern roller grand action

the key goes down (frequently 9·5 millimetres = $\frac{3}{8}$ inch) and the distance the hammer covers (typically 47·5 millimetres = $1\frac{7}{8}$ inch) to the string. An average weight of touch is 52 grammes (1·83 ounces). Touch weight is normally heavier in the bass than in the treble, the bass hammers being heavier, the damper springs necessary to quieten the thicker bass strings being stronger and overstringing causing the back sections of the bass keys to be longer and thicker. These factors can be overcome only partially by weighting of individual keys. Of the six thousand pieces in a piano some four thousand five hundred are in the action, which incorporates two different leathers and four grades of felt, requiring different degrees of firmness and smoothness to assist in the attainment of a smooth touch.

The main object of the action, apart from impelling the hammer to the string and achieving an agreeable touch, is to obtain rapid repetition. Good repetition should enable the note to be repeated six times per second. To play the same note twice very quickly, the set-off button (Pl. 18) causes the jack to slip out from under the butt before the hammer hits the string, so that the hammer travels 2–3 millimetres ($\frac{1}{16} - \frac{1}{8}$ inch) under its own impetus. On the rebound the hammer is checked about 15 millimetres (c. $\frac{5}{8}$ inch) from the string (Pl. 19) and when the key begins to rise, the jack aided by a spring slips quickly back into position. The note now can be repeated more swiftly than otherwise would be possible, as the key has not risen to its original rest position and the hammer does not travel the full distance.

Changes of humidity affect the action at its most critical points, the moving centres. In dry conditions the wood (in Europe usually hornbeam), in which a circle or bushing of cloth is inserted and in which the flange pin (Pl. 19) moves, dries and in so doing contracts away from the pin which becomes loose, causing a clicking noise. The looseness causes the hammer to wobble and to strike the string with a different part of its face, giving tonal unevenness. In humid, damp conditions the opposite happens, expansion causing the wood and cloth of action and key to tighten around their respective pins, so that notes stick. This common experience may make old and new pianos difficult to play when weather conditions change rapidly. Plastic flanges on the other hand, introduced by some manufacturers in the last fifteen years to replace the clothbushed centres, have overcome the problem which had troubled piano makers since the instrument's invention as they are unresponsive to humidity changes. Variations in humidity also cause the action felts and leathers to swell and shrink, resulting in unevenness of touch. The action, like the engine of a car, needs regulation to maintain it in first-class condition.

Modern controlled drying, or kilning, of timber before processing in the factory has helped to diminish the havoc precipitated by changes of climate. Moisture from the timber's cell cavities and walls can be removed by natural air seasoning or by forced kiln drying. Prior to the Second World War sawn planks used to be left for up to seven years in the open air, drying gradually and evenly. The humidity contained in the air, however, saw to it that drying by this method seldom brought the moisture content of the wood below 16 per cent. Beech destined for tuning planks, and resonance wood then were dried for a further spell inside the factory near the ceiling to take advantage of the old dictum that hot air rises. Some still prefer this method arguing that forced artificial drying robs wood of its 'life'. Since 1945, however, the practice of kilning has become widespread, partly as few manufacturers can afford to keep several years' supply of timber seasoning in the open. Kilning dries wood more rapidly (typically between two and five weeks, depending on species and thickness) down to lower moisture contents than are otherwise possible. It is considered still desirable to air-dry freshly sawn timber, a fairly rapid process, to a moderate moisture content, but many believe that kilning is in no way harmful, providing that it is carried out at a speed which dries out the complete cross-section of the timber uniformly—if the outer section loses its moisture more rapidly than the inner section it tries to contract, but because the inner section has not shrunk, the outer section unable to do so, splits. To control this process kilns use heat, moisture provided by steam, and ventilation to control humidity and thereby the speed at which the wood's moisture is surrendered to the surrounding air.

Soundboard wood is dried by modern kilns to moisture contents as low as 4 per cent and because the planks re-absorb moisture in the atmosphere after kilning, the made-up soundboard is baked immediately prior to the glueing of the soundboard bars. This treatment obviates splitting in the driest parts of the world to which pianos find their way.

The kilning process, however, presents a miniature of what may happen to furniture and musical instruments in centrally-heated homes, where the moisture present in the air is so little that it endeavours to suck moisture from objects in the room, should these contain more moisture than the air. This process ceases only when both are equally moist and equilibrium is attained. When moisture is surrendered before equilibrium (in centrally-heated England typically between 8 and 10 per cent moisture content) is reached, little significant harm is done to furniture made from kilned wood—this is the primary reason for kilning.

The absence of controlled drying causes wooden skirting boards (often at moisture contents of over 20 per cent since builders frequently leaves timbers exposed to rain) in new houses to shrink objectionably. Pre-war pianos may be little use in centrally-heated rooms because, prior to the acceptance of central heating and kiln drying, the wood was dried inadequately before manufacturing. Soundboards may shrink and split, and tuning planks contract, causing loose tuning pins and instruments which refuse to stand in tune. The casework may split—an experience common with antique furniture. One means of alleviation is to place humidifiers near radiators so that the dry air draws moisture from them. Better still if the central heating is maintained at a temperature which holds relative humidity at 50–60 per cent—a pleasant level avoiding headaches and throat irritations caused by excessively dry air. All natural materials, even carpet and curtain fibres, as they dry become brittle, causing extra wear as the individual fibres split more easily.

Similar movements of moisture cause pianos to need tuning two or three times annually. Soundboards are sealed and varnished to prevent as far as possible moisture entering or leaving, but when humidity increases the board absorbs moisture, causing swelling which raises the bridge (Fig. 15) and increases the strings' tension so that pitch rises. In extreme central heating the opposite happens—the soundboard contracts and pitch falls. Temperature changes without humidity changes have little effect on a piano— humidity is the vital factor. Providing humidity changes are gradual minimum harm is done; it is rapid changes which are harmful.

Like most things mechanical a new piano takes time to settle down. Most of the wire's initial stretch is removed during tunings in the factory. In addition when the instrument is newly strung many makers rub a wheel along the wire, forcing it downwards and thereby stretching it. The average piano receives two 'chips' and two tunings in the factory to a slightly higher pitch than that to which it settles ultimately. 'Chipping up' acquires its name from the 'chipper' or plectrum used to sound the strings before the hammers have been inserted. The longer the instrument is left to settle between tunings, the better.

During performance the hammers' blows tense the strings and any residual stretch may result in their going out of tune. The soundboard may 'give' slightly under the strings' downward pressure causing a small reduction in string tension and so drop

61

in pitch. Furthermore the action felts compress as they impact in other parts of the mechanism, losing fine accuracy of touch and making adjustment necessary.

It is a common belief that tone improves with age. It may be true that in the initial years the soundboard settles under the strings' down-bearing pressures to a curvature which it finds most conducive to tone production, and that the soundboard's fibres acquire facility and responsiveness in vibrating to their best advantage, forming their own patterns of response. This pattern is even more relevant to the violin, which many believe to be affected also by the composition of the varnish. The sealer and varnish applied to the piano soundboard are intended to hold flows of moisture to a minimum and to give a smooth protective finish. If the weight of varnish is excessive the soundboard's response may be retarded, but in practice the varnish is believed to have little influence on piano tone. The surface skin of the hammers receive their first indentations from impact on the strings and they too are 'played in'. These factors explain the common experience that a piano acquires greater tonal warmth after several years' use.

The average piano has up to half a century's life before its inherent virtues begin to be played out. In smaller towns grands made eighty years ago are found still in concert use, although most have acquired a coarse falseness of tone, impossible to eradicate on instruments so old. How does age destroy the instrument's tonal beauties? The soundboard loses its resilience so that the strings force its curvature to go into reverse. Losing the position it was designed to settle in, it surrenders its supple elasticity and so forfeits its sensitivity. As its grain ages its response may become uneven, distorting the overtone patterns. The wire loses its flexibility and becomes stiffer, causing further distortion. Unless the hammers are renewed or satisfactorily refaced, they wear, the hammer nose losing its roundness and a flatter section striking the string. The felt's lower levels normally having been toned less, they are also harder and both flatness and hardness alter the overtone structure.

Age takes its toll of action and keys. The bushings surrounding the key pins and action flange pins wear and need replacing. Felts subject to friction—prime examples are the butt leather (Pl. 18) and lever felt (Pl. 18)—need replacing. Bad design accentuates friction which, due to the angles which are established, results from unavoidable compromise in reducing the height of the low upright. Compression and wear affect felts which impact in one another—for example the balance head (Pl. 19) and check (Pl. 19). Wear means replacement, as otherwise sloppiness of touch results from lost motion caused by wear and sensitivity of touch is destroyed.

The choice of timber for the casework influences the tonal character of clavichord and harpsichord. The tone producing components of these instruments are weak compared with the piano and their casework is thin. The vast majority of sound is transmitted by the soundboard, the casework material having only a small beneficial effect on volume, but depending on design a considerable effect on overtone content, tonal quality and stability of tuning. The piano's case is more robust and is not designed to give added resonance. Consequently although theoretically it may affect tonal richness (the rim (Pl. 25) of any good grand vibrates to the lower bass notes to an extent which can be felt), in practice it has little influence. The same is true of plastic parts introduced in recent years to the action in place of horn-beam, a very hard timber used for butchers' chopping blocks and chosen for the facility with which it can be drilled with an engineer's precision. The cabinet of the upright piano, however, subdues tonal volume and if the lid is opened the sound is better able to escape.

Veneers have been used for thousands of years, but often prejudice ensured that a veneered article was viewed as inferior to an item constructed of solid timber alone. Veneering was rediscovered when glues were developed and as glues have gained in reliability so veneering techniques have acquired respectability. Many solid timbers—for example walnut or palisander (rosewood, so called because of the aroma the veneer gives off)—are exorbitantly expensive, but by conversion into veneer the species becomes readily available. A further advantage of cutting into veneers is that decorative effects can be obtained, which would be incapable of achievement in solid timber. These are grain effects—figure, growth markings and grain peculiarities. The most common method of producing decorative veneers is to slice the log across the grain. Individual pieces differ only in minutest detail from neighbouring pieces, making matching effects easy.

63

Additional decorative effects may be obtained by inlay and marquetry (the former defined as inletting small pieces of wood or materials like mother-of-pearl or ivory into cavities cut in solid wood; the latter as patterns formed by several woods inlaid into a veneer, so that veneer and inlay form one sheet which then is mounted on a solid surface), both crafts practised today by a handful of surviving highly skilled craftsmen.

Plastic substitute veneers and grain printing of cheap plain veneers to obtain desired patterns have won increasing popularity in the last decade and may have deadened public sensibility to highly exotic veneer effects. On the other hand these new techniques are unlikely to make substantial headway in piano manufacture because of the large variety and comparatively small quantities of piano finishes required, but more importantly because the moment it is understood that the piano is finished in a man-made substitute for original veneer, the public rejects it, knowing instinctively that there is no substitute for genuine veneer on what should be the best-finished item of furniture in the home.

Variable colouring of genuine veneer can cause concern to the piano owner and can be overcome partially by time-honoured staining techniques. The purple tint contained in American walnut compares unfavourably with the brown colour of traditional French walnut and more recently to remove it a bleaching technique has won some acceptance.

'Fading' is a frequently misunderstood natural phenomenon because depending upon species, often it is darkening and not fading. It is particularly irksome on a piano, where the lid over the keys alternates between open and closed positions. The ultra-violet rays contained in natural and in strong artificial light cause certain woods to darken with age. Usually the process is gradual and noticed little, but in an extreme case if the piano lid is open for a long time and the instrument subjected to strong light, when the lid is closed a line is visible along the top door (Pl. 20). The lower part of the top door, concealed by the open lid which protects it from the light, has not darkened to the same extent as other exposed parts. If the lid is closed, eventually the previously protected area darkens naturally and catches up. Experimental work has produced a barrier application to shield the veneer from penetration by ultra-violet rays, but it is expensive and

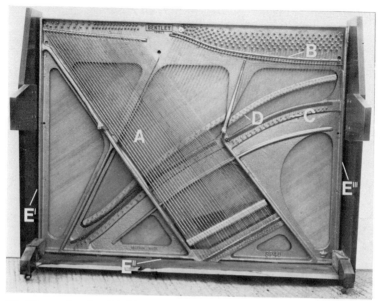

16. Strung back of 1·09 metres (43 inches) upright by Bentley of Stroud, England. Key: A, Bass strings cross over middle strings (over-stringing); B, pressure bar; C, hitch pin table; D, string portion on non-sounding side of bridge; E′, E″, E‴, additional outer rims used in 'backless' frames

17. Soundboard and barring of 0·97 metres (38 inches) upright by Bentley. Key: A, soundboard bar

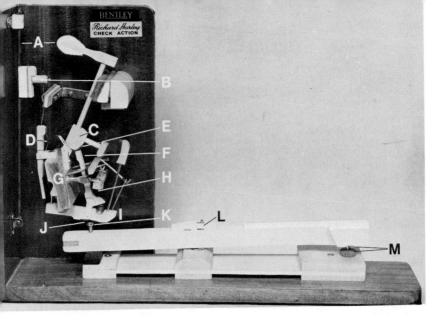

18. Bentley 'Richard Harley' upright action—key at rest. Key: A, 47·5 mm ($1\frac{7}{8}$ inches) blow; B, damper drum; C, butt; D, damper spring; E, butt leather; F, jack; G, action beam; H, set-off button; I, lever; J, lever felt; K, pilot; L, chasing; M, 9·5 mm ($\frac{3}{8}$ inch) touch depth

19. Bentley 'Richard Harley' upright action—hammer in checked position. Key: A, *c.* 15 mm (*c.* $\frac{5}{8}$ ins) checked distance; B, balance head; C, check; D, jack spring; E′ E″, E‴, E⁗, flange pin in flange

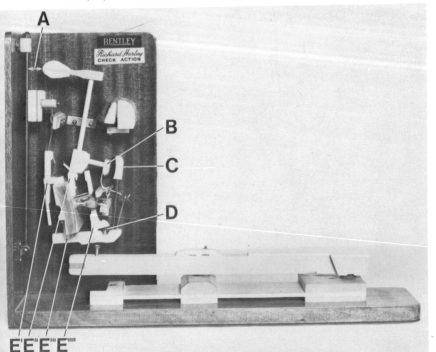

20. Upright piano. *c.* 1976. 'Apollo' model by Bentley. Key: A, bottom door; B, lid or fall; C, top door; D, treble end

21. Square pianoforte. 1767. By Johann Zumpe of London

22. Grand piano. 1775–80. By Heilmann of Mainz. Viennese action

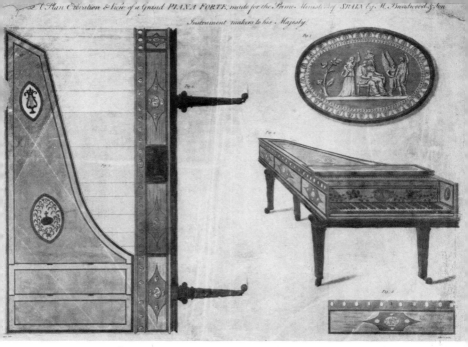

23. Design for a grand piano by Thomas Sheraton. 1796. Made by Broadwood of London and sold for £223 13s. 0d. to the Prime Minister of Spain. Sheraton omitted the pedals which he considered objectionable

24. Square piano. 1800–15. By Muzio Clementi & Co. of London

25. Grand piano. 1806. By John Broadwood & Sons of London. Showing separate bass bridge introduced by Broadwood. Key: A; horizontal veneer on rim; B; separate bass

26. 'Portable Grand Pianoforte'. 1801. By John Isaac Hawkins of Philadelphia. One of the first uprights with strings extending below the keyboard to ground level

27. The same instrument with case work. The panelling below the keyboard is a Venetian Swell. The inscription above the keyboard reads: "J. I. Hawkins Invenit et Fecit. Patent. No. 6. 1801. Philadelphia"

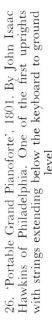

28. Cabinet upright piano. 1800–12. Maker unknown. Height 1·89
metres (6 feet 2½ inches). Mahogany casework with elaborate inlay
depicting birds, butterflies and plants

complicated and so has won little acceptance. Inspection of the underneath of a dining-room table convinces—light wood underneath contrasts with the table top, darkened by exposure to a stronger light.

Since 1945 there has been considerable growth in the use of wood in forms other than the solid. First came plywood, formed by glueing layers of wood veneer together and offering enhanced strength. Chipboard followed some years later and currently is applied widely despite often inappropriate criticism, for correctly treated it offers outstanding stability of shape in changing humidity conditions. Formed of small wood chips glued together under high pressure, chipboard offers the advantage that, so long as both faces are treated equally (otherwise a stress or pull is set up on one face), no warping or twisting takes place because there is no grain. Chipboard often is lipped round the edges with solid wood as means of concealment and of ensuring that screws and mountings are fastened to solid wood. Numerous manufacturers of expensive furniture and illustrious pianos use chipboard, undetectable to the eye.

Glue was employed to bond pieces of furniture three thousand five hundred years ago, but after the Roman Empire fell glue was not used extensively. Dry joints were utilized and much superb wooden roofing—a severe test—was constructed using mortice and tenon joints and wooden (often oak) pegs. Such glues as were available employed 'natural' components—bone, skin and fish offal, animal blood and protein from milk (casein). Veneering was not introduced widely until the sixteenth century and subsequently experience was acquired. The art of cross-banding, for example, glued three veneers together, the grain direction of the centre veneer at a right angle to that of the two veneers either side of it—an attempt to prevent warping and indeed the earliest attempt at plywood. Glued joints were reintroduced and the first glue factory was established in the early eighteenth century, growing demand leading to attempts at improving the properties of animal glues. In the early twentieth century the manufacture of laminated (i.e. glued together) timber parts was growing and so also was the aircraft industry. Both made substantial use of casein glues, recently developed and at the time offering the best resistance to water. Vegetable starch, blood albumin and soya bean glues followed. Synthetic resin adhesives were to prove the most important new type, however, and their introduction commenced in the 1930s.

The term 'synthetic resin' often gives rise to misunderstanding because 'synthetic' suggests artificial production of chemical or plastic-based products, but these in their turn frequently derive from natural materials. Resins, obtained from trees, the ground and insects, are also natural. With the rapid development over the last thirty years of the chemical and plastic industries, synthetic resin glues, of which there are now numerous categories, largely have replaced natural 'animal' glues as the former are able to offer superior properties in demanding conditions.

Animal glues offer resistance to hot dry conditions but not to the humid conditions encountered in many tropical areas. Casein glues offer greater but still inadequate resistance to moisture. Consequently pianos exported to the tropics were 'tropicalized' involving casework which was frequently solid and unveneered, and hammer felt impregnated to resist insect attack. The natural key coverings and chasings (Pl. 18) were pinned and the sharps were screwed, both to prevent the pieces falling off if the glue joint failed due to excessive humidity in the air. In addition soundboard bars and bridges were screwed, although if the glue fixing them to the soundboard failed, while they did not fall off, a discordant tone resulted. The planks in a soundboard needed to be tongued and grooved, rather than glued by a flat butt joint as is usual with modern glues, because animal glues were unable to provide a joint which would hold fast under the strain to which the soundboard is subjected when heavy chords are struck.

Those synthetic resins which set by hardening under the influence of a catalyst causing chemical change, did not suffer from these disadvantages as the change could not be reversed by adverse climatic conditions.

The pianist and scientist often differ about the artist's ability to vary tone by the manner used to depress the key. Many pianists maintain stoutly that their method of touch affects the tone colour produced by the instrument. The scientist argues that this is impossible as from the moment the jack flies out from underneath the butt, the finger loses contact with the hammer and so has no means of controlling it when it strikes the string. The resulting note depends solely on velocity, which the player controls by striking the key with varying force.

The pianist influences other factors, which may lead him to conclude that his touch determines tonal qualities. The degree of legato influences tone, as it effects the way one note flows into the next and so the resulting overtone pattern. The sustaining pedal adds to the note being played the sympathetic vibrations of other strings. Effects obtainable by judicious use of the pedal may be thought to originate in finger touch. The scientific view concludes that finger touch can determine the volume, but not the tone colour.

It is surprising how little attention is given to the proper use of different pedalling methods. The sustaining pedal raises the dampers from the strings. When a note is struck its overtones, closely corresponding with the fundamental pitch of strings above, cause those strings to vibrate and so to sound in sympathy. This phenomenon is demonstrated simply. Press down a' and e'' so gently that they do not sound and hold them down so that their dampers are held away from the strings. Then play note a with a short sharp impact. After the damper has silenced it, a' and e'', first and second overtones of note a, continue sounding. Pedalling therefore adds volume and resonance by introducing further notes and overtones.

Until the mid-nineteenth century the pedal was depressed usually at the same instant as the note was struck. Liszt, Kullak and others propagated syncopated pedalling, or depression of the pedal slightly *after* the note was struck—by this time the impure mechanical noise contained to greater or lesser degree in piano notes has faded but the overtone content, summoning into sound the higher strings, is still present. Syncopation produces clear, pure sounds. In the early twentieth century pedalling *before* the attack (the anticipated or acoustic pedal) was first mentioned. The note attains maximum tonal volume instantaneously and therefore the attack achieves greater effect although mechanical noise may be magnified. Pedalling *after* the note is played has become the most common method.

Two additional pedalling accomplishments may be mentioned. Half-pedalling comprises raising the pedal rapidly and quickly depressing it again, the dampers touching the strings only briefly and lightly damping the weaker treble strings while merely reducing the volume of the bass strings. Half-pedalling is employed also to cut back a mass of tone and Liszt was probably one of its earliest masters. Pedal-tremolo involves small rapid movements of the pedal avoiding its total release. The effect is rapidly to disperse dissonant sounds into consonant ones without deadening resonance.

VI

The Piano's Beginnings in Europe, 1710-1800

Literary references to several instruments, their details often veiled in obscurity, show that the idea of fitting keys to an instrument whose strings are set in motion by striking with hammers, had been thought of probably as early as the fourteenth and certainly in the fifteenth century. In the former century mention is made of an instrument known variously in Spain as *'exaquir'* and in France as *'échiquier'* or exceptionally as the *'eschaquier d'Angleterre'*. Why in France it should have been associated with England is uncertain, but it is known that the English King Edward III, who for five years had held captive King John II, *'le Bon'*, presented an *échiquier* to the French monarch in 1360, the year of his release. Although in poetry, accounts and correspondence of the same period several references are made to the *échiquier*, little is known of its nature. It is believed to have been a stringed instrument possessing a keyboard. It has been suggested that the string was plucked or that the key propelled a wooden block which in free flight struck the string. The latter at any rate coincides with an action described by Henri Arnault of Zwolle in the Low Countries writing in about 1435, although scholars are far from certain that Arnault was describing an *échiquier*. *Échiquier* means 'chessboard' and 'exchequer', and although it is hard to associate the instrument's name with monetary administration, it has been surmised that either its black and white keys or the pattern of the casework suggested the chessboard.

As the sixteenth century drew to a close greater musical lyricism produced the invention of the cantata, a secular song in the style of a recitative, accompanied by a single instrument. The cantata grew out of discussions held at a meeting in Florence of amateur musicians, the participants determining to attempt a revival of classical drama founded on tragedies of the Greek poets. At this meeting Vincenzo Galilei, father of the astronomer Galileo, referred to an attempt at producing tonal variety by bowing the strings of a harpsichord. The *'Nürmbergisch Geigenwerck'* was founded on this principle, the key pressing the string against a revolving wheel. Doubtless the idea was suggested either by the bowed string instruments (*Geige* means 'violin', coming to the fore at the time), or by the hurdy-gurdy. Hans Haydn made such an instrument in about 1600 in Nürnberg and it was described in considerable detail by Michael Praetorius in 1618–1620. Similar attempts at a successful *'Geigenwerck'* continued in Germany into the eighteenth century.

A step nearer to the piano may have been the *'Piano e Forte'*, so called by its maker, an Italian called Paliarino, who mentioned it in letters dated 1598 to the Duke of Modena. Although a further attempt to introduce tonal variety, it is not known whether it had hammers. In the fifteenth century a drawing was made of a dulcimer with keys and in 1610 a kind of keyed dulcimer was made, of Dutch origin and with minute hammers joined to the keys, which provided four octaves.

Despite these intimations it was not until the eighteenth century that conditions evolved which were to make possible the victory of the piano over its domestic rivals, the clavichord and harpsichord. The initial development of the new instrument was inevitably slow.

The credit for the invention of the piano is given to Bartolommeo Cristofori, a Paduan harpsichord maker responsible for the care of forty harpsichords and spinets belonging to Prince Ferdinand de' Medici. He made the first known piano in about 1709 in Florence, calling it *'gravicembalo col piano e forte'*, the phrase "with soft and loud" indicating that its distinctiveness lay in the variety of tone gradation it offered. It differed from the harpsichord in its action mechanism, for deer leather hammers took the place of the harpsichord's jacks.

By 1726 Cristofori had built about twenty *'gravicembalos'*. The action of the later ones (Fig. 18) made in the 1720s had a padded check, an improvement on Cristofori's earlier spring, to catch the hammer. Also introduced was the una corda system, whereby the keyboard moves sideways so that hammers striking two or three strings to a note strike one string fewer. This mechanism was operated by two levers under the keyboard.

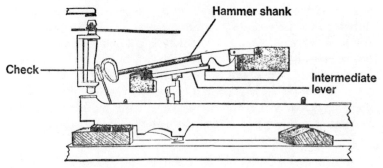

Fig. 18. Improved action by Cristofori

Whether the clavichord, whose tangent strikes the string, or the idea of the keyed dulcimer led to Cristofori's use of hammers is uncertain. It could be that he had heard about a kind of primitive keyed xylophone with hammers travelling upwards to strike tubes of wood, which was described in 1637 by Father Mersenne. The essential difference of the piano is that, due to the 'escapement' the finger has no contact with the hammer at the moment it strikes the string. If contact were maintained as in the case of the clavichord, the hammer would remain pressed against the string until released by the key, transforming the note into a dull thud. The force of the finger striking the key determines the hammer's impact on the string, enabling notes to be played softer or louder at will, creating the distinctive expressiveness of the piano.

Cristofori's mechanism was already more complicated than the clavichord's. His action shows that he recognized the problems which were to occupy piano designers for the next hundred years and more—the 'escapement' allowing the hammer to rebound from the string and the necessity of then catching the hammer before it falls back to its original position, so that the note can be repeated more quickly than would be possible if the hammer had to cover the greater distance.

Numerous problems emerged as the piano developed. For example, the impetus of the hammer striking the string could cause the shank (Fig. 18) to snap; until the check was perfected, the hammer tended to bounce back on to the string a second and even a third time, causing unwanted sounds; in due course the

71

strings need to be thicker to prevent breakage under the hammer's impact, thus necessitating a more substantial soundboard and frame to carry them. These changes gradually developed the '*gravicembalo*' out of all recognition, so that it bore no resemblance to the 'harpsichord with hammers'.

Scipione Maffei, writing in 1711 in the *Giornale de' Letterati d'Italia*, defended Cristofori's instruments from their detractors and seems to have had a remarkable grasp of the possibilities of the infant piano:

> Some professors have not awarded to this instrument all the approval it warrants; firstly, as they have failed to comprehend the skill necessary to conquer its complexities, nor the marvellous nicety of hand needed to fulfil the task with such accuracy; secondly, as they thought the sound of such an instrument, differing from that they were familiar with, was too subdued and dead. This sensation, however, arises only when the hands encounter it for the first time, as we are accustomed to the silvery tone of the other harpsichords. . . . Furthermore it has been objected that this instrument lacks great tonal volume, nor does it possess the whole forte of other harpsichords. The reply could be given that, firstly, it possesses much more tone than is commonly realised, when he who desires to, and knows how to, brings it forth as he strikes the keys energetically;. . . . In fact, however, the most important opposition which has been placed before this new instrument, is the general lack of knowledge at the first encounter concerning how it should be played, for it is not enough to be able to perform fluently upon conventional keyboard instruments. As it is a new instrument, it demands someone who, comprehending its possibilities, has studied it particularly, so as to regulate the strength of the blows necessary to be imparted to the keys to produce gracious contrasts at the appropriate moment, and to choose suitable pieces. . . .[8]

Organists and harpsichordists clearly found difficulty in varying the force which they used to depress the keys. The new kind of touch which piano playing demanded, was to emerge slowly, but the time was not yet ripe.

Nonetheless in 1732 the first published work written specifically for the new instrument appeared in Florence—Ludovico Giustini's twelve sonatas 'for soft and loud harpsichord, commonly called mallet-harpsichord'. The instructions '*forte*', '*piano*' and even '*più piano*' showed the player where to vary his tone (Fig. 19).

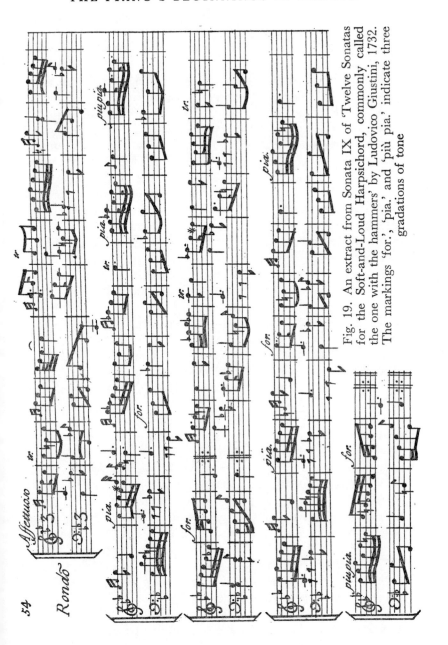

Fig. 19. An extract from Sonata IX of 'Twelve Sonatas for the Soft-and-Loud Harpsichord, commonly called the one with the hammers' by Ludovico Giustini, 1732. The markings 'for.', 'pia.' and 'più pia.', indicate three gradations of tone

73

Although Cristofori's new piano did not take root in Italy, it is easy to understand why it was made first in the country where musicians had long valued expression. They were first to write expression marks into music at least a hundred years before the piano was invented. Hence Italian usually is used for this purpose to this day. Secular song, leading to the birth in Italy of opera, gave greater scope for expression. In addition the more dramatic style, which already by the seventeenth century was replacing the older dignified type of counterpoint, showed the value of accentuation. The instruments built by Cristofori coincided with the peak of Stradivarius' achievement. The rise of the great Italian violinists showed the value of 'espressione' and the string orchestra, which was introduced even into church services, was used for experiments in expression. The gradations of tone available on the violin's bowed string came to be desired for the plucked string of the harpsichord.

Because expressive playing leaves so much to the sensitivity and good judgment of the performer, the eighteenth century was to witness the growing importance of personal interpretation, which for a time in the following century was to become all important in the art of piano playing.

Within a few years of Cristofori building his first 'gravicembalo' experiments made by others show the continuation of the search, now more persistent, for an alternative to the precise tone of the harpsichord.

In 1716 in Paris Jean Marius, who may have heard Hebenstreit perform when the latter visited Paris in 1705, made several models of an action mechanism for a 'clavecin à maillets'. He submitted his designs to the Académie Royale des Sciences, but they received little attention beyond polite praise. Marius had to wait for posterity to recognize his achievement, which later appealed to French pride, for as late as the Paris Exposition of 1855 it was claimed that Marius without contradiction beat Cristofori and Schröter to the invention of the piano.

Shortly after the submission by Marius of his models, Christoph Schröter, a musician of Leipzig, having heard Hebenstreit play his pantaleon, had the idea 'to invent a keyboard instrument upon which one could play loud or soft at will'. Not being a practical man he enlisted the help of his cousin, a cabinetmaker, and between them they produced a double model incorporating two different designs of hammer action. Schröter could not afford to have an instrument made utilizing his designs and he lacked the necessary skills to make it himself. So Schröter took his double model to the Court at Dresden, but although the king led him to believe that a complete pianoforte would be made according to one of his two designs, it never materialized. After the hammer action principle became well-known and every instrument maker worth his salt was claiming the invention for himself, Schröter became embittered and proclaimed in print that the invention was his, that Silbermann, the 'ingenious man at Dresden', and even Cristofori had copied his design, and that the differences between the action designs were accounted for by their miscomprehension of his invention! At any rate no less a personage than Beethoven believed that the piano was conceived in Germany : '. . . Hämmer-Klavier is certainly German and it was also a German invention. . . .'[9]

Germany was to be the home of the next developments following Schröter's model. Gottfried Silbermann maintained Hebenstreit's pantaleon and clearly had thought of operating the fast-flying mallets by keys instead of human muscle, so that the effects obtainable on the pantaleon would be placed within reach of a larger number of players. A translation of Maffei's article appeared in Hamburg in 1725. Silbermann certainly read it as it was published by a friend of his, König, the Dresden court poet. The action mechanism of his instruments shows that Cristofori's influence was considerable.

In 1736 Silbermann apparently showed his instruments to J. S. Bach, who was visiting Dresden. The master criticized their heavy touch and weak treble. Johann Agricola, who studied with Bach and who later was appointed court composer by Frederick the Great, recounted that Silbermann was 'angry with Mr Bach for a long time'. Silbermann subsequently improved the action so that in 1746 Frederick accepted one and by 1747 owned fifteen. It was believed that Bach found acceptable Silbermann's pianos during his famous visit to the king at Potsdam in 1747. Bach, however, did not grasp the potentiality of the infant 'Forte and Piano', and showed no further interest in it.

Silbermann was a renowned practical joker in his youth. One sympathizes with villagers who, so the story has it, unwittingly brought into action hidden guns fired by a trip-rope, a trap which

the youthful Gottfried had constructed before persuading them to
dig by night for non-existent treasure. Shortly after he escaped
to Strasbourg! In later life Silbermann became the renowned
builder of forty-seven church organs and the first person to be
successful enough to make piano building his leading activity.

Others besides Silbermann and the Saxons were starting to
make pianos. A group of makers grew up in Bavaria. A square
piano made in the Allgäu by Johann Socher in 1742 is the oldest
surviving example of this type, which contrary to its name is
rectangular. The square, its shape modelled on the clavichord,
was cheap to make and took up less space than a grand, to which
it became the main alternative until the vertical upright was
developed more successfully in the next century.

In the 1750s the piano began to receive favourable mention in
musical treatises, its superiority over the harpsichord for obtaining shading often being noted. At this time pianos were made
and played in Germany alone. By the 1760s, however, the experience of a piano was confined still to comparatively few citizens, partly because it was still a poor aid to musical expression.
Its strings, strung at low tension, were not much thicker than
those of a harpsichord. Therefore small hard hammers were
necessary to produce maximum tone, which was light, but duller
and softer in volume than that of a harpsichord. The instrument
could be played '*forte*' and '*piano*', but the action was unable as
yet to manage subtle tonal variations. Most Germans still preferred the cheaper clavichord to make music in the home, while
C. P. E. Bach gave the musician's view:

The more recent pianoforte, when it is sturdy and well built, has
many fine qualities, although its touch must be carefully worked
out, a task which is not without difficulties. . . . Yet, I hold that
a good clavichord, except for its weaker tone, shares equally in
the attractiveness of the pianoforte and in addition features the
vibrato and *portato* which I produce by means of added pressure
after each stroke. It is at the clavichord that a keyboardist may
be most exactly evaluated.[10]

Meanwhile changes were hastening the development of musical
life and ultimately the spread of the piano. That interpretation
of the world which satisfied an inward desire for order and cer-
tainty had been reflected in fugue and counterpoint. In early

eighteenth-century Germany, however, Pietist religious attitudes advanced, influencing many to discard logic for a cult of sentiment which did not reach its climax until the 1770s. It was paralleled in some ways by the English Wesleyan movement.

From the 1730s opinion spread that polyphony was over-laboured, and musical feeling hitherto overshadowed by intellectual principle acquired greater influence. The contrapuntalists' intricate compositions were discounted gradually in favour of plain but prominent broad melody with softer accompaniment and delicate gradations of volume able to move the senses in a manner previously unknown. Ornaments, which had stressed a note's importance on the harpsichord, lose their point on the piano, for to produce an accent the finger strikes the note harder. Haydn and Mozart became supreme masters of the new style. Nonetheless the view that the music of the mighty Bach, the supreme polyphonist, was 'forgotten' is over-emphatic. Although little played in public for some eighty years following his death, references to him by many leading pianists (John Field, Beethoven and J. B. Cramer, to name but three), show that his influence was profound.

The new style, suited to the piano, demanded changes in fingering. Harpsichordists played with bent fingers stationed directly above the keys, the principal movement coming from the finger joints. The thumb, positioned below the keys, was kept in reserve and brought into use only in difficult passages. To play scales longer fingers crossed over shorter (for example third finger over second or fourth), making speed difficult. J. S. Bach, although relying heavily on the old fingering, probably worked out the principles of the modern, and was among the earliest executants to allow more extensive use of the thumb, as his son, Carl Philipp Emanuel explained :

My deceased father told me that in his youth he used to hear great men who employed their thumbs only when large stretches made it necessary. Because he lived at a time when a gradual but striking change in musical taste was taking place, he was obliged to devise a far more comprehensive fingering and especially to enlarge the role of the thumbs and use them as nature intended; for, among their other good services, they must be employed chiefly in the difficult tonalities. Hereby, they rose from their former uselessness to the rank of principal finger.[11]

77

The new technique, finding some acceptance in the mid-eighteenth century, positioned the hand further in from the front edge of the keyboard with the thumb resting over a natural. Eventually the keys were lengthened to accommodate it. Neither thumb nor little finger was permitted yet to play a raised sharp key, but the former was allowed to pass under the middle fingers,* making the playing of scale and arpeggio passages over several octaves smoother and more rapid. Arpeggios and scales soon became the foundation of piano technique. The superficial sparkle which they assisted became another factor working against complex polyphony.

C. P. E. Bach, whose work was treated with the greatest respect by Mozart and Beethoven, codified the principles of the new fingering in his 'Essay on the True Art of Playing Keyboard Instruments', welcomed by pianists.

Prosperity in eighteenth-century Germany broadened, leading to a growing demand from moderately well-off partially-educated burgher families for a clavichord or later a piano in the home. Keyboard instruments enabled ladies to preserve their feminine decorum. The 'cello and wind instruments had obvious disadvantages in this respect and even the violin was long regarded as unladylike—an important reason for the piano's long reign as a highly desirable activity of the middle-class female, who became the principal performer on the domestic pianoforte.

The majority of these worthies thrived on music that was undemanding. Many understood little or nothing of harmony and counterpoint and were unable to tune their instrument. Consequently tuning became a separate occupation, and the Broadwood Journal shows 5s. as a representative charge. Few mastered extemporization or figured bass, which from the 1760s became less influential except in the professional world. Amateurs welcomed catchy dance tunes and single line melodies with straightforward left-hand accompaniments. Melodies could be sung and the piano became the ideal accompanying instrument.

Wealthy and better-educated German amateurs became known as 'Kenner und Liebhaber' (connoisseurs and amateurs). Their

---

* '. . . we learn that the thumb is never placed on a black key, that it may be used after the second finger, after the second and third fingers, or the second, third, and fourth, but never after the fifth'. C. P. E. Bach, 'Essay on the True Art of Playing Keyboard Instruments'.[12]

enduring influence was to help establish music as an art almost to be revered. They formed clubs for musical performances—first of all at members' homes and then in taverns, their meetings being graced with the title *'collegia musica'*.

Concerts given by child prodigies proved an attraction. The promoters' motives were less disinterested than those of the Kenner und Liebhaber meetings, but both enabled concerts, attended by the middle-classes prepared to pay for tickets, to become a regular feature of musical life.

Developments in printing assisted the spread of amateur music-making. Before 1750 professional musicians usually copied music by hand. Even later, Mozart, like many others, often prevented his manuscripts circulating widely, so that they would not be copied. He did not sell his compositions to publishers too often, for there was no Copyright Act ensuring protection after publication.

Early printing impressed staff and notes by two separate processes. In the sixteenth century it was discovered how to set type combining small sections of staff with the notes. By the early eighteenth century this movable type virtually had been superseded by engraving—the punching of staff and notes on to metal plates from which impressions were taken.

In the mid-1750s Breitkopf, the Leipzig publisher, gave printing from movable type a new lease of life by breaking note-type into tiny sections, so that notes forming chords, of growing influence in keyboard music, at last could be printed clearly over one another. This improvement remained important until lithography, the most popular process of music printing today, developed a half century later. Shortly after Breitkopf perfected his method, C. P. E. Bach was preparing for publication Part Two of his 'Essay'. He referred to Breitkopf's improvement in its Foreword: 'My original intention was to engrave the musical examples on copper plates. . . . However, I changed my mind later and chose the excellent invention of music printing so that illustrative matter might appear in the text. . . .'[13]

Greater prosperity helped music publishing develop into a viable business. In the early 1760s Breitkopf commenced issuing catalogues of music held in stock—the first time a German publisher had been prepared to print first and sell after, rather than to obtain advance subscriptions before printing. He was able to

79

accept the risk because there was an improved chance that music printed would be sold within a reasonable time and because a buoyant demand for keyboard music had grown up.

Musical life in early eighteenth-century England was more extensive than in Germany. Commerce was expanding rapidly and there was a larger 'comfortably off' element. As early as the seventeenth century London possessed a considerable public with a fair degree of musical ability, and in the 1650s the bookseller John Playford became the first man to make a separate business of music publishing. The earliest public concerts anywhere commenced in 1672 when John Banister, at one time Charles II's leading violinist, mounted regular performances at his home at 'a shilling a head and call for what you please'. By the 1730s Handel was able to act as impresario for his own opera and oratorio performances—unimaginable in his native Germany at the time. Tavern concerts followed Banister's innovation and, together with popular light opera and pleasure garden performances, led to a lowering of standards. They induced also a desire to play popular tunes at home. Serious suites and sonatas often were called 'lessons', suggesting that they were regarded by some as an infliction, like the music teacher's visit.

Owing perhaps to the decline in standards, proficiency on an instrument became less acceptable socially in the early eighteenth century. The view spread that a gentleman wasted valuable time learning to play well and risked falling into bad company when he should have been pursuing his chosen activity with single-minded diligence. Serious music suffered and as it became a less acceptable pastime for the gentry, foreigners and the fair sex should supply it! Consequently native musical creativeness lay dormant for nearly two hundred years. German and Italian musicians, sensing a ready market, hastened to London. Soon they provided the majority of concert artists, and from the second quarter of the century leading harpsichord makers were immigrants.

So far as is known, the earliest piano to enter England returned with Samuel Crisp in the 1750s. He claimed to have bought it in about 1752 in Rome, where according to tradition it had been made by Father Wood, an English monk, in 1711! Crisp sold it as a curiosity for one hundred guineas to Fulke Greville, Dr Burney's friend.

The Seven Years' War halted piano-making in Saxony and twelve instrument makers, among them several from Silbermann's workshop, crossed to England in 1760. They are called sometimes the 'twelve apostles'. One of them, Johann Zumpe, took employment with Shudi, who in 1761 was joined by John Broadwood. English piano-making, following the Silbermann-Cristofori tradition, commenced in 1766 when Zumpe established his own workshop to make small square pianos (Pl. 21). His action (Fig. 20), a simplified version of Cristofori's mechanism,

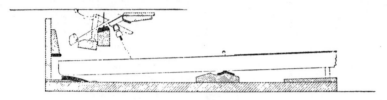

Fig. 20. Square piano action by Zumpe

was crude. The hammers were attached to a separate rail, but there was neither escapement nor check and the instrument was difficult to control. Due to the simplicity of the action, the hammers tended to bounce back on to the strings again after the initial impact and this resulted in the tone being dull and subdued.

In May 1767 the pianoforte made its public début during an interval in the ever popular *Beggar's Opera* at Covent Garden, when Miss Brickler sang a song 'accompanied by Mr Dibdin, on a new instrument, called Piano-Forte'. On 2nd June 1768 the first piano solo at an English concert, held at the Thatched House, later a venue for meetings of The Literary Club attended by Dr Burney, Dr Johnson and others, in St James's Street, was given on a Zumpe square piano by J. C. Bach, the 'English Bach', now living in London.

As Bach, Queen Charlotte's music master, approved of the piano, it became fashionable and it was expensive enough to be attractive! Zumpe charged Bach about £50 although Shudi was asking only £73 10s. 0d. for a two-manual harpsichord. As the square, which was thought of as a new kind of spinet, was much cheaper to produce, Zumpe's profits must have been handsome and he retired to his native land a rich man.

The value placed on music by the French lay somewhere between German enthusiasm and English cynicism. The first '*Concert spirituel*' given in 1725 was the earliest Paris concert without restrictions on whom could be admitted and at which an entry charge was made with the aim of making a profit. Dependent on royal licence, the holding of a *concert spirituel* was permitted only on those church holy days when opera performances were forbidden.

References to the piano appear from the late 1750s. At a concert spirituel held on 8th September 1768 it was played in public. Prior to this the few pianos in France must have been German, but the late 1760s saw the arrival of Zumpe squares, boosting the instrument's growing popularity. London was regarded as trend-setting and '*les pianos anglais*' retained prestige and ready saleability for half a century.

An interesting reflection on comparative values is given by a 1782 announcement in the *Affiches, annonces et avis divers*, a kind of contemporary *Exchange and Mart*, offering to exchange a square fortepiano for a violin by Stradivarius or Amati!

In the 1770s several piano-making workshops commenced business, most of the proprietors possessing German names. Sébastien Erhard, aged sixteen, arrived in the capital from Strasbourg in 1768. Later he dropped the 'h' from his name. His mechanical ingenuity soon caught the attention of the influential and in 1777 he constructed a piano at the residence of the Maréchale de Villeroi, who had taken him under her wing. His early pianos were variants of the popular English squares and soon enabled him to open shop in the rue Bourbon. A few years later the remarkably talented Erard started a series of experiments which led to the invention, completed in 1810, of the double-action pedal harp. In some respects a simplification of its forerunners, Erard's double-action provided for the raising of the pitch by two successive semitones so that the harp could be played easily in all keys. The fingering became the same for every key and the complexities of diverse fingerings for the various scales were abolished. This achievement empowered the harpist to modulate rapidly and to play passages previously beyond the facility of even the most gifted. Sébastien's instrument, known as the 'Grecian' harp, provided the basic design for the modern 'Gothic' harp subsequently developed by his nephew Pierre and which, patented in

82

1836, supplanted the more elegant Grecian instrument for concert purposes. Larger in size, it boasted a more powerful tone. The spacing of the strings was widened slightly and three additional strings were incorporated. The heavier Gothic harp, however, was less suited than its more graceful forbears to female amateurs, many finding it beyond their physical powers. Its increased size, which enabled it to hold its own with the enlarged symphony orchestra, therefore delivered the *coup de grâce* to the harp as a rival to the piano in popularity as a domestic instrument, a rivalry which had lasted some forty years. The earlier domestic popularity of piano and harp undoubtedly attracted Erard's talents in the direction of both instruments and the considerable soundboard area of the harp combined with the heavier stringing introduced by the Erards led to piano and harp having more in common than appears at first sight. Indeed the harp has been referred to unkindly as a species of half-grown piano. It is remarkable how many Erard harps are still in regular use.

In 1789 the Revolution shattered musical life. Many leading pianists settled in London, where Erard had established himself a few years before. He opened a shop selling pianos and harps in Great Marlborough Street, as London boasted a more vigorous trade than Paris. After the worst blood-letting was past Erard returned to Paris in 1796, but his family retained workshops in both capitals for over a century.

VII

Viennese and English Schools, 1770-1830

Vienna, where Mozart, Beethoven and Schubert worked, with Haydn at nearby Esterházy, became towards the end of the century a lively centre for composers and musicians, musical life focusing on the households of the nobility. For fifty years domestic chamber music flourished to an extent unequalled before or since. John Russell commented amusingly on the importance the Viennese attached to music:

> The Viennese take to themselves the reputation of being the most musical public in Europe; and this is the only part of their character about which they display much jealousy or anxiety. So long as it is granted that they can produce among their citizens a greater number of decent performers on the violin or piano than any other capital, they have no earthly objection to have it said that they can likewise produce a greater number of blockheads and debauchees.[14]

In 1777 Mozart praised enthusiastically Johann Andreas Stein's fortepianos, his endorsement leading to the instrument's near-universal acceptance. From this date Mozart's keyboard music was composed for the piano. His contemporaries regularly called the pianoforte 'fortepiano', the reversal of the two syllables causing later misunderstanding. Present-day musicians consequently know the lightly-built piano of Mozart's time, although merely the piano at an early stage of its development, as the 'fortepiano'.

Mozart, who long retained his partiality for a joke, recounted his first meeting with Stein in a letter:

> Although I had asked them to keep my identity a secret, yet Herr von Langenmantel was so thoughtless as to say to Herr Stein: 'I have the honour of introducing to you a virtuoso on the clavier',

and began to snigger. I at once protested and said that I was only an unworthy pupil of Herr Siegl in Munich, who had asked me to deliver 1,000 compliments to him. He shook his head – and said finally : 'Is it possible that I have the honour of seeing Herr Mozart before me?' 'Oh, no,' I replied, 'my name is Trazom and I have a letter for you'. He took the letter and wanted to break the seal at once. But I did not give him time to do so and asked : 'Surely you do not want to read that letter now? Open the door, and let us go into your room. I am most anxious to see your pianofortes'. 'All right,' he said, 'just as you wish. But I feel sure that I am not mistaken'. He opened the door and I ran straight to one of the three claviers which stood in the room. I began to play. He could scarcely open the letter in his eagerness to make sure. He could only read the signature. 'Oh', he cried and embraced me. He kept crossing himself and making faces and was as pleased as Punch. I shall tell you later on about his claviers. . . .[15]

Stein, working in Augsburg, was the best-known of the Bavarian school of makers and found demand sufficient to warrant his full-time devotion to the piano. His instruments employed a different action design from that used by Silbermann, the latter becoming known as the 'English' Action after further development in London. The Stein type became known as the 'German' and later as the 'Viennese' Action and was used in both grand and square pianos. These two varieties, the English and Viennese, divided two great schools of piano-making in subsequent years.

The moving centre of each hammer (Fig. 21) on a Viennese action rose with the key, in contrast to the English action (Fig. 22) on which hammer shanks were attached to a continuous rail.

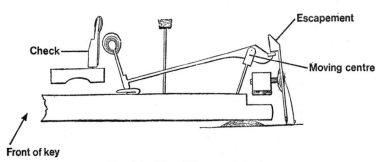

Fig. 21. The 'Viennese' Action

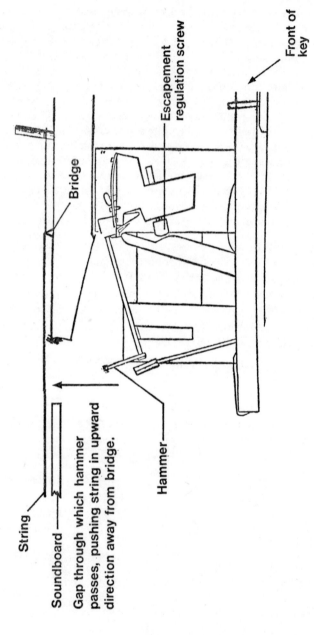

Front of key

Escapement regulation screw

Bridge

String

Soundboard

Gap through which hammer passes, pushing string in upward direction away from bridge.

Hammer

Fig. 22. The 'English' Action

The Viennese also differed from the English as the hammer on the former pointed towards the key. Stein's achievement was to add an escapement (Fig. 21) to the southern German action by cutting through the continuous rail, making a separate piece at the back of each key. The escapement moved back as pressure was placed on the key until the rear of the hammer slid out from underneath it. This refinement enabled finger to remain in contact with hammer for the greater part of its journey to the string, giving the player better control. Stein also added a check piece (Fig. 21) to prevent the hammer bouncing back on to the string a second time.

Mozart praised the sensitivity of Stein's piano in the famous letter he wrote on 17th–18th October 1777 :

Mon très cher Père !

. . . . In whatever way I touch the keys, the tone is always even. It never jars, it is never stronger or weaker or entirely absent; . . . His instruments have this special advantage over others that they are made with escape action. Only one maker in a hundred bothers about this. But without an escapement it is impossible to avoid jangling and vibration after the note is struck. . . .[16]

The Viennese action became the accustomed one for German and Austrian instruments for over fifty years until after Erard perfected his repetition action. With a light (about 28 grammes = 1 ounce), shallow (about 6·3 millimetres = $\frac{1}{4}$ inch) touch and small leather hammers, sometimes hollow, producing a bright sparkling tone, the Viennese action was suited admirably to the swift flowing music of Haydn, Mozart and Hummel.

Organists too, took to the new instrument, but it was not unexpected that they soon should think of adding a pedal board. The restrictions of the piano's compass provided a special incentive to extend the bass by means of pedals. Mozart had a pedal board added to his Walter fortepiano for this reason, and played his Fantasias on it. The well-respected Viennese organ and piano maker Josef Brodmann made a piano in 1815, placing it on a self-contained pedal board. Later, however, levers connected the pedals to the backs of the keys played by the fingers, so that extra strings were necessary no longer. The Erard firm developed its pedal pianoforte using this principle and expected it to appeal to Bach enthusiasts. On occasion the pedal board was used so that works normally requiring a second instrument could be performed on one. In 1845 Schumann became almost the sole composer of note to write for the pedal piano, his *Stüdien für den Pedalflügel*, *Op. 56* (Studies) and *Skizzen für den Pedalflügel*, *Op. 58* (Sketches) intended for it. Today they are played usually on two pianos, evidence that the pedal board addition did not prove of lasting value as the keyboard compass grew and as the piano's primacy killed the earlier orthodoxy of the keyboard trinity—that organ, harpsichord and clavichord co-existed on an equal though different footing.

Towards the end of the eighteenth century England made superlative contributions to the piano's development. John Broadwood became renowned, achieving fame for his instruments in a series of innovations.

Broadwood enlarged Zumpe's square piano design by moving the tuning pins from the soundboard to the left side at the back of the case. Then by making the case more substantial and the stringing heavier, he gave the square greater resonance. As the final step he elaborated Zumpe's crude action, which had earned the epithet of the 'mopstick' or 'old man's head'. Shortly after in 1786 John Geib, making pianos for Longman & Broderip, added the 'hopper' or 'escapement', his action becoming known as the 'grasshopper'. Geib's action soon was recognized in the best English-made squares, but for a couple of decades both 'grasshopper' and the developed 'mopstick' actions were offered, the former eventually winning the day. These improvements were greatly to the advantage of the square instrument and ensured that its popularity and subsequent penetration of the home easily outweighed that of the alternative wing-shaped instrument, although square piano tone still was feeble in comparison.

In 1783 Broadwood introduced the sustaining pedal, often miscalled the 'loud' pedal, in place of the previous knee-lever. He began to use a separate bass bridge (Pl. 25) on the soundboard of wing-shaped pianos in 1788. Rearrangement of the bridge positions enabled him to use higher tensions with shorter thicker bass strings producing fuller tone, assisted by the positioning of the strike line so that the hammer struck the string at a more favourable point (about one ninth of its speaking length). He then extended the keyboard by half an octave in the treble and in 1794 by half an octave in the bass, so that in the same year

Dussek performed on a six-octave grand in public. Broadwood's instruments knew no rivals in tonal volume and sonority.

The 'English' Action (Fig. 22) was developed by Broadwood with his apprentice Robert Stodart, who commenced manufacturing on his own account after completion of his apprenticeship, which he had combined with service as a private in the Royal Horse Guards, and the Dutchman Americus Backers. The mechanism was a modification of Cristofori's principle—his intermediate lever (Fig. 18) was omitted and the escapement was regulated by a screw (Fig. 22). Intended for grand pianos this action imparted a strong blow on the strings, but necessitated a heavier and deeper touch than the Viennese action, resulting in a loss of speed making rapid passages difficult to play. Stodart included the new action in his patent of 1777 for a combined harpsichord-piano. In this patent of his 'new invented sort of instrument or grand forte piano' the term 'grand' as a description of the wing-shaped piano is encountered for the first time. 'Grand' was accepted into general use by about 1790, so that harpsichord-shaped pianos ceased to be called 'large pianos'. The English action enabled Broadwood to draw maximum tone from his more resonant pianos, but they lacked the brilliance and sparkle of the Viennese type. The improved English pianos became the alternative to the lighter Viennese instruments (Pl. 22) until developments in the next century supplanted them.

In the last twenty years of the century the piano rapidly replaced the harpsichord as the customary keyboard instrument. In the 1770s and '80s music publishers often inscribed on the title page 'for harpsichord or pianoforte'. In the '90s the description 'for the pianoforte' became more common.

Growing demand for pianos led to the establishment of further successful producers and at least thirty makers were in business in London in the last quarter of the century. Several of the 'twelve apostles' were active still. Pohlmann, making small squares for potential customers whom Zumpe could not satisfy, continued until 1793. Christopher Ganer, who opened his business in the 1770s, was in Broad Street, Golden Square until 1809. Zumpe's business was taken over on his retirement by Schoene who continued for nine years until 1793. Beck ceased in 1794, Beyer and Buntebart in 1795. To their names must be added most notably Longman & Broderip, founded in 1767 as 'Music Sellers, Makers of Spinets and Harpsichords' at No. 26 Cheapside under the 'Sign of the Harp and Crown'. Before house numbers replaced hanging signs as means of identification, Shudi's premises had been known as 'The Plume of Feathers' after the Prince of Wales' crest which hung above the entry. By the mid-1780s the Longman & Broderip partnership was selling pianos in addition to harpsichords. As all kinds of wind, string and keyboard instruments were bought in from other makers for resale under the Longman & Broderip name, there is considerable doubt about the existence of the partnership's own production facilities. The original makers were usually in a small way of business and the names of several, in the case of harpsichords and spinets, have been found on the underside of the soundboard or of a key, the best known being Thomas Culliford. A small travelling piano which could be played in a coach was a Longman & Broderip speciality—at least one was heard on the canals of Venice, providing marked contrast to gondoliers' songs.

The principal piano-making centres were London, Paris and Vienna. England, however, with the Industrial Revolution under way, led the world in manufacturing methods and consequential purchasing power. With a large number of identical parts the piano was suited admirably to the growing practice of division of labour.

John Broadwood became the world's largest piano producer, making seven thousand square and one thousand grand pianos between 1782 and 1802. Earlier the Shudi partnership averaged nineteen harpsichords annually and about twenty pianos was the annual average which Stein of Augsburg maintained. This low figure indicated the maximum output over which a master with a handful of assistants could maintain close personal supervision.

Broadwood's development marked a transition from a 'craftsman-workshop' basis to the modern concept of factory production. In the early nineteenth century Broadwoods made use of steam power—only in England was piano production large enough to justify this.

Large outputs helped reduce prices. In the 1780s a typical Broadwood square cost £21 plus 10s. and 6d. for a packing case. In 1815 a square by the same maker cost £18 3s. and was a great quality improvement on the earlier £50 Zumpe instruments. The lower price combined with rising living standards and growing population created a wider market. In the early nineteenth century Broadwoods, employing six hundred workers, expanded to average nearly seventeen hundred pianos annually and the piano reached the lower middle classes. Its ownership soon became a desirable symbol of respectability (Pl. 29).

The piano's improved capabilities were soon explored by the musicians. Mozart's musicianship embodied classic ideals of temperance; using a light wrist he kept the fingers close to the keys. In contrast Clementi offered a foretaste of how pianism was to develop and relied increasingly on brilliancy of technique for effect. He completed his *Gradus ad Parnassum* in 1817 when interest was growing in technique for its own sake. The studies in the Gradus provided the tenets of modern pianism and remained pre-eminent until Chopin published his *Etudes*.

The sonatas which Clementi published in 1773 often are regarded as the earliest works showing a complete understanding of the new piano. Passages in his music contained remarkable foresight, foreshadowing harmonic effects obtained decades later. The fuller-toned English piano of the eighties clearly influenced his later style. His contemporaries were grouped into 'English' and 'Viennese' schools, their playing affected by the instruments they used. Dussek, for example, sat left of centre at the keyboard to impart more power to the bass. On the other hand Kalkbrenner, after additional keys had been added in the treble, positioned himself to the right of centre.

These were, however, still early days for the piano and Clementi was a product of his age. As a young man he continued to play the harpsichord and later introduced the custom of practising with a coin on the back of the hand. Moscheles went one better and taught that one should be able to play with a glass of water on the wrist.

Competitions between keyboard players were popular. Cramer pitted his skills against Beethoven's and the encounter between Liszt and Thalberg was another test of genius. In the contest arranged by the Emperor Joseph II in 1781 between Mozart and Clementi, the two greatest pianists of the day, neither was clear victor. Afterwards Clementi was generous in his appreciation of Mozart's touch and taste. Mozart, on the other hand, was terse in a letter dated 16th January 1782 :

91

Now a word about Clementi. He is an excellent cembalo-player, but that is all. He has great facility with his right hand. His star passages are thirds. Apart from this, he has not a farthing's worth of taste or feeling; he is a mere *mechanicus*.[17]

Clementi, a Roman, was 'imported' to England when fifteen by Mr Peter Beckford, M.P., a gifted talent-spotter during his travels. Clementi continued his career as a pianist for about thirty years into the first decade of the nineteenth century, but in later life devoted his energies to his music publishing and piano-making business. In 1798 he transformed the bankrupt Messrs Longman & Broderip, soon changing the name to Clementi & Co. He became a widely-travelled salesman, journeying as far as Moscow to promote his pianos and making them so well-known that in many countries they were regarded as second only to Broadwood.

John Field, apprenticed for one hundred guineas to Clementi & Co., became such an outstanding demonstrator of Clementi's pianos that his master took him on his continental travels. Both men left England in 1802, Clementi not returning for eight years despite a disastrous fire in 1808 causing £40,000 damage to his factory. (Broadwood's men magnanimously raised sufficient funds to replace their competitors' tools). Field broke away from Clementi's tutelage and settled in Russia where he enjoyed great success, although his dissipations were discussed widely. His eighteen nocturnes, a form which he invented, and his lyricism inspired Chopin.

Dussek was the earliest virtuoso to tour continually. Unlike Mozart and Clementi, who played mostly in salons, he performed regularly at public concerts in the new concert halls. Traditionally the pianist's back faced the audience but for the newly influential solo piano, re-arrangement was required. Dussek solved the problem by presenting his right side to the audience, offering two advantages—the raised piano lid reflected the sound at the concert-goers, who were able to admire Dussek's fine profile. 'Le beau Dussek', as they called him in Paris, in later life became grossly plump!

Dussek was important in other ways. He was first to mark pedallings in his published music and he anticipated Chopin by changing fingers on the key while it remained depressed, to achieve a smooth legato.

A rival, J. B. Cramer, called 'Glorious John' in his adopted England, included fairly regularly in his programmes music not composed by himself—unusual at the time. Like Clementi with whom he studied, Cramer was composer, pianist and business-man. He was a partner in the infant Chappell business, which in 1812 'begged leave to acquaint the nobility and gentry' that 'they have just opened a Ware-room, for showing a number of instruments . . .'[18] personally selected, it was stated, by Cramer himself. About thirty years later Chappells commenced making pianos in Soho. The music publishers Cramer & Co., founded by Cramer in 1824, turned to building pianos towards the 1860s.

In contrast stood another kind of pianism—that of Wölffl and Steibelt, who served the public what it wanted. Steibelt, assisted by his wife on the tambourine at the majority of his concerts, added the tremolo to the pianist's equipment and soon was nick-named 'the tremolo pianist'.

A pianist's reputation usually did not precede him. Upon arrival in a city, the ambitious reckoned to spend several weeks sallying forth from his hotel hoping to make the acquaintance of the right people and flourishing letters of introduction, his aim to procure an invitation to appear at a concert society's regular performance. Surviving this test, he hoped to be offered orches-tral accompaniment and use of the hall for a later concert for his own purposes.

Emphasis was by now on the soloist, although custom did not permit him to give a concert entirely on his own. The orchestra, in smaller cities numbering under a dozen players, customarily commenced with an overture. The soloist made perhaps three appearances interspersed between orchestral pieces and operatic arias, the latter probably with piano accompaniment. Follow-ing a concerto, his second item was perhaps a further concerto or improvisations on a theme to be worked into a potpourri. A set of variations or a fantasy might round off the pianist's con-tribution.

Some virtuosi did not deign to attend the usual orchestral rehearsal, and the orchestral parts lacked today's care. The three-movement concerto following Mozart's form, with conflict and harmony between soloist and orchestra carefully controlled by convention, was disturbed rarely. The cadenza, adopted from operatic practice, gave the soloist opportunity to display his technical prowess, concealing the theme in darting scale passages and rapidly repeated notes. Not until Beethoven's 'Emperor' Concerto was the pianist expected to play the composer's written cadenza. By 1840 concert improvization was largely a lost art.

Several pianists provided a bridge from the elegance of the classical tradition to romantic bravura. Born towards the end of the century they made even Clementi appear old-fashioned, but themselves were out-dated rapidly by Liszt and Chopin. Brought up on pianos suiting 'close to the keys' finger style, their weak tone did not stand comparison in the 1830s.

Hummel, Kalkbrenner and Czerny number among them. Hummel represented the culmination of the classical school and split Vienna into rival factions between himself and Beethoven.* Like Hummel, Czerny was at home on the light Viennese piano and disliked the more ponderous English instruments. Clementi commented on this discontent when he wrote: '. . . the price, the heaviness, and the *depth of touch* are the general objections throughout Germany to English P. Fortes; but especially the *first* (the money) sticks most confoundedly in their gizzard. . . .'[20] Moscheles attempted to overcome these objections. He borrowed Beethoven's Broadwood piano and after Conrad Graf generously carried out hasty repairs, attempted to demonstrate at a Viennese concert the distinctive strengths of the English and Viennese instruments:

> I tried in my Fantasia to show the value of the broad, full, although somewhat muffled tone of the Broadwood piano; but in vain. My Vienna public remained loyal to their countryman—the clear, ringing tones of the Graf were more pleasing to their ears. . . .[21]

With hindsight Czerny exerted a more lasting influence as a teacher than performer. Taught for a time by Beethoven, Leschet-

* Beethoven's smouldering resentment towards his rivals rose to the surface in a letter written in 1794 to Eleonore von Breuning:

. . . had I not already noticed fairly often how some people in Vienna after hearing me extemporize of an evening would note down on the following day several peculiarities of my style and palm them off with pride as their own. Well, as I foresaw that their pieces would soon be published, I resolved to forestall those people. But there was yet another reason, namely, my desire to embarrass those Viennese pianists, some of whom are my sworn enemies. I wanted to revenge myself on them in this way, . . .[19]

izky and Liszt, both dominating teachers, studied with him. In this way the later nineteenth century had contact with Beethoven. Future generations despised the drudgery of Czerny's many studies, which ran to over one thousand opus numbers—a record even when so many were writing *études*.

As the piano became serious business, group teaching was tried, offering to its practitioners a greater income than single pupils did and to its students lessons at reduced prices. John Bernard Logier taught groups of twenty in two-hour sessions. His prospectus made his system look a 'must'. Enthusing over Logier's unique teaching capabilities, it promised enquirers that if they were of ordinary capacity they could become capable of emulating Corelli, Handel, Haydn and Mozart! Logier was prepared nonetheless to sell his 'secret', providing they kept it, to other teachers for one hundred guineas.

Clementi and Cramer recommended Logier's instrument of torture, the chiroplast (Pl. 33), its guides for fingers and wrists designed to keep the hands at the correct height. Moscheles was more sceptical. After Kalkbrenner, Logier's most influential disciple, took him to hear Logier's students, he noted in his diary:

> ... I could not share his (Kalkbrenner's) admiration of this newly invented system, although I think Logier and his wife a clever and artistic couple. Would I have any one follow this system? I hardly think so. The mind should work more intensely than the fingers, and how can there be a question of *mind* when two pupils play the same piece at the same time?[22]

Commencing his campaign in 1814 from 'Chiroplast Hall' in Dublin, Logier established over eighty 'academies' in the British Isles by 1819. In 1823 he obtained a two-and-a-half-year contract with the Prussian Ministry of Education. His 'academies', however, vanished as rapidly as they had sprung up. Kalkbrenner deserted for Paris. He realized that the chiroplast finger guides made it impossible to pass the thumb under the other fingers so that not even scales could be played! Safely installed in Paris, however, Kalkbrenner soon was up to tricks in an attempt to convince the French court that his son was a child prodigy. When an improvization was arranged for the king's pleasure, the child let his father down disastrously. He played for a while, but then

Fig. 23. An extract from 'Battle of Prague' by Franz Kotzwara

stopped suddenly and turned to Kalkbrenner with the fatal words, 'Papa, I have forgotten'.

As popular music spread its average quality declined. Battle music was in demand during and after the Napoleonic Wars. The English speciality was, aptly enough, naval battle pieces, although one of the most popular battle compositions depicting military prowess was Francz Kotzwara's *The Battle of Prague* (Fig. 23). Appearing in 1790, its hails of bullets, cries of the wounded and other vulgarities ensured its popularity for decades.

VIII

Beethoven Spurs the Piano's Development, 1790-1830

Andreas Stein died in 1792. Shortly after his daughter Nanette, about whose piano playing Mozart had made pungent comments, moved to Vienna and in 1794 established with her husband the firm of Streicher, soon the leading Viennese piano-making firm, its renown upheld into the middle years of the nineteenth century by their son, J. B. Streicher. Nanette's husband, Johann Andreas Streicher, was once a friend of the poet Schiller and in 1782 had escaped with him from the military academy in Stuttgart.

The Streichers further improved Stein's action, but in general the Viennese makers were less ready to innovate than their London counterparts, as the characteristics of their fortepianos matched the music which was portrayed to its best advantage on them. John Russell commented on the Viennese propensity for inventing new instruments, witness the phys-harmonica, the ditanaclasis, the xänorphica, the pammelodicon, the davidica and the amphiona, rather than improving the manufacture of known ones. Although Stein incorporated a sustaining pedal six years after Broadwood introduced it, knee-levers were common still in 1800. Often only two unison strings were used compared with three on the heavier English instruments. The bass strings were long and thin—the wooden frame would not have withstood thicker strings—producing a bass which many maintained balanced the treble better than the fuller bass of the London pianos.

Russell writing in the early 1820s stated that there were some sixty-five pianoforte makers in Vienna. Known locally were Brodmann, whose workshop was taken over in 1828 by his apprentice Ignaz Bösendorfer, providing a foundation for his business, Joseph Moser, Z. Pohack, these two referred to by Beethoven, M. Müller, Schanz, whose instruments Haydn favoured, Martin Seuffert, Wachtl and Anton Walter.

The customary five-octave compass was sufficient for twenty of Beethoven's piano sonatas and his first two concertos. In the early nineteenth century the Viennese began to follow the London makers by adding several notes in the treble. The sonatas from the 'Waldstein' onwards demand at least six octaves range and the 'Hammerklavier' Sonata the six-and-a-half-octaves of the Viennese Conrad Graf, Beethoven's last piano, as strong as his six-octave Broadwood. Graf, who made pianos until 1841, built this piano with four strings for each note (except the lowest fourteen notes which were trichord) in deference to the composer's deafness.

Limitations imposed by the compass are noticeable in Beethoven's sonatas, notes in full flow reverting suddenly to an octave higher in the bass or lower in the treble. In the third bar from the end of the first movement of the Sonata Op. 2 No. 3 the master had little option but to omit the bottom note of the octaves in the left hand below F', the lowest note on the five octave keyboard. In Fig. 24 from the Sonata Op. 110, the composer logic-

Fig. 24. An extract from Sonata Op. 110 by Beethoven

ally would have reached beyond the top c'''' of his six-octave Broadwood. Beethoven turned such limitations to good effect, for rich discord results in bars 189–191 of the first movement from the Sonata Op. 31 No. 2 when he was unable to continue the octaves in the treble hand upwards beyond the highest f''' of the five-octave keyboard. With pitiable lack of understanding later editions sometimes have done so for him.

The unparalleled force of Beethoven's playing burst upon Vienna in 1792, his music linking classical and romantic schools. Some commentators stress Beethoven's position as the last of the great classicists continuing along paths trodden by Haydn and

Mozart, while others view him as the first romantic establishing guidelines which can be traced through to Wagner. This diversity of opinion indicates that form and harmony were assuming new complexity during Beethoven's lifetime. Normally adhering to the framework of sonata form, his later works stretched it to its limits and show that his imagination was ranging increasingly outside its restrictions. Nevertheless he maintained an intensity of expression which in consistency frequently surpassed that of later composers, and united in novel ways emotional content with forms which also satisfied the need for symmetry. It is, however, false to assess Beethoven as 'greater' than Mozart—he should be seen as 'different'.

The need to express this fresh emotional range led to a search for novel effect on the piano—a search which served as a pointer for his successors and indicated new directions. Beethoven's quest for unsullied harmonic impact and his progression beyond the smooth evenly-balanced melodies of Mozart brought the sustaining pedal into its own, one of his fundamental contributions to future piano literature. Beethoven must have relied primarily on simultaneous depression of pedal and key for normal effects although contemporary records show that his pedalling was erratic in the extreme—the result firstly of his deafness, secondly of the poor sustaining power of contemporary pianos. The repeated a″ in the third movement of the Sonata Op. 110 is a device employed partly in an attempt to overcome lack of sustaining power. It was accepted that the pedals were likely to be noisy or even to cease functioning and indeed they did not achieve reliability until the arrival of the lyre support.

The texture of Haydn's and Mozart's music requires only the most discreet pedalling and the composers themselves rarely indicated when the dampers were to be raised. Beethoven became one of the earliest composers to mark down pedalling instructions, the first occasion being in the Sonata Op. 26, completed in 1800. Nonetheless deafness sometimes made his markings inappropriate for pianos of the period, let alone for modern pianos with their enhanced sustaining capability. In a number of instances the pedal is prescribed for long sustained bass notes, easier to prolong on modern pianos than in Beethoven's day. It should, however, be borne in mind that some contemporary pianos had a 'split' pedal arrangement, one pedal raising the bass dampers and a second pedal the treble ones. When the treble dampers were raised, it was possible therefore for the treble to 'sing on', while the bass was damped in the normal way. The 'split' pedal may have led to later misunderstanding of Beethoven's intentions and might explain what was believed to be his most notorious excess—holding the pedal down occasionally for a whole movement without any intermittent damping. It is thought that he played the complete first movement of the 'Moonlight' Sonata in this way and his instructions *'sempre pp e senza sordini'* suggest it. In the Sonata Op. 31 No. 2 the pedal is to be held down through a recitative of six bars—Czerny told Kullak that Beethoven was seeking to produce a sound as if he was speaking into a cave, where resonance would cause the sounds to reverberate and merge. Opinion is divided over whether this pedal instruction should be followed on the modern piano. The blurred melody creates an effect not unpleasant, although often tempered today by judicious half-pedalling, and the soft right hand notes emerge through the reverberation, sustained by the pedal, of broken chords in the bass, creating an impression unthinkable a few years previously in Mozart's day. Such contrasts between hands were more likely as the piano attained greater variety of dynamics and touch.

Beethoven suggests nuances for which the pianos of his day were inadequate. Deafness may have caused his imagination to produce tonal contrasts which remained unheard. The infliction of deafness made a strong impression on his contemporaries. John Russell described Beethoven's playing and the tragedy of deafness :

The moment he is seated at the piano, he is evidently unconscious that there is any thing in existence but himself and his instrument; and, considering how very deaf he is, it seems impossible that he should hear all he plays. Accordingly, when playing very *piano*, he often does not bring out a single note. He hears it himself in the 'mind's ear'. While his eye, and the almost imperceptible motion of his fingers, show that he is following out the strain in his own soul through all its dying gradations, the instrument is actually as dumb as the musician is deaf.

I have heard him play; but to bring him so far required some management, so great is his horror of being any thing like exhibited. Had he been plainly asked to do the company that favour, he would have flatly refused; he had to be cheated into it. Every person left the room, except Beethoven and the master of the house, one of his most intimate acquaintances. These two carried on a conversation in the paper-book about bank stock. The gentleman, as if by chance, struck the keys of the open piano, beside which they were sitting, gradually began to run over one of Beethoven's own compositions, made a thousand errors, and speedily blundered one passage so thoroughly, that the composer condescended to stretch out his hand and put him right. It was enough; the hand was on the piano; his companion immediately left him, on some pretext, and joined the rest of the company, who in the next room, from which they could see and hear every thing, were patiently waiting the issue of this tiresome conjuration. Beethoven, left alone, seated himself at the piano. At first he only struck now and then a few hurried and interrupted notes, as if afraid of being detected in a crime; but gradually he forgot every thing else, and ran on during half an hour in a fantasy, in a style extremely varied, and marked, above all, by the most abrupt transitions. The amateurs were enraptured; to the uninitiated it was more interesting to observe how the music of the man's soul passed over his countenance. He seems to feel the bold, the commanding, and the impetuous, more than what is soothing or gentle. The muscles of the face swell, and its veins start out; the wild eye rolls doubly wild; the mouth quivers, and Beethoven looks like a wizard, overpowered by the demons whom he himself has called up.[23]

Louis Spohr was struck by the master's decline :

. . . It was hardly an enjoyable experience; for, to begin with, the piano was badly out of tune, a circumstance which troubled Beethoven little as, in any case, he could not hear the music, and secondly scarcely anything remained of the artist's once so greatly admired virtuosity, also because of his deafness. In the *forte* passages the poor deaf man struck the instrument with such violence that the strings rattled, while in the *piano* passages he played so softly that whole bars were inaudible and the music became unintelligible if one was unable to follow the pianoforte part in manuscript. I was overpowered by a feeling of deep sorrow when I considered this hard fate. . . .[24]

By 1817 Beethoven was writing to Frau Streicher in an effort to obtain one of her husband's pianos, specially modified because of his deafness :

. . . Now I have a great favour to ask of Streicher. Request him on my behalf to be so kind as to adjust one of your pianos for me to suit my impaired hearing. It should be as loud as possible. That is absolutely necessary. . . . Only Streicher would be able to send me the kind of piano I require. . . .[25]

Beethoven's physical prowess was clearly too great for contemporary pianos, whether of the robuster English or the lighter Viennese type. Ferdinand Ries commented that

Beethoven was very clumsy and awkward in his movements; his gestures were totally lacking in grace. He seldom took up anything without dropping or breaking it. Thus he repeatedly threw his inkwell into the piano that stood next to his writing-desk. . . .[26]

Stumpff wrote of the composer's sturdy Broadwood (Pl. 37), presented to him by its manufacturers in 1818, making the journey via Trieste to where it was shipped:

Beethoven complained of the imperfection of the grand pianoforte, upon which one could not perform forcefully and effectively under present conditions. 'I myself possess a London instrument, which, however, does not live up to my expectations. Come along, it's in the next room, in a most miserable state.' When I opened it, what a sight confronted me! The upper registers were mute and the broken strings in a tangle, like a thorn bush whipped by the storm [sic]! Beethoven begged me to advise him as to what should be done to it. 'Do you think that the pianomaker Stein could repair it, if you consulted him in this matter?' I promised to do my best. . . .[27]

Even before his deafness became acute, Beethoven struck the keys far harder than was usual and early pianos needed re-tuning half-way through an evening of only 'normal' playing. The master of voluminous crescendos and stabbing accents urged piano makers to produce more durable and sonorous instruments. As Beethoven broke new ground (his earliest sonatas could be played on harpsichord or piano) it became clear, as he put it in a letter to J. A. Streicher in 1796:

There is no doubt that so far as the manner of playing it is concerned, the *pianoforte* is still the least studied and developed of all instruments; often one thinks that one is merely listening to a harp. And I am delighted, my dear fellow, that you are one of the few who realize and perceive that the time will come when the

103

harp and the pianoforte will be treated as two entirely different instruments. . . .[28]

The reason for the piano's shortcomings was that it was not yet strong enough to withstand forceful experiment.

Beethoven exchanged ideas with the Streichers over a number of years. 1810 found him complaining impatiently to Streicher:

> . . . But I do ask you to ensure that the instruments do not wear out so quickly—You have seen your instrument which I have here and you must admit that it is very worn out; and I frequently hear the same opinion expressed by other people—. . . .[29]

The understanding Frau Streicher on occasion provided medicines and servants to ease Beethoven's domestic plight.* He demonstrated the interaction of the composer's needs with the instrument maker's craft. The fury of the 'Hammerklavier' Sonata with in excess of twenty thousand notes made it urgent that the piano's frame should be sturdier and the action more reliable, and so Beethoven's compositions marked a turning-point in the instrument's progress. Exposing its inadequacies beyond any shadow of doubt, his prompting led to quicker development of the instrument than otherwise would have been the case. At the same time, if the expressive capabilities of the piano had not reached the stage they had in Beethoven's lifetime, the ethereal atmosphere of the last sonatas stretching the emotional range of the instrument would have been incapable of attainment.

The matching of the instrument with the composer's requirements poses a dilemma illustrated more vividly by Beethoven than by anyone before or since. Does the instrument determine the music composed for it or do composers' demands spur piano makers to design instruments which offer the desired characteristics? Scholars usually uphold that an instrument's improvement has not created music of a new dimension, but that composers in advance of contemporary taste provided the stimulus

---

* "Dear Friend!

I am making use of your permission to send you the laundry so that you may kindly attend to this . . ." Letter of May 16, 1817 to Frau Nanette Streicher.[30]

". . . Forgive me. I have no scissors, no knife, nor anything. I think that the rags are too bad and that it would be better to buy some linen—The neckcloths too need *to be mended*—. . ." Letter of 1817 to Frau Nanette Streicher.[31]

necessary before an instrument's radical development would be undertaken. They maintain that it is incorrect to claim, as a few writers have, that because the instrument preceded the music, the nature of the available instrument guided the composer's inspiration.

The exchange between Bach and Silbermann is unusual, as Bach was disapproving of the instrument, rather than essentially sympathetic towards it; nonetheless his criticisms provoked Silbermann to improve it. It is said that early pianos sounded like harpsichords because their makers, having little conception of any other tone quality, wanted them to resemble the familiar timbre of the plucked string. Mozart gave little impetus, writing generally within the limitations of contemporary Viennese forte-pianos. It was natural for him to commence with accepted tone-colour and to add to it the piano's greatest strength, that of dynamic gradation. Furthermore the light tone suited the light construction of contemporary instruments, which was all that the current state of technical knowledge permitted. Wiser by far to gain experience based on contemporary capabilities before undertaking radical experiment. Beethoven acted as a spring-board, his impetus largely coinciding with awakening knowledge, won during the Industrial Revolution, of materials applied in new ways and with renewed willingness to undertake radical experiment. These fresh factors were as much dependent on experience gained gradually in increasing stringing stresses and strengthening the framework, as on knowledge that there was a demand with a composer of Beethoven's stature providing a continuous incentive.

As the piano developed during the first part of the century, pianists still became builders of pianos, although after 1850 when the piano was largely a mature instrument, this double role ceased. Later makers were attempting still to provide larger more versatile pianos, but they were also increasingly anxious for testimonials. As growing commercialism in sales techniques became the rule and as the factory system grew to require the full-time skills of those engaged in it, it is possible that pianists came to shun the makers. The eagerness of piano makers to supply him, before his reputation as a piano destroyer was widespread, irritated Beethoven as early as 1802 when he wrote to von Domanovecz:

Well, my dear Z(meskall), you may give Walter, if you like, a strong dose of my affair. For, in the first place, he deserves it in any case; and, what is more, since the time when people began to think that my relations with Walter were strained, the whole tribe of pianoforte manufacturers have been swarming around me in their anxiety to serve me—and all for nothing. Each of them wants to make me a pianoforte exactly as I should like it. For instance, Reicha has been earnestly requested by the maker of his pianoforte to persuade me to let him make me one; and he is one of the more reliable ones, at whose firm I have already seen some good instruments—So you may give Walter to understand that, although I can have pianofortes for nothing from all the others, I will pay him 30 ducats, but not more than 30 ducats, and on condition that the wood is mahogany. Furthermore, I insist that it shall have *the tension with one string**—If he won't agree to these conditions, then make it quite plain to him that I shall choose one of the others to whom I will give my order and whom I shall take later on to *Haydn* to let the latter see his instrument. . . .[32]

After the piano became accepted as a mature instrument, few composers tried seriously to change it. Consequently many experiments appear as isolated incidents which never stood any chance of lasting success. Instead composers have turned to stressing different aspects of the instrument's nature—Debussy its blurred resonance, Bartók its percussive aspect. In the twentieth century theories of composition advance without troubling whether the instrument in question is able accurately to reproduce the sounds heard in the composer's imagination, which frequently appear to threaten the quality of the instruments. Therefore the electronic age, which many regard as hostile to the piano, has neither passed it by nor changed it. It is a tribute to the piano's versatility that it still retains its place as a respected and relevant instrument in composition of an electronic nature.

It may be said therefore that the qualities of contemporary instruments influenced the range of nuances and effect capable of realization, even although composers were able to think beyond these. Therefore, certainly in Beethoven's case, the instrument provided no straitjacket for the imagination. For lesser men now largely forgotten it frequently restricted their thoughts. If it is

---

* 'The tension with one string' probably refers to the propensity of bi-chords and trichords to go out of tune rapidly.

accepted that composers regularly thought beyond the capabilities of available pianos, it is then only a short step to accepting the argument that it is beneficial to perform their compositions on mature twentieth-century instruments.

Meanwhile to meet new demands for a harder initial blow imparting greater resonance and sustaining power, constructors set about improving the responsiveness of the action mechanism and the size and strength of various tone-producing components.

Experiments with iron tension bars were commenced by Broadwood as early as 1808 in the treble section of grands. Wooden braces became heavier as the compass in the treble was extended and as pitch gradually rose (higher pitch enabling wind instruments to achieve enhanced brilliancy), but the supports became overcumbersome and their effectiveness was in doubt. The piano Broadwood sent to Beethoven possessed no metal, but in 1821 his grands employed between three and five separate metal strengthening struts parallel to and above the strings. Broadwood was experimenting also with iron struts *underneath* the sound-board, replacing the wooden bracings. In the same year 1821 a Broadwood employee, Samuel Hervé, arranged in a square piano a metal hitch pin table (Pl. 16) to which the bottom ends of the strings were attached and which formed a support for resistance bars. From 1822 these tables were used regularly by Broadwood, who in 1827 took the next step by patenting solid metal bars *combined in one piece* with a fixed metal hitch pin table. Shortly afterwards Erard, experimenting with metal supports at the same time as Broadwood, introduced a similar arrangement, giving rise to a lively correspondence in *The Times* at the time of the 1851 Great Exhibition, to determine who had been first to utilize metal bracing bars. The letters which appeared established that Erard brought into general use in 1824 steel support bars running parallel to the strings, but as Broadwood's had in their possession a piano dating from 1823 with steel tension bars, it seemed clear that Broadwoods had beaten the French firm to the winning-post by a short head.

As the tension of the strings, now supported at the hitch pin end, tended to pull the tuning pins down (Fig. 25), attempts were made to make a solid metal plank in which the tuning pins could be embedded. This did not prove practicable, and iron

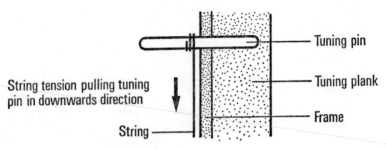

Fig. 25. Tension on a tuning pin

over the wooden tuning-pin plank eventually became the accepted means. Other experiments introducing metal components followed and patents were registered by makers as far apart as Vienna and Canada.

These experiments with solid bars and plates had as their object the creation of resistance to the bending strains and enabled tensions to be carried, which never could have been supported by wooden casing. Meanwhile James Thom and William Allen, workmen of William Stodart whose firm had incorporated metal struts in a piano as early as 1788, had been experimenting with metal tubes of similar material to the strings positioned below them, i.e. brass tubes above brass strings and iron tubes above iron strings, bearing on metal plates resting on the rear surface of the soundboard (Pl. 35). The principle was that of compensation as fluctuations of pitch caused by temperature variations still were serious. It was intended that as the wire expanded or contracted, the metal framework and with it the attached soundboard would do so commensurately so that pitch would remain constant. This compensation frame was patented in 1820.

As the keyboard compass was extended (Herz already was writing alternative parts for a piano with seven octaves and Pape by 1844 had experimented with an eight-octave grand) and heavier stringing at higher tensions came into use, resistance became a more serious problem than temperature compensation. The idea of resistance eventually won universal acceptance, although as late as the Great Exhibition of 1851 Stodarts exhibited a piano with compensation frame.

English makers were first to adopt generally the metallic bracing bars, using most frequently cast and wrought iron, while even gun-metal was brought into service as wedges. The next step was to unite the various metal components into a single solid casting. To this end American makers made their vital contribution using cast iron.

IX

The Piano Matures,
1770-1850

The American colonies were unimportant in the history of the clavichord and harpsichord, but the eastern seaboard flourished and enabled the United States to contribute to the piano's evolution. The first reference to the piano occurred in the early 1770s. Then in 1775 John Behrent of Philadelphia, apparently the first piano constructor on his side of the Atlantic, announced that he had 'just finished an extraordinary instrument by the name of Pianoforte, made of mahogany'.

English and soon French musicians added to the numbers of eighteenth-century German settlers who had stimulated a taste for music. Immigrants brought with them European ideas of 'enlightenment' and concert life developed. A sudden demand for music in the home led to considerable imports from Europe, followed by the rapid establishment of native music publishing.

American craftsmen acquired experience of the new instrument and Englishmen such as Isaac Hawkins and Thomas Loud were able to contribute to the piano's progress in America. For over twenty years Charles Albrecht, for example, copied English pianofortes, regarded as unrivalled and selling well until the mid-century. Clementis found readier favour than Broadwoods.

Boston became the liveliest centre. In 1813, Appleton, Hayts and Babcock established a piano business, soon known as Franklin Music Warehouse. By 1819 the Franklin firm was finishing two pianos weekly, but this was not to last. Alpheus Babcock broke away and in 1825 cast the first one-piece iron frame. For a square piano, it united the portion covering the tuning plank with the hitch pin plate and bracing bars. A one-piece frame was the logical conclusion to the experiments with metal support bars. It determined the future course of piano-making, for it

110

was the *sine qua non* for the success of other developments with heavier strings necessary for the piano's maturity to be achieved. The later triumph of the American piano rested on the gradual elaboration of Babcock's achievement.

The succeeding years witnessed numerous experiments with cast iron. Patents for cast-iron frames were taken out by Pape in 1826 and by Petzold, another Parisian maker whose instruments Moscheles played in the early 1820s. Allen, who eleven years before had invented the compensating frame with Thom, took out a patent in 1831. That late-comers often claim an invention as their own proved true when Conrad Meyer claimed that his frame cast in 1832 in Philadelphia had been the earliest one-piece cast frame. In fact Babcock, seeking makers to take up his idea, had persuaded Meyer and a few others in Philadelphia to give it a try. In 1836 Isaac Clark of Cincinnati patented a frame design which could be constructed of either wrought or cast iron. Other overall iron frame schemes appeared in the 1830s in London, Paris and Vienna before in 1840 Jonas Chickering patented his own complete metal frame for square pianos and then applied the knowledge he had gained to the grand.

In the 1830s, however, the one-piece frame had still to gain widespread acceptance, which it did not achieve finally for a quarter of a century. Earlier prejudice against metal, believed to be detrimental to tone and out of place in the home, died slowly. But iron, in the age of the steam engine, eventually was associated with wealth-producing progress and even seemed attractive. Broadwoods described their grands employing cast and wrought iron, displayed at the 1862 International Exhibition as 'Iron Grand Concert Pianofortes' and were proud to do so. Introduced in 1847, the 'iron grand' was Broadwood's first with a full iron frame and was believed also to be the first English grand of this type. Nonetheless it was not cast in one piece. It incorporated a diagonal bar which replaced the straight resistance bars producing, its makers claimed, improved evenness of tone and touch as strings and action no longer were diverted by the straight bars. Enhanced tonal purity and nobility also were attained.

Moscheles' comments following an 1822 concert when he played a Broadwood instead of his usual Clementi show that metal was not accepted fully :

111

The strong metal plates used by Broadwood in building his instruments, give a heaviness to the touch, but a fulness and vocal resonance to the tone. . . . I, however, use Clementi's more supple mechanism for my repeating notes, skips, and full chords.[33]

Sébastien Erard was always in the forefront of progress and contributed several improvements, among them the perfection of the repetition action. The main French contributions to piano construction were made at this time. Erard attempted to unite the best qualities of the English and Viennese actions—the firmness of the former with the lightness of the latter—with reliable rapid repetition. Swift repetition was difficult to obtain when involved rhythm was required, which it was increasingly in contemporary music, as the key had to revert to its highest position to accent a repeated note. The action required development to obviate this defect.

With these aims in mind Erard completed in 1821 his Repetition Action (Fig. 26). It had taken some thirteen years to

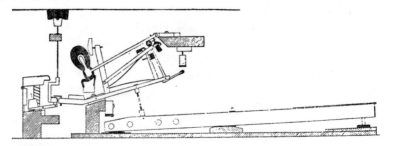

Fig. 26. Repetition action with double escapement by Erard, 1821

develop, his earliest repetition action appearing in 1808; although initially the first action created a favourable impression, with the passing of time irritating noises appeared and the touch proved unreliable. Erard continued to seek means of overcoming the drawbacks, but not until 1821 was he sufficiently confident to unveil his improved action. It retained the layout of the English action, but small levers and springs were added to enable the hammer to rebound not to its original position of rest but to a point closer to the string, where it remained until the finger either released the key totally or propelled the hammer against the string a second time. Speed of repetition was improved as for a

29. "Farmer Giles & his Wife showing off their daughter Betty to their Neighbours on her return from School". Published 1809. Etched by J. Gillray. The square piano is by Longman & Broderip

30. Upright grand. *c.* 1815. By
Clementi of London. The
doors when open reveal book-
shelves at the top right

31. Fortepiano. *c.* 1810. By
Frederikus Jahn of St Gallen,
Switzerland. It is believed,
however, that Jahn did not
make, but placed his name on
instruments made in Vienna.
Length 2·43 metres (8 feet).
Casework figured walnut. Rare
'Biedermeir' example with
'Empire' legs. Viennese action.
5 pedals include drum and
bell effects; the bell is visible on
far side of case

32. Giraffe cabinet piano
c. 1810. By Van der Hoef
of Amsterdam

33. Chiroplast in position
on the keyboard, showing
wrist and finger guides.
Inscribed "Royal Patent
Chiroplast. No. 1446.
Manufactured by J. Green,
Music Agent, 35 Soho
Square, London"

34. Cottage upright piano. 1816. By Wornum & Wilkinson of London. This rosewood specimen probably was made for a boat

35. Grand piano. 1825–30. By William Stodart of London. Short compensation tubes. Three brass tubes over brass bichords and trichords in the bass and four iron tubes over iron trichords

37. Grand piano. 1814. By Broadwood of London. Similar to the instrument presented to Beethoven in 1818

36. Clockwork barrel piano. 1800–20. Maker unknown

38. (*above left*) Lyre grand. *c.* 1830. By Schleip of Berlin

39. (*above right*) Upright piano. *c.* 1840. By Henri Herz, Rue de la Victoire 36, Paris. Casework rosewood. Oblique stringing

40. (*below*) Cottage upright piano. 1840s. By I. H. R. Mott, 76 Strand, London. Inscribed "Makers to Her Majesty"

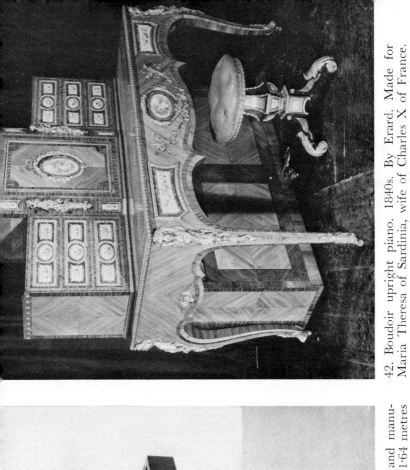

41. Pocket grand pianoforte. *c.* 1840. Invented and manufactured by Robert Wornum of London. Length 1·64 metres (5 feet 4¾ inches)

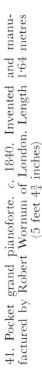

42. Boudoir upright piano. 1840s. By Erard. Made for Maria Theresa of Sardinia, wife of Charles X of France. Casework of kingwood with inset Sèvres centre medallions depicting pastoral scenes and inset Sèvres side panels depicting birds and flowers

43. Albion square piano. 1840s. Invented and manufactured by Robert Wornum of London. 0·91×0·91 metres (3×3 feet). Down-striking action. The tuning pins are at the front between the keys and the lockrail

44. Upright piano. 1850s. By Erard of London. Inscribed "Great Exhibition the only Council Medal for pianofortes to Erard of London"

repeat blow the hammer travelled under half the initial distance. This system was known as 'double escapement'.

Sébastien's nephew, Pierre, patented the new action in England where in the late 1820s considerable hostility, almost amounting to a campaign, was shown towards the Erards. When the action patent expired they decided on the unusual step of seeking its renewal. The Erards were men of refinement; before the Revolution Sébastien was on an excellent footing with French aristocrats and after he transferred his activities to England he put his talent for mixing to good effect making useful contacts among the English nobility, for no man spurns friends in high places. A Privy Council inquiry presided over by Lord Lyndhurst in 1835 vindicated the Erards' cause and subsequently the request of Pierre Erard, in control following his uncle's death in 1831, for a renewal of the action patent was granted.

At first the new action was felt to be over-complicated to be reliable, but with later modifications it became the one used in grands by most makers to this day. In 1821 Moscheles commented:

> Young Erard took me today to his pianoforte factory, to try the new invention of his uncle Sébastien. This quicker action of the hammer seems to me so important that I prophesy a new era in the manufacture of pianofortes. I still complain of some heaviness in the touch, and therefore prefer to play upon Pape's and Petzold's instruments; I admired the Erards, but am not thoroughly satisfied, and urged him to make new improvements.[34]

In 1830 he was finally converted: 'The touch in particular is vastly improved, I begin to revel in these instruments.' One of few pianists able to develop his style to keep up with the times, Moscheles gave part of the credit for this ability to the new Erard and the following year he abandoned the Clementi for Erards. Shortly afterwards Thalberg and others chose Erards which now were held to possess greater responsiveness and fuller tone than their competitors. Delicate nuances and powerful bravura display could be achieved on the same instrument. The action for the romantics had arrived.

Erard's principle of double escapement was seized upon by other constructors who sought to improve it. A repetition action invented in 1844 by Kriegelstein, a pupil of Pape, was held to be both simple and effective and was taken up by others. Antoine Bord, a piano maker who had gravitated to Paris from Marseilles via Lyon, brought out his own repetition action in 1846, while Broadwoods employed their own design of a repetition action. Pleyel and Collard also soon possessed their own modified versions. But it was Erard's great invention which won the day. After overcoming the initial scepticism, the Erard family decided during the 1830s to incorporate it in all their grand pianos and by 1860 virtually all makers were using it in the horizontal grand, although often in one of its modified forms.

A worrying problem was the danger that the hammer's blow might modify the horizontal instrument's tone and reduce stability because the hammer travelled upwards to the string which it pushed away from the bridge (Fig. 22). Another defect was the reduced area of soundboard, cut away so that the hammer's upward progress was unimpeded, but weakening the wooden frame. As the hammer's blow became more powerful, these disadvantages were magnified. Clearly Erard's action was to overcome most difficulties except these.

Earlier attempts were made with a down-striking action with the hammer pushing the string towards the soundboard. That gravity could not be relied on to bring the hammer back from the string proved an insuperable obstacle. Counter-weights or springs had to be used. J. B. Streicher, Jean-Henri Pape, Robert Wornum (Pl. 43), whose father was a violin maker and publisher, and others experimented along these lines. An ingenious attempt at a satisfactory answer was Wornum's 'Pocket Grand' (Pl. 41). The soundboard was placed *above* the strings, so that when the piano top was raised soundboard and strings rose with it. This principle was tried also by Henri Herz, an Austrian settled in Paris and another virtuoso-composer turned piano maker.

This was not to be a solution and other problems made it more vital than ever to improve the bedding of strings on bridges. The strings gradually became thicker than those used in the early nineteenth century, so they needed to be strung at higher tensions to maintain required pitch.

The early nineteenth century saw the introduction of a copper covering spun on to steel wire for bass strings, the copper increasing elasticity, aiding a purer louder sound compared with uncovered thick strings which tended towards inflexibility. The copper covering wire sometimes was given a protective coat of silver to prevent corrosion. The principle of wrapping copper round another string was not new, for even clavichords, lightly strung in comparison, had covered strings although the wire was not wrapped closely together. Soon no space was left between the closely-wrapped coils of the piano string and a heavier string was achieved. One experimenter substituted india-rubber and cat-gut for copper.

The invention of the telegraph led to improvements in wire drawing and during the phase in which techniques developed rapidly, various makers' wire gained preference. In Germany wire made in Nürnberg and then Berlin was praised and Viennese wire also acquired a reputation. In England Broadwoods strung with German and English steel wire, and Webster of Birmingham built up a name for cast steel wire. The steel wire replaced brass wire in the bass and in the treble the iron wire which sometimes had been used. Patents for tempering steel wire appeared early in the century although tempered strings did not come into general use until later. Pape may have been first to use them regularly from 1826. A patent for tempering granted in Paris in 1840 appeared to include the ingredients of a witches' brew! The wire was to be dipped in a solution of white suet, beef suet, olive oil, yellow wax, hartshorn and chamouny honey, and then immersed in milk mixed with charcoal dust. Modern tempered wire strung at high tensions withstands the most punishing demands and possesses the required tonal properties. In 1821 tension on a six-octave grand was $c.$ 6,600 kilogrammes (about $6\frac{1}{2}$ tons); by 1844 the tension on pace-setting French grands by Erard, Pleyel and Pape had reached $c.$ 10,650 kilogrammes (some $10\frac{1}{2}$ tons), still insufficient to prevent strong blows breaking strings.

In 1808 Sébastien Erard invented the agraffe, a brass stud for the wire to pass through (Fig. 27) with a hole for each unison string in the note, so that there was one agraffe to each note. It fixed the speaking length at the tuning plank end and provided a firm bedding. Pierre Erard devised in 1838 the harmonic bar, a metal bridge through which the high treble strings passed and which, like agraffes, on grands prevented the hammers forcing the strings upwards and away from the bridge. It served to

Fig. 27. An agraffe

space the strings and also determined the angle they took from the termination of their sounding length to the tuning pins. The harmonic bar became widely used on grands, there being barely adequate space in the treble for agraffes. In 1843 the '*capo tasto*' or 'pressure bar' was invented by Antoine Bord. Its blunt edge pressed on the string between the upper bridge and tuning pins (Pl. 16), helping to keep it securely in position and adding firmness to it. Cheaper than agraffes, most uprights employ it to this day.

The method of fixing the string at the hitch pin end also was altered. Previously the eye of each string hooked over a hitch pin (Fig 28). The disadvantage was that eyes broke. Also when there was more than one string per note, the wires were often

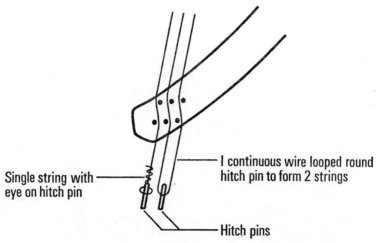

Fig. 28. Alternative methods of fixing string to hitch pin

116

neither the same length nor the same tension, and therefore re-acted differently to temperature changes. In 1827 James Stewart, Chickering's original partner, registered a patent that abolished two eyes by using one piece of wire of double the length, passing it round a single hitch pin (Fig. 28). Friction at the hitch pin was sufficient to prevent the string on one side of the hitch pin being affected when tuning altered the tension of the string on the other side. When the wire formed the third unison of one note and the first of the next, this still held true. Some years later Stewart's innovation won universal acceptance.

These developments enabled the tension to be increased further. On Erard's seven-octave grands of the 1850s total tension had risen to 22,000 kilogrammes ($21\frac{2}{3}$ tons) and on the seven-octave grands exhibited by Broadwood in 1862 it was over 16,250 kilogrammes (16 tons), the highest tension on an individual string reaching 159 kilogrammes (352 pounds). Two similar 1852 grands, jointly played at 918 concerts in their first ten years of use, each lost only one string over this period.

It proved necessary to thicken the soundboard to withstand the demands of heavier stringing. 4–6 millimetres ($3/16$–$\frac{1}{4}$ inch) was a typical thickness on early pianos and contributed to their light tone. Greater thickness aided the production of a mellow powerful tone. Mozart recorded that Stein simply left the soundboard in the open air to dry and to split as much as it would, the splits then being glued up. Now renewed experiments were carried out to remove the resin content and to bake the board in order to obviate as far as possible later splitting.

Several materials had been used for covering hammer heads. Sheepskin and buckskin were long popular in the German-speaking lands—the latter proved most durable but variations in thickness and elasticity frequently were troublesome. In England, famous for its wool, a coarse woollen cloth was tried and so also was cloth arranged as an outer layer on top of leather. Experiments had been conducted with cork and also with sponge, and when difficulties in obtaining the correct texture were encountered, with wood tinder. Conventional leather hammers, hardened by age, produced dry pitched tone. A softer more durable material was necessary and in 1826 Jean-Henri Pape, after experiments with hat felt, patented felt hammers blending sheep's wool with rabbit hair. The surface of the softer felt hammer remained in contact with the string for longer before rebounding, enhancing fuller rounder tone in contrast with the shrillness produced by leather. The extra weight of larger felt hammers imparted greater energy to the thicker strings. The value of Pape's discovery was quickly recognized and while numerous experiments in other directions in succeeding years showed that all were not yet convinced, in the second half of the century felt hammers superseded leather. Specialist felt manufacturers followed the trend and soon devoted their energies to producing hammer felt, perhaps the most highly critical felt of any. R. R. Whitehead, aptly located since 1770 in textilian Lancashire, was the earliest firm to specialize in producing hammer felts and in 1859 E. V. Naish founded his felt business near Salisbury. In the twentieth century wools selected from several sources are blended in the production of hammer felt and both firms possess worldwide reputations for their piano and hammer felts.

With the notable exception of cross-stringing, all technical features of the mature grand had been introduced by 1830, if not yet accepted and exploited. The grand was now suitable for the romantics, although not yet master of all situations. Despite the metal frame the instrument was barely able to withstand onslaughts from hard hitters and occasionally strings broke. Liszt was notorious, leaving a trail of shattered pianos behind him. Often a reserve piano was held in the wings during his performances to meet the eventuality of the piano on stage requiring first aid. In 1852 Moscheles in Leipzig wrote of modern pianists:

One plays in a style cold and clear as a bright December night, and just as frosty; another, with his crashing chords, shakes, and arpeggios, is really too merciless on my unfortunate Erard, which is not only beaten out of tune, but somehow or other has been severely injured. I know the culprit. . . .

The damage could not be put right locally and he turned to Erards for advice and inquired how long he would have to be without his piano. Pierre Erard answered:

. . . just long enough for one of our best grand pianos to be sent to you; you have had yours for seven or eight years already; since those days we have made great improvements, and you ought to have our very best instrument.[35]

During the years of French dominance Erard and Pleyel were names found frequently on the concert platform. Ignaz Pleyel, born near Vienna, the twenty-fourth of thirty-eight children, founded his piano-building enterprise in 1807. Publisher and prolific composer, his later music became increasingly monotonous. Camille Pleyel took over his father's business in 1824. His wife, a famed pianist, as Marie Moke had been engaged to the composer Hector Berlioz. When she broke off the engagement, he stormed from Rome intent on murder to be followed by his own suicide. Kalkbrenner the pianist became a partner in the concern and with his skilful promotions the fortunes of Pleyel flourished, the firm soon sharing the leadership with Erard, now directed by Sébastien's nephew Pierre. A curious coincidence connected the Pleyel and Erard families. The founders of both firms died in the same year, 1831, and their respective successors in 1855.

Businessmen replaced craftsmen at the head of piano firms and commercial considerations played a larger role in marketing. Communications were influential. Much railway construction was undertaken in the 1840s and trains speeded artists and often their pianos from concert to concert. Moscheles was a pioneer in 1831 and described with relish his first railway journey:

On the 18th I went by rail from Manchester to Liverpool; the fare was five shillings. At 1.30 I mounted one of the omnibuses, which carried all passengers gratis to the great building called the 'station'. Eight to ten carriages, each about as long as an omnibus, are joined closely to one another; each carriage contains twelve places, with seats like comfortable arm-chairs; at a given signal every traveller takes his place, which is marked with the number of his ticket, and the railway guards lock the carriages. Then, and not before, the engine is attached to the foremost carriage; the motion, although one seems to fly, is hardly perceptible. . . . Words cannot describe the impression made on me by this steam excursion on the first railway made in England, and the transports I felt with an invention that seemed to me little short of magic. . . .[36]

The new means of transport promoted factories with large outputs and industrial nations over non-industrial. Previously Erards had exported pianos along canal and river, but now they

119

were sent by rail to neighbouring countries—a far cry from the early days when Zumpe's porter carried squares on his back to customers. French and English provincial makers declined as output was concentrated in larger factories in the metropolis.

Pleyel and Erard developed rapidly. In 1827 Pleyel employed some thirty men making one hundred annually. Seven years later Erard's 150 men made some four hundred pianos. By 1855 both makers employed upwards of four hundred men and produced fifteen hundred pianos each. There were nearly two hundred makers in Paris alone—this rapid growth assisted by population increase.

Pape and Herz were two further influential figures in Parisian piano-making. Pape's favourite instruments appear to have been medium-sized with a pleasant tone, less powerful than the new ideal many makers were striving towards. In this respect Pape was behind the times and consequently his pianos never gained a lasting niche for concert work. Pape claimed 137 inventions, including one in 1834 for a circular piano, during his long career. An inventor before he was a businessman, many of his fantasies appeared impracticable but satisfied his desire for schemes of mechanical ingenuity. His vision is illustrated by two extremes. On the one hand he reduced the weight of the average piano by restricting or rejecting altogether various parts; on the other he developed very large pianos, exported to America and known as 'sarcophagi'. Pape also developed a saw for cutting veneers and, delighted to find that he could cut ivory into long sheets, he soon veneered a piano completely with ivory. In the 1840s he ran a piano business in London in addition to his Parisian activities.

Henri Herz of salon fame opened his piano factory in 1828. Eleven years later an imposing concert room followed, which at the outset encountered considerable difficulties as some artists attempted to stipulate that they play on an instrument other than a Herz. When contraptions aimed at assisting the acquirement of technique enjoyed their short-lived success, Kalkbrenner of chiroplast disrepute introduced his *'guide-mains'* or 'guide for the hands', in effect a chiroplast without finger holes. Seeing that its inception fell on fertile ground, Herz soon introduced his 'Dactylion', as useless as Logier's chiroplast because neither scales nor arpeggios spread over several octaves could be performed.

A spring was provided above each finger, which passed through a ring attached to the bottom of the spring. It was maintained that precision was assisted as the tension on the spring helped the finger to rise quickly once it released the note. Doubtless it increased the likelihood that the key would be released involuntarily too soon! Herz's American concert tours were beneficial to his piano-making business, for observing defects of various piano constructions during his journeys, he revised the Herz models and changed manufacturing methods. His tours promoted sales of his pianos in many parts of the globe and he even established a depôt in California. Herz is remembered primarily for his modifications, today incorporated in most grand piano actions, to Erard's double escapement principle.

Boisselot et Fils of Marseilles was regarded as rivalling the Parisian houses in reputation and merit. Situated by the Mediterranean, M. Boisselot specialized in exporting to Spain, Portugal, Italy and America. He strove to ensure that his pianos withstood temperature changes in severe conditions and in these markets his success rivalled that of the English pianos. Wolfel et Laurent Soufléto, and Kriegelstein et Plantade were further piano-makers recognized in the French capital as leaders in the middle of the century.

Mid-century France, however, made only one-third as many pianos as England. Broadwood, the largest maker in the world, made some 2,300 annually and Collard, the old Clementi firm, some 1,500. The total English output in 1850 was about twenty-three thousand. Viennese pianos no longer were considered foremost in design and tone, although surviving specimens suggest that they were fuller-toned than they usually are given credit for. In the 1840s the largest of the capital's 108 makers achieved only two hundred pianos in any one year.

Larger outputs and swifter transport fostered the founding of specialist-parts manufacturers and by the mid-century actions, hammers, keys and soon casework, soundboards and iron frames sometimes were made in separate factories.

Actions and iron frames are components presenting the piano maker with the most daunting manufacturing problems. At the piano's conception the action with the phenomenon of the hammer in free flight was the decisive agent determining the new instrument's character. The action's parts, repeated many times in each mechanism, lent themselves as output of pianos increased to mass production by machines, reducing cost. Furthermore experience acquired as the instrument matured gradually weeded out many action types so that a smaller range of actions remained in everyday usage. These additional factors promoted the growth of specialist action factories and indeed determined that the action became the first component to attract the attention of specialists aiming to supply the piano makers. In 1810 Henry Brooks founded in London the first business to concentrate on manufacturing actions for others to install in their pianos. L. Isermann founded the first German action factory in 1842 and two years later Jean Schwander commenced making actions in Paris, his company known by the name of his son-in-law, J. Herrburger. In 1920 Brooks and Herrburger united, the production of 'Schwander' actions continuing in Paris until 1953 and thereafter in England only. In the later nineteenth century when the composite frame at last was vanquished, the number of foundries casting piano frames grew, so that in the early twentieth century in England alone it reached double figures.

X

Virtuoso Fireworks, 1830-1850

The 1830s and 1840s witnessed a frenzy of romantic piano-playing with Paris acting as international host, a role it took over from London, which forty years earlier had become the pianists' mecca. The concert virtuoso became the equivalent of today's pop idol. Playing had to captivate and superlatives were in—fastest, loudest, richest, most unexpected contrasts—all accommodated by the progress the makers had made. A round, mellow sound lacking sharp corners finally stilled the remnants of baroque tone. The Victorian organ underwent a similar tonal transformation. In eighty years the value placed on a neatly defined world had been replaced by fluid thought acknowledging fewer decisive frontiers and taking the idea of revolution in its stride. Emotional spontaneity was preferred to careful premeditation and the ego with its inner world became of primary importance. In the world at large, man aided by science and products of industrial growth was extending his control over his surroundings. In the virtuoso he glorified his own image.

Pianists flocked to Paris to make their reputations. Liszt, the boy wonder soon to be known to Parisians as 'le petit Litz', arrived during the 1823 season. Pixis came in 1825 and Hiller in 1828, followed by the delicate Chopin in 1831. Liszt and Chopin left the most permanent impression of all romantic pianists.

Frédéric Chopin was in some ways least typical. As tuberculosis weakened him he scarcely was able to play forte and relied upon delicate nuances to compensate for lack of volume.* Liszt reviewed a concert which Chopin gave in 1841 :

* 'His soft playing being a mere breath, he requires no powerful forte to produce the desired contrasts; . . .' (Moscheles noted in his diary after first meeting Chopin).[87]

. . . Speaking to a society rather than to a public, he could safely show himself as what he is—a poet, elegiac, profound, chaste and dreaming. He had no need to astonish or to shock, he sought delicate sympathy rather than noisy acclaim . . . but for fear of increasing the fatigue already obviously betrayed in his pale countenance, the crowd would have demanded again every piece on the programme.[38]

Chopin's style ended the hold of classical values which paradoxically he prized greatly, Bach and Mozart being two formative influences. He and other romantic composers, determined not to be hampered by musical form, devoted less energy than their predecessors to four-movement sonatas, exploring instead new single-movement pieces favoured by Schumann and later Brahms. Chopin created the Ballade, expanded the Scherzo and won recognition for the Mazurka, Polonaise and Nocturne as distinctive art forms.

Chopin adopted the easiest fingering. The Viennese school disapproved of his involvement of the thumb with black keys and allowing fingers to slide to adjacent notes. His pedalling assisted the achievement of nuances and of dreamy sounds, unequalled until Debussy seventy years later perfected a novel impressionistic pianism. Chopin's preference was for Pleyel's square pianos. Liszt wrote that Chopin favoured Pleyel's instruments 'because of their silvery, somewhat veiled, tone and easy touch. It permitted him to draw therefrom sounds that might recall one of those harmonicas of which romantic Germany held the monopoly. . . .'[39]

Franz Liszt on the other hand was a superlative showman to whom everything seemed clear-cut. Liszt heard Paganini, who his contemporaries believed was in league with the devil, at his Paris début in 1831 and vowed to be the stupendous virtuoso of the piano. He allowed his sentiments free rein in a letter:

'And I too am a painter!' cried Michael Angelo the first time he beheld a *chef d'oeuvre*. . . . Though insignificant and poor, your friend cannot leave off repeating those words of the great man ever since Paganini's last performance . . . what a man, what a violin, what an artist! Heavens! what sufferings, what misery, what tortures in those four strings![40]

The hysteria Liszt caused was devastating. Garlands of laurel were placed on his forehead, while pieces were cut from his clothing. Countesses hurled their jewellery at the stage. Relics—snuff box, cigar stub, gloves (often deliberately left on the piano for the purpose) or broken hammers—were fought for and treasured until death. Women counted in their hundreds wore gloves bearing his image, while in Paris it was rumoured that he abducted Countess Marie d'Agoult inside his grand piano. The procession which escorted him when he left Berlin in 1842 after giving twenty-one public concerts was near-regal. Julius Kapp described it :

> The University had resolved to provide Liszt with a farewell escort. A coach pulled by six white horses awaited him in front of his hotel. When Liszt appeared he was greeted by the cheers of a thousand-headed crowd. He took his seat beside the senior members of the University. 30 carriages-and-four followed his, escorted by 51 horsemen in festive academic dress, representatives of the various student fraternities. Hundreds of private conveyances joined this official retinue, to conduct him in a festive procession through the town. All the streets are tight-packed, thunderous cheers announce the approach of the celebrity. The court itself had travelled into town, to view the jubilation. 'Not like a king, but as a king he departed, surrounded by the exultant throng, as a king in the immortal realm of the spirit. . . .'[41]

In the first flush of excess Liszt became accustomed to such fêting, for the citizens of Cologne, in appreciation of his fund-raising efforts directed towards the completion of Cologne Cathedral, determined to give visible expression to their gratitude :

> A steamer, festively decorated with flowers and flags and with three hundred and forty members of the Philharmonik on board, proceeded to Nonnenwerth to provide an escort of honour to Cologne. . . . At 7 o'clock the Philharmonik Society set Liszt in its middle and boarded the boat, decorated with gay Chinese lanterns, to the accompaniment of thunderous cannons . . . rockets and many-coloured fireworks flew heavenwards, while flaming torches magically surrounded the ship. Music and hurrahs were heard on shore. Cologne in its entirety was assembled. Some 15,000 people attached themselves to the Philharmonik procession slowly winding through the illuminated streets and conducted Liszt to his hotel, where a splendid banquet . . . concluded the festivities.[42]

Liszt transferred technique from hand to arm and even trunk as never before, assisting the victory of showmanship. He pushed piano playing to new horizons and his *Twelve Etudes of Transcendent Execution* rarely have been equalled in their technical demands. Liszt's improvization was legendary and he was accredited with being the best sight-reader of all time. Mendelssohn once placed before him the freshly completed but illegible manuscript of his G minor Concerto, which Liszt sight-read to perfection. As Mendelssohn enthusiastically told Hiller : 'It couldn't be played better than he played it—it was wonderful!' Liszt (Pl. 48) retired from regular concerts in the 1840s to compose and teach. His last pupil died only after the Second World War.

Other pianists abounded, worthy competitors and poor imitators. Sigismond Thalberg was Liszt's greatest rival. With a quieter platform-manner he achieved his effects without swaying his body. He said that he acquired an attitude of self-control by smoking a Turkish pipe while practising exercises, the length of the tube calculated to keep him upright and motionless. Thalberg's trick was to make two hands sound like three. He achieved this by emphasizing the melody with his two thumbs and surrounding it with arpeggios. New at the time, it earned for its exponent the title of 'Old Arpeggio'.

Thalberg was one of the earliest pianists to visit the United States. American journeys soon became an established part of the touring pianist's life. Leopold de Meyer, called the 'Lion Pianist' owing to his mane and dramatic treatment of the keys, toured in 1845 followed in 1846 by Herz, a master of the salon. Salon pianists playing a lighter kind of music had considerable success in the early romantic period. de Meyer used fists and elbows as key-hitters. Sometimes he sat at the keyboard, decided he did not like the positioning of the piano and had it moved, whilst making speeches to his audience. de Meyer and Herz learned quickly the importance of employing agents to organize their American tours with extravagance, publicity and regrettably false claims. Public relations soon came to the fore. Herz acquired Bernard Ulmann as his press agent. A stunt tried by Ulmann was to light the hall with a thousand candles, curiosity selling all tickets in under a day. After Herz had played his first piece a sonorous voice announced that there were not a thousand candles. The objector could count only 992.

Inevitably de Meyer and Herz, who performed on successive days in Baltimore, crossed swords spurred on no doubt by their agents. After de Meyer who performed first failed to remove his Erards from the hall, a long exchange of letters in the press gave invaluable publicity.

In the 1830s the conventional orchestral backcloth for the piano was encountered less frequently. Singers' accompaniment, still an essential feature of every concert, often was provided by piano with possibly string quartet. Moscheles planned to give a concert in 1837 of music for piano alone. He dispensed with the usual orchestral assistance, but was persuaded to take the precaution of blending vocal music with keyboard to avoid monotony. The newspaper critics were generous in their praise, finding fault only with the interruption caused by introducing the voice! Two years passed before Liszt took the plunge and gave in Rome the first concert anywhere without supporting artists. He described it in a letter to the Princess Belgiojoso:

. . . I have ventured to give a series of concerts all by myself, affecting the Louis XIV style, and saying cavalierly to the public, 'The concert is—myself.' For the curiosity of the thing, I copy one of the programmes of the soliloquies for you:
1. Overture to William Tell, performed by M.L.
2. Reminiscences of the *Puritani*. Fantaisie composed and performed by the above-mentioned!
3. Etudes and Fragments by the same to the same!
4. Improvisation on themes given—still by the same.[48]

Liszt referred to 'soliloquies'. It seems that Frederick Beale first applied the description 'recital' to an evening for solo piano. In 1840 he arranged Liszt's appearance at the Hanover Square Rooms, undisputedly London's leading concert venue after the Argyll Rooms were burnt down in 1830, and placed an advertisement for 'Liszt's Pianoforte Recitals' in *John Bull*, the plural s suggesting the several compositions billed. In 1841 Liszt gave the first piano recital held in Paris without supporting cast as part of his campaign to recapture his public from Thalberg. Later the 's' was left off and 'recital' passed into the language as applied to the piano.

The fuller-toned piano, expected to resound in a fair-sized

hall,* aided these developments. The halls opened by the Parisian firms, Pleyel, Erard and Herz, each held three to four hundred concert-goers, although the Hanover Square Rooms absorbed about six hundred. Liszt's concert in the Peers' Hall, St Petersburg, was attended by nearly four thousand—to remain an exceptional number.

Virtuosi still arranged programmes round their own music, commonly based on a popular tune or an opera medley. Thalberg played at the Théâtre-Italien to an audience of fifteen hundred, his *Moses* fantasy and his fantasy based on Meyerbeer's new opera, *Les Huguenots*. Composers frequently played in the 1820s included Mayr, Paër, Pixis, Weigl and Winter, names now seldom heard. Haydn, Mozart and Beethoven appeared increasingly after 1830.

From the mid-1830s multi-piano performances, possibly started after Kalkbrenner's return to Paris in 1823, were fashionable. Three, six or more pianos were used, often with two players at each. In the United States Herz remained adamant and composed a piece for eight pianos, rather than the forty pianos Mr Ulmann thought necessary! Further south at a concert in Rio de Janeiro in 1869 forty young ladies seated at twenty-five pianos performed the National Hymn. Famous pianists were acclaimed when they performed together, weaving their own fantasies from the operatic ones. The *Hexameron*, variations for six pianos and orchestra on a march from Bellini's *I Puritani*, was performed first at a charity concert given in Paris and was revived at a 1972 Promenade Concert. Master-minded by Liszt, variations were contributed and played by Chopin, Czerny, Herz, Pixis and Thalberg, while Liszt poked fun at the last three in his introduction and finale.

Marathon orchestral concerts of typically two symphonies, two overtures, two grand instrumental and four vocal pieces were given. Moscheles listed twenty-nine items performed at one concert. With programmes of such length the audience could not be taken to task for chatting, laughing and eating. Few artists demanded silence. While the orchestra enjoyed its moment of

---

* Moscheles observed in his diary, that invaluable commentary on contemporary trends, of a concert in Birmingham in 1834: 'The powerful tones of the Erard were heard all over the colossal and crowded hall, which was not intended for solo instruments; . . .'⁴⁴

45. The overnight popularity of American pianos in Europe. 1867
cartoon from *Le Charivari*

46. Concert grand. 1868. By Erard. Casework satinwood with inlay depicting flowers, and with cross-bandings and ormoulu in Louis XVI style. Composite frame. Parallel strings. 7 octave

47. Perpendicular piano. 1878. By Percival of Bayswater. The left hand was intended to play the bass on the keyboard reflected in the mirror, and the right hand the treble on the second keyboard

48. Liszt in 1886 seated
at an upright piano by
Schiedmayer & Soehne
of Stuttgart

49. Upright piano by
Ibach of Schwelm,
Germany, in Liszt's
room at Weimar

50. 'Gothic' upright piano. Late nineteenth century. Maker unknown

51. Leaflet showing Pesaresi street pianos. Late nineteenth century. This firm was listed as still in business in 1939 in Camden Town, London

PESARESI & SON,

Manufacturers of Piano Organs and the Improved Automatic Coin-in-Slot Pianos,

30, WARNER STREET, CLERKENWELL, LONDON, E.C.

Orders promptly attended to.   Marking of Cylinders a Specialit

THE "PESARESI" STREET PIANO.

READY FOR USE

INTERIOR VIEW.   EXTERIOR VIEW.

LOWEST PRICES (NETT CASH) FOR PIANOS, COMPLETE WITH BARROW AND COVER:

			HEIGHT.	WIDTH.	LENGTH.	
Class A	40	Hammers	4 feet 4 inches	1 foot 11½ inches	2 feet 10 inches	£16
" B	44	"	4 " 5 "	1 " 11½ "	3 " 1 "	£17
" C	48	"	4 " 6½ "	1 " 11½ "	3 " 3½ "	£18
" D	55	"	4 " 7½ "	1 " 11½ "	3 " 9 "	£21

ALL PIANOS ARE WITH TEN TUNES OF YOUR OWN SELECTION.

52. Street piano (mandoline piano). Late nineteenth century. By D. Antonelli & Sons of Manchester. Inscribed 'Manufacturer of Automatic Pianoforte with Penny-in-the-Slot"

53. Reproducing piano. c. 1927. By Grotrian-Steinweg of Braunschweig, incorporating Hupfeld 'Tri-Phonola' reproducing system. The note pneumatics are situated under the back of the keys. To the left of these may be seen the dynamic valves and underneath these, the expression box with plastic windows controlling both the accompaniment and theme notes. With this model the suction pump is provided in a separate cabinet, with roll storage above

54. 'Pianola' player-piano unit. *c.* 1903. By The Orchestrelle Co. of London and New York, mounted on an Erard grand. Example of the early player-piano, a separate attachment which could be positioned at the keyboard of any piano. The harmonium-type bellows, soon replaced by electricity, are visible on the left

55. The same instrument showing the pierced paper music roll. The white label on the left indicates 'on' and 'off' positions for the 'accent' effect controlled by the operator. The white indicator visible beneath the paper roll enabled the operator to regulate the tempo

56. Electropiano Instruction Laboratory. 1975. By Baldwin of Cincinnati, USA. Miss M. Jefferson (facing camera) at the master instrument, using the Electropiano Laboratory at the Guildhall School of Music

57. American 'spinet' upright piano. c. 1976. By Kimball of Jasper, Indiana, USA. Casework Spanish pecan

58. Paderewski at the height of his fame playing the Steinway. Newspaper caricature of unknown date

59. Piano in Highgate Cemetery, London. Inscribed "To the memory of my beloved husband Harry Thornton, age 35. A genius who died Oct. 19th, 1918"

glory in the tuttis, Liszt stamped the floor and rattled his decorations. Earlier the continuo player or the leading violinist directed the orchestra. In the 1820s Spohr popularized the baton and within twenty years the conductor as we know him today was encountered frequently as a separate entity, a pre-condition for the establishment of modern orchestral concerts of symphonic works with one or two concertos.

The scene, however, still differed greatly from today's. Compositions were altered without conscience and Liszt once proposed replacing the composer's libretto for Schubert's opera *Alfonso and Estrella* by another. Sentimental programmes were adapted to music. Schumann found he could fit the story of Hero and Leander to *In der Nacht* from the *Fantasiestücke*. Liszt gave the eccentric pianist de Pachmann, who appeared to have an endless supply of dressing-gowns in which he received visitors and which like the socks and gloves he wore had, he assured inquirers, belonged to Chopin, a programme for Chopin's F minor Fantasy involving Liszt, Camille Pleyel, and George Sand, the latter pleading for Chopin's forgiveness.

Such riots of the imagination cannot be judged by today's standards, for the romantics based their actions on the opposite of present-day precepts and thereby earned their contemporaries' praise. Only in this century has self-restraint in expression and faithfulness to the written note won acceptance.

Leading pianists arranged their concertos and divertissements in simplified two or four-hand arrangements to be played by the amateur at home, and many symphonic works appeared in duet form. The piano (and sometimes pianos) in the home was for many the only means of introduction to music which otherwise would remain unheard. Much popular music was arranged for piano. *Spinning Songs* and *Hunting Songs* were followed by *Elfin Dances* and *Witches Dances*, selections soon appearing in volumes.

As study at the piano became compulsory for an ever-wider circle of young ladies and as the ambitious wished to emulate the fireworks of the virtuosi, so the idea evolved that learning the piano was drudgery. Years of slavery on scales, arpeggios and double octaves were regarded as an essential prelude. If the untalented desired to become proficient, it was maintained that persistent practice would achieve success and they became additional grist to the mill for piano teachers.

XI

The Upright Piano, 1730-1850

The development of the upright with strings running vertically instead of horizontally commenced in the piano's early years, but a century elapsed before the vertical instrument replaced the square as the alternative to the horizontal grand.

Christian Friederici in Gera was an early constructor of vertical pianos. In similar fashion to an upright harpsichord he turned a wing-shaped instrument on end, the strings running upwards in front of the player. Diagonal arrangement of the strings enabled the tallest point of his instrument to rise symmetrically in the middle and in 1745 he called it a 'Pyramid Grand'. Essentially a modification of Cristofori's principle, the escapement on Friederici's action (Fig. 29) was modified into a jack and the intermediate lever omitted. Friederici was not alone, for in 1739 at about the time when he was experimenting with his vertical piano, a pyramid-shaped piano was made by an Italian, Domenico del Mela of Gagliano. After Silbermann's death in 1753 and the departure of the 'twelve apostles' to England, Friederici became for some years the best-known piano and harpsichord maker in Germany.

The space between the keyboard of early upright instruments and the floor was wasted as the strings ended at the keyboard. Little serious thought was devoted to a vertical piano until the end of the eighteenth century, when the pianoforte appealed to a larger public and the potential of the upright for saving space in cramped city dwellings was attracting attention.

The Londoner William Stodart registered his 'Upright Grand' in 1795—'an upright piano in the form of a bookcase' in which 'both the hammers and dampers are returned by weight', as the patent stated. Haydn, who saw one of the novel upright grands in Stodart's shop, was pleased with its musical and orna-

Fig. 29. Upright
action by Friederici

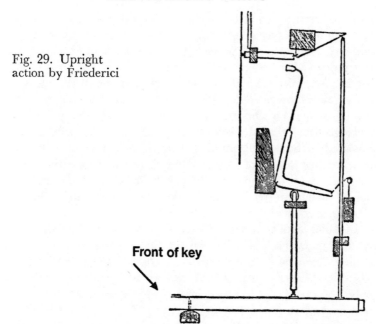

Front of key

mental potential. A grand was erected vertically on a stand and inserted in a rectangular cupboard. Doors opened and shelves were positioned in the space on the right. The upright grand achieved little success abroad, but retained some popularity in England until the 1820s. Broadwood, producing 940 from 1799 to 1831, and others (Pl. 30) made upright grands, which were 10–15 per cent more costly than conventional grand pianos. Its height of over 2·45 metres (8 feet) caused the instrument to become perilously top-heavy. The usual horizontal grand action, adapted for the less advantageous striking angle, was employed.

In 1798 William Southwell, a Dubliner working at St Martin-in-the-Fields in London, patented a square placed upright on a stand. The hammers were positioned close to the instrument's highest point and were connected to the keys by rods or 'stickers', a primitive form of the later popular 'sticker' action. Southwell's idea was unsuccessful, but in 1811 he returned to it placing a square piano vertically on a stand. The strings and soundboard sloped backwards away from the player resulting in Southwell's awkward appellation—'piano sloping backwards'. The instrument tapered to a narrow width at the top, creating a distance between the player's face and the piano, for its designer was endeavouring to avoid projection of the voice directly into the instrument when the pianist was also a singer. The 'piano sloping backwards' appeared gauche but offered one further novelty, a foot pedal operated an attachment to turn the pages of the music. Singers, it appears, never were satisfied and years later were grousing that the silk front of the cabinet piano, a form invented by Southwell, muffled their voices. These criticisms led to a further family of instrumental shapes in which the centre was cut away for the voice to penetrate through the gap, the height to left and right retained so that the bass string lengths were unaffected and symmetry upheld.

In 1800 two continents saw the omission of the stand, the vertical piano itself standing on the floor so that the strings extended downwards to ground level reducing the overall height. Matthias Müller's *Ditanaklassis*, devised in Vienna in 1800, was only 1·84 metres (72·5 inches) high. A clever down-striking action was devised to avoid leaving a gap in the soundboard for the hammers to strike the strings from behind and a tape was employed to help bring the hammer back from the string—the last feature predicting the tape-check action. However Müller's true upright met with little success—possibly he could not keep the price low enough to attract potential customers.

In the same year Isaac Hawkins, an engineer of English parentage, unveiled in Philadelphia his 'Portable Grand Pianoforte' (Pl. 26, 27) only 1·38 metres (54·5 inches) high as the bass strings were formed like springs to obtain the required weight from shorter length. The soundboard was suspended in a metal frame supported from behind with metal rods and the tuning plank was covered by metal. Like the 'Ditanaklassis' and modern uprights, Hawkins' action was positioned on the keyboard side of the strings. The keyboard itself folded away, Hawkins possibly having in mind a ship's cabin. Resort is made by a few twentieth-century manufacturers to the collapsible keyboard, not for marine entertainment, but to save freight when packed pianos are despatched overseas. This instrument by Hawkins, who also won renown as the inventor of the ever-pointed pencil, showed the ingenuity of the engineer's mind. Its ideas were developed during the next forty years.

The next attempt to improve the upright was English. Thomas Loud, who later like Hawkins emigrated to Philadelphia, patented oblique stringing (Pl. 39) from the top left-hand corner to the bottom right in 1802. It provided either longer bass strings or a reduction in the height of the instrument for the former string length, for Loud envisaged that a bass string length almost the same as the instrument's height could be achieved. The potential of his idea, however, which had been tried occasionally earlier, was not realized for some years.

An unknown Viennese maker introduced the 'Giraffe' upright (Pl. 32). The style became popular in the German-speaking lands, its vogue lasting forty years. Although nearly 2·45 metres (8 feet) high, the action was below key-level. Its shape exposed the curve of the horizontal grand and the right-hand side above the treble strings frequently made a shelf, on which statues or glossy brass ornaments were stood. Higher flights of fantasy allowed caryatids or Apollo complete with lyre, or during the Turkish fashion dark-skinned boys with expensive plumes. Gaudiest fancies were exploited on the giraffe, satisfying the desire of the *nouveaux riches* to impress.

The introduction to military bands of the Turkish drum, triangle and cymbals popularized effects activated by the generous number of pedals provided on Viennese fortepianos and giraffe uprights. A drumstick was made to strike the soundboard. Brass strips struck the lower strings to give a cymbal effect. A further pedal commonly produced 'triangle' or 'bells' (Pl. 31) and a bassoon effect was achieved by a parchment strip resting against the strings of the three lowest octaves. These gimmicks were useful for Turkish and battle music. They supplemented the sustaining pedal (called the 'forte' pedal) and on grands the 'una corda' pedal, the two pedals which survive on grand pianos.

The una corda pedal functions by moving keyboard and action to the right for each hammer to strike two strings in place of three or one string instead of two, the unstruck string vibrating sympathetically. Thereby the volume is softened and hence the pedal is commonly known as the 'soft pedal'. More significant is the changed tonal colour resultant from the hammer's movement towards the treble. The string is set in motion by a different portion of the hammer's felt nose, a portion less compressed and less worn as it receives the full impact only when the una corda pedal is in use. The distinctive tone produced by this method is more noticeable than the half-blow effect on the vertical piano. The una corda principle generates complications—the pedal action may be heavy and mechanical irregularity coupled with uneven wear of hammers and action can occur. Furthermore one string of two and three string notes remaining unstruck may cause the other strings to go out of tune more quickly. The tonal contrast dependent on the extent of the hammer head's wear varies from piano to piano and during the lifetime of each instrument. Ravel indicates that the una corda pedal should be held down for the whole of 'Le Gibet' from *Gaspard de la Nuit.*

The pedal on some early instruments was able to be pressed progressively deeper for the hammer to strike first one and then two strings fewer. Beethoven refers to the device in the slow movement of the 'Hammerklavier' Sonata when he instructs *'una corda'* and later *'poco a poco due ed allora tutte le corde'* ('gradually two and then all the strings'). In the third movement of the Sonata Op. 101 the player is instructed *'nach und nach mehrere Saiten'* ('more and more strings'). This contrivance gave greater gradation of pianissimo, for the una corda device was more dramatic on early nineteenth-century pianos than on modern ones and doubtless helped harpsichordists not yet masters of the piano, who varied volume by use of the pedals rather than by finger touch. An interesting device of this nature to imitate the swell of an organ was contrived for his combined harpsichord-piano and patented in 1774 by Joseph Merlin, an ingenious inventor who also made mechanical tea-tables pouring a dozen cups simultaneously and who invented a wheel-chair and roller-skates. His shop known as 'Merlin's cave' achieved a fashionableness, while James Cox's museum of mechanical novelties was another, popular in London at the time. Contemporary fascination with fanciful automata extended even to the construction of a life-sized musical silver swan, a plaything believed to have been made for Thomas Weekes' 'museum'. Its articulated neck swooped down to seize a fish, which then appeared to be swallowed to the accompaniment of the tune the swan produced.

It proved difficult to apply the una corda principle to the upright piano and Czerny for one questioned the change of tone colour resulting from the hammer striking one string fewer. Consequently the left-hand (or more accurately left-foot) pedal of the modern upright is a half-blow—the hammers on their shanks are moved forward in order to travel a reduced distance before striking the strings. Their impact is lessened and a softer note results, but the tonal contrast associated with the una corda mechanism is lost. The 'half-blow pedal' of the upright fails to attract the attention devoted to its sustaining pedal.

A third or middle pedal known as the 'celeste' is favoured on modern uprights in certain countries. A strip of felt is lowered between hammers and strings to produce a muffled tone likened by the famous teacher Tobias Matthay to a 'dog with its head in a sack'. Despite this description it is useful as a practice pedal when neighbours wish to remain undisturbed. As early as 1800 the felt strip was the subject of experiment by Hawkins in the production of graduated increase and decrease of volume by tapering the thickness of the felt which then is raised and lowered gradually.

In the 1820s the 'lyre grand' (Pl. 38), principally a Berlin form and a variation of the giraffe, appeared. Obliquely strung, it achieved the symmetry which the giraffe lacked. J. C. Schleip was the best-known maker of lyre grands and was said to have designed the form.

Southwell's 1·83 metres (6 feet) tall 'cabinet piano', a type to remain popular for some years, appeared in 1807. Bass strings rose vertically from floor-level. Front panels sometimes were covered with silk and a pair of 'carved pillars' impressed the pretentious. The 'sticker' action (Fig. 30) was completed by further alterations to escapement and damping and could be used for tall or short pianos, its convenience ensuring for it a long life. The cabinet piano overcame a familiar problem of grands and uprights—the necessity to cut through the soundboard to allow action parts, usually hammers or dampers, to reach the strings. This weakening of the soundboard caused instruments to go out of tune more readily. Southwell's cabinet piano stood in tune better.

The large 'cabinet' (Pl. 28), however, looked bulky in a small room and listeners saw only the pianist's back. Continuing attempts therefore were made at a *small* upright. Most influential was Wornum's design of 1811 with diagonal strings stretching to the ground and a projection on the jack activating the dampers.

Fig. 30. The sticker
action

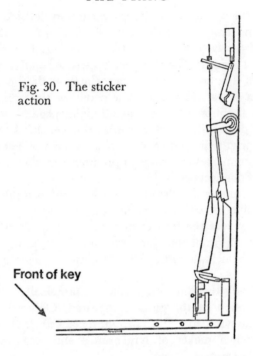

Front of key

0·99 metres (39 inches) high with a five-and-a-half-octave keyboard, the ends (Pl. 20, 34) extended a considerable distance
beyond the first and last keys to accommodate the diagonal strings
in the bass. In 1813 Wornum produced a further small upright,
this time vertically strung. Wornum called his small upright of 1826
a 'professional pianoforte' and in 1828 he completed his 'cottage'
piano about 1·17 metres (46 inches) high and vertically strung;
the overhead check was replaced by one mounted on the lever.
The tape (Fig. 31) was included in Wornum's 1842 patent of
his tape-check action, which is substantially the action now used
universally in upright pianos.

The hammer on an upright action cannot rely solely on
gravity for its return and must therefore be more dependent
upon strings and tapes, its speed of repetition presenting grave
difficulties compared with the grand piano's repetition facility. It
was observed by Wornum's contemporaries that these problems
would cause the inventor of a successful upright action to shed
drops of sweat. Continued attempts were made to achieve sig-

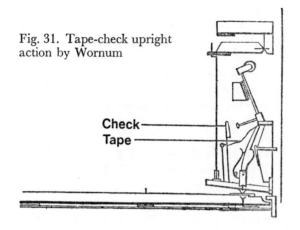

Fig. 31. Tape-check upright
action by Wornum

Check

Tape

níficant improvements by incorporating Erard's double escapement principle into the very different vertical action of the upright.
As recently as 1973 the German piano maker Sauter displayed in upright pianos a double repetition device comprising an
additional spring built into the jack; this firm is now offering it
in certain models.

Robert Wornum was to the upright action what Sébastien
Erard was to the grand action. Pleyel copied the tape and check
of Wornum's action and Wornum's design with some alteration
was found shortly after in Germany and the United States. In
Paris it was made soon in such quantities that in Germany and
ironically England, where some makers purchased the French
versions, it became known as the 'French' action, while the
French continued to know it as the *'mécanique anglaise'*
('English action').

English designers therefore were indispensable in bringing the
upright to commercial feasibility. The French followed shortly
after and stimulated Germany and Austria to produce eventually native versions of the 'pianino', as Pleyel called Wornum's
small instruments (Pl. 34). At the time it was believed erroneously
in Germany that the upright had been invented in France. As
early as 1815 Pleyel had been instructing Pape, still in his
employ, to supervise the making of cottage pianos on the
Wornum pattern. Continuing along the guidelines shown by
Wornum, Blanchet et Roller, a Parisian firm directly descended

137

from the eighteenth-century harpsichord maker Blanchet, exhibited in 1827 at the Louvre an upright only 1 metre (39 inches) tall, smaller than Wornum's instruments. Obliquely strung, whereas many of Wornum's instruments were strung vertically, it gave to its makers the opportunity to achieve for a given height a better tone than was possible with vertical stringing. The piano was the most talked-about instrument exhibited and the firm's miniature uprights assured its success in the decades which followed.

In 1828 Pape made the first of his 'console' uprights 1 metre (39 inches) high. The instrument took the logical next step from oblique stringing and introduced over-stringing, now accepted practice. The bass strings crossed over the treble ones (Pl. 16), enabling the maker to obtain longer bass strings stretching from corner to corner and mounted on a separate bridge. It was taken up by isolated makers in England (John Godwin registered a patent in 1836), the United States (in 1830 Babcock added over-stringing to the iron frame of his square piano and in 1833 Bridgeland and Jardine exhibited an over-strung piano in New York), Germany and Austria in the 1830s. In the later 1840s it became widely used. Wheatley Kirk, a Yorkshireman, patented in 1836 the earliest complete metal, apparently cast iron, frame for an upright and by 1839 Pape had introduced the iron frame to his 'piano consoles'.

The vertical piano developed later than the grand and as greater variation was conceived in its shape and technical features, it took longer to decide which of its many forms ultimately would prevail. By the middle of the century, however, a definite pattern was visible. The action was so arranged that the hammers pressed the strings on to the bridge, obviating the cut through the soundboard. The low upright, which did not overpower a small room and which allowed the singer's voice to carry, had won widespread acceptance. Nonetheless for the duration of the century and into the next, the upright of intermediate height, lower than the cabinet pianos but taller than the diminutive instruments, remained the most popular. On the other hand, the vogue for taller upright grands, cabinet pianos and giraffes passed together with the desire for ornate impression and the wish to attract attention by presenting in vertical form a piano reminiscent of the horizontal grand.

In 1851 only 5–10 per cent of English output was accounted for by grands compared with 80–90 per cent by uprights. The English-made square piano was virtually obsolete, only about fifteen hundred being produced, the majority for export to India. It had, however, undergone some development in the preceding years. An iron frame frequently replaced the wooden one and Pierre Erard even introduced double escapement. Although the square's resonance was added to, it still lagged behind the dramatic tonal improvements made to the grand so that in comparison it sounded deficient. The French nicknamed the square instrument 'the kettle'. Pierre Erard had realized its ultimate fate when in 1824 he foresaw that the square instrument's awkward shape would kill its sale as rooms became smaller. Promptly he set about designing upright models to replace the large percentage of squares in his output. As the keyboard grew to a compass of six octaves so did the square instrument's size. Its casework became more ornamented and by 1840 inventive minds had produced writing-desk and hexagonal table-topped squares, and even a table from which the piano could be detached (Fig. 32).

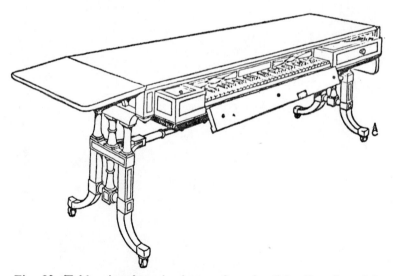

Fig. 32. Table pianoforte in drawer form by John Broadwood & Sons, 1803. The piano can be removed entirely from the table, like a drawer

Victorian mechanical ingenuity recognized few limits (Pl. 47). In 1866 Millward patented a 'combination of piano, couch, closet, and bureau with toilet articles'. The stool housed a work-box, a writing-desk, a looking-glass and a set of drawers. In the same year a patent by J. Macintosh stretched the imagination still further. The tone was to be magnified by compressed air created inside a trumpet-shaped covering positioned over the pianist or singer. Even more bizarre was Daniel Hewitt's patent of 1854 whereby the strings were attached to the wall of the house to save the expense of the piano frame!

XII

The United States, Germany and Modern Concert Programmes, 1830-1914

Babcock's one-piece iron frame, more economical and offering the only practicable long-term solution to problems of stability, soon found adherents in the Boston area, but the New York makers preferred to retain European metal structures of several distinct pieces.

Piano-making in the United States grew considerably, diminishing the European makers' share of the market. In the 1830s Jonas Chickering rose to pre-eminence, assisted by his partnership with a wealthy sea-captain John Mackay, who ensured until he was lost at sea in 1841 that there was no shortage of money. Earlier Mackay had financed Babcock during the period when he carried out his momentous casting. After they parted company the sailor transferred his aid to Chickering whose original partner, a Scotsman called James Stewart, had left him in 1825 to return to Europe, taking with him it was said the idea, which he patented in 1827, of looping one wire round the hitch pin to serve for two notes. It seems plausible as this device was tried next by Babcock in 1830. Mackay, a sea-dog able to put a love for pianos to practical benefit, was an unusual combination. With financial worry behind him, Chickering adapted Babcock's cast-iron frame principles with his own patented modifications including one in 1843 for the earliest complete cast-iron frame for a grand.

With the growth of concerts the grand came into its own in the following decade. Previously few American makers devoted much energy to it, but at a time when the preference for fuller tone was growing, tended to concentrate improvements on the square which fitted readily into a covered wagon, but which in Europe rapidly was becoming obsolete. In America the pretentious still regarded the large square's superiority over the cabinet upright as unquestionable. Steinway's square added an octave to the European square piano compass of six octaves while the largest square piano, which the American public rejected, was 1·83 metres (6 feet) long. The casework of these large squares extended considerably beyond the extremities of the keyboard, causing such instruments to appear insufferably long. The American square became a cumbersome heavy-legged box, its appearance to modern eyes extremely gauche. Its tone, however, was surprisingly full. Soon it was appreciated that these great squares consumed more materials than the upright, which required less floor space, and so the former became no longer suitable for a poor man's piano. As the piano spread to less well-to-do families in smaller homes, it was only a matter of time before the rectangular square was ousted by its vertical rival and in the last quarter of the century the square lost favour, its lingering extinction nearly complete by the 1890s. By 1903 their construction had ceased, but there were so many in circulation that the American makers bought up and burnt a large number on a 15 metres (50 feet) high bonfire in Atlantic City.

In the early 1850s about nine thousand instruments were made annually, Chickering, his iron frame giving his grands great power of tone, producing thirteen hundred.

Many Germans, threatened with ruin from the unrest which produced the 1848 Revolution, arrived, among them Heinrich Steinweg, who showed a youthful interest in musical instruments winning a medal for bugling in the face of the enemy at Waterloo! He anglicized his name and in 1853 founded Steinway & Sons. Steinway and his offspring soon took the final steps in perfecting the modern concert grand. Henry Jr introduced overstringing (Pl. 16) to the one-piece grand frame in 1859. The bridge was lengthened to give it more curvature and was brought in from the outer edge of the soundboard. In the 1870s Theodore Steinway, the last of the family to arrive from Germany (the business he left behind to become known as Grotrian-Steinweg), and a trained scientist in touch with the famous Berlin acoustician Helmholtz, increased the stress on the frame to its present figure of nearly 20,000 kilogrammes (19·7 tons) and strings again were struck harder by heavier hammers. The double escapement action was modified further so that the touch weight was acceptable. The duplex scale, a further product of the exchange of ideas between Helmholtz and Theodore Steinway, was introduced in 1872. Helmholtz established the principles for our modern understanding of overtones, of which Steinway made use. The portion of the string on the non-sounding side (Pl. 16) of the bridge usually is deadened. Steinway calculated the length required for its pitch to coincide with that of an overtone produced by the speaking length and allowed these newly-calculated back lengths to vibrate in sympathy with the note, thereby adding to the fullness of tone.

Steinway's grands offered unrivalled volume combined with incredible sensitivity and responsiveness. The nineteenth-century ideal of ringing, abundant tone, suitable for sustaining thick blocks of chords, had at last been realized fully, Steinway adding additional volume to the warmth of tone present on grands of the mid-century. By the end of the Civil War Steinways were making over two thousand pianos a year and shortly after overtook Chickering's output.

In 1874 Steinways perfected the 'sostenuto' pedal, to hold the dampers aloft from any notes already depressed at the time the pedal is brought into action until the latter is released. Meanwhile ensuing notes could be played normally, unaffected by the sostenuto pedal. This effect, the subject of experiment thirty years previously when Boisselot et Fils exhibited an instrument incorporating it at the Paris Exposition of 1844 followed by an improved version in 1849, is useful in the widespread mysterious chords of Debussy and others, sustaining a bass note when the left hand moves from it to notes higher up. It became popular on American grands as the middle pedal of the three, but was never adopted universally for European pianos. Josef Hofmann, afraid that he might accidentally press the pedal, insisted on its removal from the Steinway instruments he played.

News of American progress circulated in Europe in the mid-1860s and the accolade of success soon was achieved at frequently-held international exhibitions. Steinway was awarded the first gold medal at the Paris Exposition of 1867 (Pl. 45), Chickering also winning a gold medal. Neither firm spared any publicity expense and it was said that their total costs during two months' duration reached 400,000 francs each. Steinways obtained a testimonial from the composer Rossini stating that Steinway pianos were 'powerful as thunder and the tempest and melodious as the fluting of the nightingale on a spring night'.[45] Chickering, not to be outdone, set up a grand in Liszt's Rome apartment. The master obliged and prayed that before dying he wished to see three things: the prairies of America, Niagara Falls and Chickering's pianos.

Great significance attached to 'collecting' testimonials and to victory at regularly-held exhibitions. Self-satisfaction was discernible in the listing of diplomas and medals awarded to piano producers at exhibitions as geographically varied as Amsterdam, Brussels, Calcutta, London, Philadelphia, Rome, Rotterdam, St Louis, St Petersburg, Sydney and Turin. Pride of place, however, went to the Paris International Expositions of the Arts and Manu factures promoted by the French government and held in 1867, 1878, 1889 and 1900, the latter the last of these great exhibitions.

A Paris award was a respected distinction of international worth, although the award policy became partially exclusive. To an exhibitor showing for the first time a silver medal was normally the highest that could be awarded, however excellent his pianos. On the second showing eleven years later the maker might aspire no higher than a gold medal and only at a third appearance, twenty-two years after the first, could an exhibitor contemplate winning the most highly coveted award of all, the Grand Prix. At the 1900 Exposition there was an innovation as each international jury was allowed to decide whether to follow time-honoured custom, which suited long-established firms well enough, or to make awards irrespective of previous appearances so that a new exhibitor could win eligibility for the highest award. The international music jury presided over by Gustave Lyons, head of Pleyel, decided to abandon custom and award solely on merit, the foreign members of the jury outvoting M. Lyons and his French colleagues. Baldwin, the Cincinnati maker exhibiting for the first time after ten years' experience of making pianos, was awarded the Grand Prix. Earlier, before the Paris expositions were opened to international entries, makers on occasion were declared *hors concours* after several notable successes—an achievement (or fate) awarded to Pleyel in 1844 after winning gold medals in 1827, 1839 and 1844, and to Blanchet et Roller in 1849.

A list of medals won in all parts of the world appeared on their proud possessor's notepaper and also as a transfer on the soundboard. The most impressive achievement, however, was to supply royalty and if a string of crown princesses and archdukes could be added, so much the better. Germany with many small principalities struggling to retain their old customs proved a happy hunting ground, and as their *Hoflieferant* (supplier to the court) Bechstein could boast of most success.

By the time of the American international success Erard, Pleyel and Broadwood were past their years of inspired innovation, their position with the world's great, overdependent upon past glories. To stay in the vanguard of progress it was apparent that European makers would have to build pianos along American lines. This decision entailed final relinquishment of the composite frame, which had been employed by most European makers into the 1850s, and adoption of the one-piece cast-iron frame, whose advantages had been proved conclusively at last by the tonal power of Steinway's over-strung square instrument with full iron frame exhibited at the 1855 American Institute Fair held in New York's Crystal Palace. Grands built by Erard in 1870 continued to employ a composite frame while Broadwood retained until 1895 the 'Iron Grand' with the introduction of a further bar and other modifications. In the early part of the century German makers modelled their instruments on English pianos and then by the 1840s on French, but now after a century of sending its geniuses overseas to find favourable conditions, German piano making once more came into its own and rose to the challenge.

In the later nineteenth century Germany became a leading industrial nation. Prussia's rise consolidated small principalities into a united country, creating one currency, strong government and improved communications. The land of romantic poets and abstract speculation was converted to practical technology. Coal and iron resources were exploited producing improved tools and readier supplies of steel wire and iron frames. Political stability induced capital investment, which with expanding commerce enabled the piano industry to grow on native soil.

Bösendorfer in Hapsburg Vienna, Ibach (Pl. 49) and Schiedmayer, all old-established firms, prospered. The youthful Bechstein, whose first grand was inaugurated by Hans von Bülow only in 1856, and Blüthner, both lacking established reputations, were in the best position to benefit. Realizing that American developments pointed to future dominance, their grands followed the American in pattern and they flourished. Blüthner's 'Aliquot' scaling demonstrated that new awareness of acoustics could be turned to good account. A fourth string was added for each treble note, intended to vibrate in sympathy and to produce the octave (first overtone) when the adjacent trichord was struck. By the 1870s Bechstein's concert grand was favoured by the majority of European concert artists. Steinways opened their Hamburg factory in 1880, but only slowly rivalled Bechstein on European concert platforms. Until 1914 Bechstein, Blüthner and Ibach supplied the best-known concert grands, contracted artists helping each firm to maintain its position, grands from three or four leading makers often being available in the same hall for the pianist's selection.

Despite these successes some German manufacturers sent their sons to America to receive their technical training, and the German theorist Hansing wrote late in the nineteenth century that Germany followed the American system of piano construction and that American cast iron frames were superior to all others in quality and artistic construction. Considerable quantities of German pianos, however, were exported throughout Europe and beyond. By 1910 Germany was the second largest world maker with an output of 150,000. The United States produced 360,000 (far removed from the nine thousand of sixty years previously), England 75,000 and France came fourth with 25,000. The period prior to the Great War coincided with the piano's most widespread popularity, extensively accepted as a source of home amusement by all classes.

While the masters of piano histrionics enjoyed their finest hour, an alternative unexplosive pianism was conceived. By the 1860s it had won unobtrusively virtual acceptance for the modern recital programme and replaced the virtuoso reliant on the superficial dazzle of his own fantasies. The new arbiters of taste sought the 'best' music, which usually implied the compositions of others in preference to their own, and stressed the interpretation of its inner worth in place of characteristics lending themselves to showy execution. Nonetheless judged by their own contemporary standards they possessed superhuman finger dexterity. Fantasias and potpourris were replaced by Scarlatti, Bach, Beethoven, Mendelssohn, Chopin and Schumann, and the sonata regained its rightful place. In addition the fashionable compositions of the day were performed and a light-hearted piece sent the audience home with a feeling of well-being.

Mendelssohn, popular with Queen Victoria, helped to initiate the change. He revived the public fortunes of Bach's compositions and may have been the sole pianist among his contemporaries *never* to perform operatic fantasies or salon pieces. Beethoven's cause was promoted by Hallé, who in 1861 was, it appears, the first to play publicly the complete cycle of thirty-two sonatas, giving eighteen recitals in St James's Hall, London. Incurring the displeasure of *The Times* for daring to play without the printed music, he positioned the score on the desk from the third recital onwards, although continuing to perform from memory.

In the 1840s it still was considered disrespectful to the composer to play his music without the score and it won Clara Schumann, probably the first pianist to play regularly from memory in public, much criticism. Frau Schumann became the acknowledged guardian of the 'classical' tradition and demonstrated that wrist once more could predominate in place of arm and elbow. Her dislike of Liszt, the seeds of which were sown in the early 1840s during the initial acquaintanceship of Robert Schumann and Liszt, reached morbid extremes—at the mention of his name she scrupulously collected herself together and walked away. After her husband Robert's death she again earned her living on the concert platform, his acknowledged interpreter, and finding also a new cause to champion—Brahms' music against that of the Liszt–Wagner lobby.

The conflict between Brahms' admirers and the champions of the 'music of the future' was one of the great mid-nineteenth century controversies. Brahms was seen by many as a mild traditionalist and so was placed on the classicist side of the fence, although hindsight judges him a late romantic at heart. Critics have assessed him as reconciling elements usually regarded as 'intellectual', for instance counterpoint (his hallmark was the attainment of perfect independence of fingering combined with frequent use of thirds and sixths and an interest in cross-rhythms), with the heart demanding 'romantic' melody. Like Schumann,

Mendelssohn and others he forsook the piano sonata, his chosen path variation form and later short lyrical pieces which he called intermezzi. The more forceful and impassioned pieces he called capriccios. In these short piano pieces he explored the particular qualities of piano tone, finding the instrument's intimacy a relaxation from larger symphonic composition. He chose to explore these avenues when other composers in the 1880s and '90s at last were beginning to comprehend that quality should not be sacrificed to cheap effect achieved through the piano's loud tone. Brahms' unusual blend of conservative and modernist traits caused a variety of judgements—his near contemporary Busoni criticized his music with its seeming failure to confront novel problems as 'too comfortable', while Schoenberg described him as progressive.

These contradictions point to growing uncertainty as the restless spirits of the late nineteenth century started to tire of romanticism but were uncertain which way to turn. The twentieth-century progressives deserted the romantic movement and consequently it often is misunderstood.

One avenue of pursuit, that of folk interest, commenced in a climate of growing national consciousness. As nations strove for political independence, so they re-explored their respective heritages and sought to develop their distinctive musical cultures. Folk-song helped to revive Spanish musical life, Albéniz and Granados introducing a nationalist element. In Norway Grieg performed the same service, his short piano pieces with titles like 'Norwegian Bridal Procession' and 'Norwegian Peasant Dance' stressing his native folk idiom. In Russia it was Balakirev, founder of a group of composers known as 'The Five' and also of an establishment in St Petersburg, the Free School of Music, which helped to spread the dogmas of nationalism. Although nationalism caused much political strife its musical side-effects were less belligerent.

National concepts of piano playing emerged in the 1860s—the rigorous German style, the warm-blooded Russian, the refined French and, as befitted a nation subject to foreign influence in forming musical judgements, the selective English. Von Bülow did much to assert the primacy of the German school of playing for some decades. Touchy, pedantic and determined to establish his pre-eminence, he was the embodiment of the

'*Tonkünstler*' ('tone-artist'). He married Cosima, his master Liszt's daughter, who after twelve years left him to conquer Wagner. He was gifted with a prodigious memory and gave 139 concerts without using printed music on an American tour—playing from memory was accepted at last! (It is curious that pianists today normally are expected to play from memory, but organists seldom do so.)

Amy Fay, a young American, graphically described the 'mini-invasion' of Germany mounted by her compatriots a century ago. She arrived in Berlin in 1869 and in the years following, like many others from the 'new world', took lessons from most of the great teachers then resident in the Kaiser's capital. A fellow American, Edward MacDowell, rose to become chief piano teacher at the Darmstadt Konservatorium proving that Americans could win acceptance by the German establishment. It was estimated that there were almost two thousand American music students in Berlin and that one-fifth of the average concert audience in any German city was composed of Americans—the latter situation recreated in the American Zone after the Second World War.

The pioneer in compelling European pianistic circles to listen to the voice of the United States and then in creating public demand in America for piano concerts on European lines, had been Louis Moreau Gottschalk. In Paris after a director at the Conservatoire had refused him a hearing on the grounds that America was only a country of steam engines, he performed his fantasies, among them *Bamboula*, *Le Bananier* and *La Savana*, employing American folk music and rhythms and invoking the atmosphere of New Orleans. From 1853 until his death in 1869 he travelled throughout North and South America and perhaps encountered those pianos which could be split into two, especially designed to be carried across the Andes by mule. His own words describe his success :

I am daily astonished at the rapidity with which the taste for music is developed and is developing in the United States. At the time of my first return from Europe I was constantly deploring the want of public interest for pieces purely sentimental; the public listened with indifference; in order to interest it, it became necessary to astound it; grand movements, *tours de force*, and noise had alone the privilege in piano music, not of pleasing, but of making it patient with it. I was the *first* American pianist, not by my artistic worth, but in chronological order. Before me, there were no piano concerts except in peculiar cases—that is to say, when a very great name arriving from Europe placed itself by its celebrity before the public, which, willing or unwilling, through curiosity and fashion rather than from taste, made it a duty to go and see the lion. Now piano concerts are chronic, they have even become epidemic : like all good things they are abused. From whatever cause the American taste is becoming purer, and with that remarkable rapidity we cite through our whole progress. . . .[46]

Conditions in Latin America were arduous at the best of times, but the Civil War in the north occasionally created a bizarre touch :

The other day in the car, there being no seat, I took refuge in the baggage car, and there I smoked for two hours, seated on the case of my piano, alongside of which, O human frailty ! were two other cases also inclosing instruments, now mute, since the principle that made them vibrate, under a skillful touch, like a keyboard, has left them. They were the bodies of two young soldiers killed in one of the recent battles.[47]

Miss Fay and those like her who flocked to Berlin were tribute to Gottschalk's work, even though the menu he served was going rapidly out of fashion in Europe.

The leader of the Russian school of pianism was Anton Rubinstein. As a youngster he imitated Liszt, hands descending from on high, but the grandeur of his playing was marred by wrong notes. Those who put spirit before cunning adored him. In the United States where he was nicknamed 'Ruby', he was lionized more than any other pianist before Paderewski, affectionately known as 'Paddy'. Rubinstein's resemblance to Beethoven was a psychological factor in his favour and produced rumours that Beethoven plausibly could have fathered an illegitimate child. His historical recitals covered the development of the piano repertoire in seven lengthy programmes, one comprising eight Beethoven sonatas including all repeats, plus encores which on one occasion consisted of the complete Chopin B flat minor Sonata !

After 1850 numerous pupils emerged from Liszt's studio, to which pianists from far and wide flocked to attend his masterclasses. With Leschetizky's pupils they produced the second age of romantic pianism and dominated the late nineteenth and early twentieth centuries. Leschetizky's pupils wrote much about his 'system' but showed complete disagreement over the characteristics of their master's teaching. It appeared to possess no inflexible method, its greatness lying perhaps in Leschetizky's ability to assess each pupil separately and vary the essence of his instruction to meet individual needs. In addition he paid close attention to muscular manipulation, a facet which stirred theorists to voluble debate.

Analysis of muscular movement aimed to achieve optimum relaxation by treating the limb from shoulder to finger-tip as an integrated whole. In England Tobias Matthay codified the elements making up touch which he defined as 'the act of levering weight upon the key during the latter's descent'.[48] Finding that there were six different methods of employing the arm, he built up a daunting system. Weight and relaxation theories, a reaction against heavy-shouldered virtuosi, retained their hold in the present century until the impossibility of playing without muscular tightening was recognized—subsequently muscular analysis has been considered largely irrelevant.

Leschetizky's reputation was cemented for all time by his pupil Paderewski, the embodiment of pianism to the Americans (Pl. 58), from whom he earned a large proportion of the ten million dollars he is believed to have amassed during his career. His technical equipment was not outstanding and on several occasions during his New York début in 1891 he practised for seventeen hours daily! Nonetheless his stylistic sense and glamour gave him a remarkable hold over his public recalling that of Liszt. Women queued to worship his hands, insured for one hundred thousand dollars. Like royalty he journeyed in his private railway carriage with his retinue, among them chef, masseur and private doctor. The earliest revelation of Paderewski's magnetism, however, the rush to the stage, was invented by his secretary at his early New York concerts by giving fifty tickets to students on the understanding that they charge the platform—a ploy to which Liszt never sank. In 1970 Edward Heath followed him as a Prime Minister who was also a musician—Paderewski returned to the concert platform in 1923 after a term as Premier of Poland.

Concert artists did much to improve amateur taste, making it no longer necessary to relax the audience between movements by inserting a piece of lighter disposition. The new awareness was reflected in home music-making. Mendelssohn's *Songs Without Words* and the more appealing Beethoven sonatas began to be familiar by the fireside, alongside selected Chopin pieces and Rubinstein's *Melody in F*. New means of entertainment had not yet arrived while the Victorian moral code maintained its grip, and so musical evenings with the daughter of the house at the piano and other members of the family most likely singing, were commonplace. A piano was found in every parlour and more were played than were left unplayed!

Transcription of earlier works both for the concert platform and in easy arrangement for the less-gifted on the family piano had an obvious justification as the instruments for which they were composed originally, the harpsichord, clavichord and even the organ, were not readily available. Bach was acceptable again and if the master's compositions were to be heard at all, it was argued that they needed rewriting into a form more suitable for the piano. These ideas agreed with the readiness of concert artists to alter music to suit their fancies and to allow their virtuosity to impress, but they transformed music of previous styles into contemporary tonal concepts. Bach/Busoni, Bach/Liszt and Bach/Tausig became widely known, converting clear polyphonic lines into the thick harmonies of the late nineteenth-century piano. Notes were added to chords to thicken them and double octaves and other contrivances were introduced to increase volume. Busoni, writing in 1913, summed up in his usual reflective manner the position of arrangement :

Transcription occupies an important place in the literature of the piano; and looked at from a right point of view, every important piano piece is the reduction of a big thought to a practical instrument. But transcription has become an independent art; no matter whether the starting point of a composition is original or unoriginal. Bach, Beethoven, Liszt, and Brahms were evidently all of the opinion that there is artistic value concealed in a pure transcription; for they all cultivated the art themselves, seriously and lovingly. In fact, the art of transcription has made it possible for the piano to take possession of the entire literature of music. Much that is inartistic, however, has got mixed up with this branch of the art. And it was because of the cheap, superficial estimation of it made by certain men, who had to hide their nakedness with a mantle of 'being serious', that it sank down to what was considered a low level.[49]

As Busoni hinted many preferred lighter fare and pieces sporting titles akin to *Maiden's Prayer*, *Warblings at Eve*, *Monastery Bells* and *Moonshine Elegies* supplied their needs, providing sentimental melodies built on harmonic schemes limited to a handful of chords.

As the aspirations of lower-income groups were aroused and a foretaste of present-day standards was afforded by quantity being adjudged a virtue, American piano production reflected higher living standards in North America than in Europe.

Factories producing soundboards (Dolge in 1880 produced over forty-one thousand), frames, tuning pins and other components by virtue of specialization helped to reduce the price of commercial pianos, but it was insufficiently appreciated that quality also declined. Rapid strides were made towards the 'mass-produced' instrument. In the 1860s Joseph Hale, knowing nothing of the craft, purchased every component and by assembling more efficiently than others was able to market pianos at prices lower than most producers could contemplate. Hale introduced the system of supplying different names (for example 'Valley Gem' was used by one of his imitators) to order, and soon other makers bought his pianos under their own names. For all the defects of his products, he helped make the attainment of a piano feasible to a wider population.

The more subtle marketing methods sometimes found in Europe are illustrated by John Brinsmead and Sons, the London manufacturer, in a description of the perils confronting an engaged couple in choosing the conventional piano:

How often when a marriage is on the tapis and the happy couple *in posse* are discussing the question of ways and means will the natural query arise, 'What about a piano?' The consistencies of chairs, tables, and the general furniture of a house need not give rise to much quibbling. Their merits or faults can be seen and judged by an ordinary pair of eyes, and the outlay of a certain sum of money will nearly always in their case assure to the bride and bridegroom a substantial return, but it is frequently otherwise with the pianoforte. A handsome price does not invariably mean a sound and lasting instrument. There are makers who, having no reputation to sacrifice, will not scruple to place before their patrons instruments which present to the eye the very acme of perfection; the filigree work and carving is beyond reproach, the keyboard is a dazzling white, . . . and so the sale is made, and the lady who, like most of her sex has an economical eye, is proud to think of the saving she has effected. Yet pay that youthful pair a visit twelve months, or, at the most, two years later, and turn the tap of conversation on to the subject of music. The lady will first of all tell you that she does not play so much now as she used to, she is horribly out of practice. 'The fact is'—here she will lower her voice and look unutterable things—'the fact is, George and I bought our piano in a hurry; it seemed very nice and pretty, but—well, it is of no use mincing matters, it was not the instrument we thought it was. Our tuner gave us his candid opinion the other day, and it was far from flattering, so George is trying to sell it for an old song, and we are going to Brinsmead for one which can be depended on.' This waste of money is a sad commentary on the commercial morality of the times, and the ease with which all but professional musicians can be deceived. . . .

Such firms as Messrs John Brinsmead and Sons are content to wait for the erring couple to call and expatiate upon their wrongs, knowing that the contrast between the instrument they are then selecting and the one which has caused them so much tribulation will be a life-long advertisement for the firm which has left no stone unturned to enhance the merit of pianos in the eyes of the musical world. *Apropos* of such a provision, it is worth a moment's fleeting thought to consider how much enjoyment a sterling piano affords to the leisure hours of the softer sex, setting aside the mere accomplishment as an accomplishment. How many homes where the lord and master has perforce to be absent, it may be, in these railroad and Cunard times for days and weeks, nay, months together, are brightened by the cheery sounds which proceed from the boudoir or the drawing-room. A listless, enervated life ceases to exist in the presence of a really good piano. . . .[50]

Nearly ninety years later with equality of the sexes an acknowledged fact, who would dare refer to the husband as 'lord and master'?

From the mid-1850s virtuosi visiting the United States had been content to use American instruments, firstly Chickerings and soon Steinways. Gottschalk, the first American concert pianist, travelled with his Chickering, maintaining that the best American pianos were the equal of the best European instruments and that he could obtain greater variety of tonal tints on Chickering's grands. The new-found eminence of American pianos in Europe and their greater reliability in the severe American climate led to remaining imports of European instruments dwindling rapidly. The Steinways realized that a piano's excellence could be promoted if artists' patronage could be publicized widely and in 1872 signed Anton Rubinstein, who following a taxing schedule gave over two hundred concerts at the rate of nearly one daily! Chickering responded by engaging von Bülow. Rivalry between makers made the piano manufacturer into a kind of latter-day patron of music (a role fulfilled in an earlier age by the aristocracy), promoting tours by artists who performed, understandably, on one make of concert grand only! Additional publicity was procured by placing a large sign announcing the piano's make on the side of the instrument—much to the disgust of von Bülow, who once publicly threw the placard to the floor.

At the century's turn further expansion was under way. Factories were established in the interior and Chicago became a centre as the piano's popularity spread westwards. The practice of manufacturers supplying models under several names added to the strains created by competition in marketing methods and cut-throat prices, and made it likely that the industry would consolidate. In 1903 the new Aeolian undertaking aimed to make various qualities of piano in different factories and absorbed the Weber name, which had enjoyed short-lived success on the concert platform. Another large combine, the American Piano Co., was formed in 1908 with Knabe and Chickering as leading names. It soon produced fifteen thousand pianos annually, but even this large figure was exceeded by Wurlitzer and Kimball. The large-scale piano factory had arrived. Success was growing also for D. H. Baldwin, whose concert grands to this day rival those of Steinway on the American concert platform.

Tempering this apparent confidence were danger signs evident for those who could interpret them. The cinematograph and phonograph, as they were known, were still in their infancy. Shortly before his death in 1897 Brahms made an early cylinder record despite the extremely poor reproduction, playing at the piano one of his Hungarian Dances. Soon pianists added melody to the silent movies, but it was new habits of entertainment which ended the piano's heyday.

XIII

The Piano in Europe, 1850-1914

After the technical development of the grand piano was complete, renewed attention was devoted to the problems presented by its appearance. The simple lines of Regency (Pl. 24) disappeared in the 1830s and '40s to be succeeded by years of forced ostentation. Special commissions presented opportunities for elaborate but often tasteful inlay (Pl. 42)—perhaps an outlet for the imagination, the shape of the piano prescribed by musical considerations allowing little scope for radical experiment. Mother-of-pearl, jasper, marble, tortoise-shell and ivory-covered specimens were produced and artists Burne-Jones, who portrayed the Orpheus and Eurydice legend on an 1880 Broadwood Iron Grand, and William Morris, like designers Robert Adam, who normally planned all the furniture and fittings for his buildings, and Thomas Sheraton (Pl. 23) in a previous generation, were attracted to grand pianoforte cabinet decoration. An ebony piano by Herz ornamented with gilt-bronze mouldings chiselled by the French sculptor Froment-Meurice found its way even to the Caribbean, while Erard exhibited in 1855 a grand decorated with paintings in the style of Watteau by M. Guichard and with bronzes by Victor Paillard.

The structure necessary to support the greatly increased weight of the grand gave it a bulky appearance and the enlarged compass of seven-and-a-quarter octaves added to the width, both detracting from the graceful curve. To some modern eyes the late Victorian grand appears over-ornate. In the opening years of this century straight legs appeared, eventually to replace their bulbous predecessors, the fretwork desk was rejected and so too were twisty gothic lettering, candlesticks, the tasselled cloth (the Victorians delighted in enveloping tables and cabinets in red, purple or green velvet) draped over the top of the piano, and the

156

framework for the pedals, the lyre, which was replaced by straight pillar supports.

The Greek lyre was regarded as a symbol of music for it was Apollo, god of music and heavenly musician, who with his seven-stringed lyre livened the banquets of the Olympic deities. Apollo's son Orpheus descended into Hades armed only with his father's present, a golden lyre, and with its strains won Eurydice's release. In the early Middle Ages King David was portrayed sometimes playing a lyre in place of the more usual harp. The lyre's shape has been employed frequently as a motif for the decoration of musical instruments, enjoying a special vogue in the nineteenth century when the Empire style promoted a fashion for antique forms evidenced by the lyre grand (an upright), Eulriot's upright shaped like a lyre and patented in 1834, music stands and the height of ingenuity, the lyre-shaped guitar. When piano-makers developed a structure to give the pedals effective support, it had been the lyre which was adopted widely (Pl. 31).

The styling of the Victorian upright piano reinforced the impression of excessive ornamentation (Pl. 50), creating dust-traps and encouraging the attachment of statuettes of revered composers. The Victorian era marked the heyday of the 'cottage piano' which, its suggestive name arousing visions of the tranquil countryside, became a popular term rather as 'minipiano' became for a spell in the mid-twentieth century. The semi-cottage and boudoir cottage pianos were variations on the same theme. The typical cottage piano height of about 1·22 metres (4 feet) continued to be most favoured in the early years of this century while rosewood remained the most popular timber for the cabinet.

The standing of the English piano had declined by the turn of the century. Earlier, England regularly introduced new developments, but latterly she followed, often belatedly, trends set by others. Southwell's 'sticker' action still was made in the 1890s, the decade witnessing its final disappearance, long after Wornum's upright action had been adopted widely overseas. As the height of the upright became less imposing, the sticker (Fig. 30), an additional lever essential to tall cabinet pianos, became superfluous, sufficient linkage obtained through pilot (Pl. 18), lever and jack alone. When the sticker was used in the smaller upright, however, although its length was reduced it introduced an additional coupling and usually was weighted with lead detrimental to sensitivity of touch. Meanwhile some manufacturers of high-grade grand pianos continued with single escapement actions, giving an easy strong blow but prone to wear and maladjustment. Some actions of this type were described as 'spring and loop' actions, their installation in some cheap grands continuing until as recently as the 1950s. Because musical taste was slow to develop, English makers were tardy also in accepting the one-piece cast-iron frame, which affected the potential tonal fulness of their products. The composite frame instruments of Broadwood (Fig. 33) and Erard (Pl. 46) were considered superior for performance of Mendelssohn, Chopin and others who composed for them, and the absence of over-stringing imparted specific tonal qualities. In line with some other industries, inclinations to rely on past successes and, unlike competitors overseas, failures to attract maximum benefit from modern science were noticeable.

Consequently as taste developed, demanding the brightness and tonal strength of the new German grands, Germany made inroads into the English market and established a reputation for unassailable quality, which only recently has been put in perspective. Leading German producers made outstanding pianos, but hosts of cheap low-grade pianos invaded England (even the names Bradwood and Erart were offered) on the strength of the good ones. The belief that foreign instruments and musicians were necessarily superior contributed to their success. In 1865 the bulk of England's piano imports came from France which supplied over two thousand four hundred pianos, mostly Erards and Pleyels, for many regarded the Erards of the period as fuller-toned than English-made pianos. In addition S. & P. Erard made pianos and harps in England, only closing their London piano factory in 1890. By the early twentieth century some twenty thousand German pianos were imported annually and Ibach and other leading German manufacturers had opened London showrooms. Bechstein Hall, opened in 1891, was later renamed the Wigmore Hall, still prominent in London concert life. Despite imports, in the years prior to 1914 English makers produced more pianos than at any time previously, although only a small proportion of output, in 1913 amounting to 9,250 pianos, was exported.

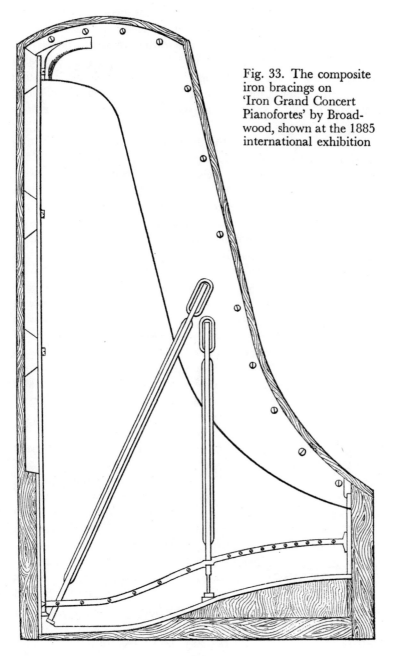

Fig. 33. The composite
iron bracings on
'Iron Grand Concert
Pianofortes' by Broad-
wood, shown at the 1885
international exhibition

In 1915 the McKenna Duties were imposed in time of war, raising a 33⅓ per cent import duty on selected goods, among them musical instruments and cars. The duties represented the first significant reversal of long-standing free-trade policies. Repealed in 1924, they were reimposed in 1925 by Churchill and although protection of home industry had not been originally the prime intention, aided by anti-German sentiment they reduced the flow of imported pianos.

Intense competition aided by growing mechanization and larger scale production caused prices actually to fall in the early decades of the century. A new piano of straight-strung design could be delivered to the home for £20 or even less. In 1929 a typical commercial 1·17 metres (46 inches) over-strung upright retailed at £45, not far removed from the prices of Zumpe's day, but now an infinitely more complex instrument was produced.

Numerous names associated with the pioneering years had languished as the nineteenth century progressed. Merlin, an experimenter of erratic genius rather than a consistent maker, died in 1804, while William Southwell continued into the 1820s. The Mott and Stodart businesses ceased in the 1860s, the latter on the death of Malcolm Stodart, son of William and grandson of Robert Stodart who had founded the business in 1775. Robert Wornum died in 1852 but Robert Wornum & Sons continued until 1900. Such firms were replaced, however, by many makers whose pianos are encountered still and which were founded at the outset of the Victorian period, rising to prominence in the middle or latter part of the century, although two, Chas. H. Challen in 1804 and W. G. Eavestaff & Sons in 1823 were founded earlier. On Clementi's death in 1832 Clementi and Collard became Collard and Collard, remaining prominent until absorbed by Chappell in the present century. At the end of the last century Collard absorbed Kirkman, the old harpsichord firm which turned to piano making, and in the present century Collard took over the Allison name, founded in 1837. John Hopkinson and J. Strohmenger & Sons both commenced manufacture in 1835. The John Brinsmead & Sons business was established in 1837 and was absorbed in the first part of the present century by Cramer. George Rogers & Sons was founded in 1843 and Monington & Weston in 1858. Numerous firms offering basic quality at basic prices did not stay the course, for intense rivalry developed as demand expanded alongside Victorian prosperity alluring yet more firms to the piano's manufacture. It is surprising how many survived for a mere five, six or even fewer years, especially in the 1840s and '50s.

Several of today's leading makers, among them Barratt & Robinson, Bentley, Kemble and Zender, were founded in the period following 1877. London at this time possessed over two hundred piano-making firms, about three-quarters of them located in north London where Camden Town, drawn into London's urban net in Victoria's reign, became a centre as outputs increased, making it impracticable to manufacture and retail from the same building. Some 'factories', however, were in reality small assembly shops completing a handful a year with a couple of men in a back-room after collecting all parts from supply houses offering pianos in 'kit' form.

The outbreak of hostilities in 1914 reduced output, factories turning to war work and seasoned timber being acquired for the doleful necessity of lining trenches. Throughout Europe the war took its toll. In Vienna Bösendorfer's production reached its highest point in the year 1913–14 when 434 instruments were despatched, but in the first year of fighting the figure fell to 136. The havoc wrought by the war contributed to the death in 1919 of Ludwig Bösendorfer, whose top hat had been welcomed in earlier years by Viennese cartoonists. Although famous he remained true to the simplicity of the craftsman's life to the end, instructing that his coffin should be borne to the cemetery in a piano van driven by his own workmen. His wish was observed.

Small producers supplied local demand in Belgium, Switzerland and the Scandinavian countries, while lack of interest in the piano in the Spanish peninsula and the Balkan lands stemmed from a different musical culture and the absence of a sizeable middle-class. In Italy where the piano had been invented, it was largely forgotten. A 'Ministerial Inquiry into the Condition of Manufactures in Italy', which commenced work in 1871, noted that over eight hundred pianos were made yearly in Turin which supplied almost the entire Italian markets, besides the few exported to South America.

Throughout the nineteenth century men of German stock produced pianos in St Petersburg, its name changed following the Revolution to Leningrad. The Diederichs brothers and

Tischner were two early makers. Concert grands made by Becker and Schroeder were accepted by Anton and Nikolai Rubinstein, trend-setters of the Russian musical establishment, and in the second half of the century by foreign touring artists who previously had transported their own instruments around Russia. By 1910 Russian production did not exceed ten thousand pianos annually.

On the European fringes the Crimean War made the piano better-known in Turkey. It even made its way into harems where it was raised on short legs to a height enabling the performer to sit comfortably on cushions on the floor. Stories, a number of them initiated by the concert artist de Meyer, told of mislaid grand piano legs, the pianist being expected to perform with the instrument held aloft on Turkish backs.

The ardour of would-be inventors continued unabated. They were not to realize that the piano by the last quarter of the nineteenth century had achieved maturity and they continued their attempts to improve diverse parts and by their rearrangement to introduce new possibilities, so that the twentieth century may claim with some justice that nearly every conceivable design change was the subject of experiment in the previous century. Like English, French and German designers before him, a little-known experimenter, Thomas Machell, who owned music warerooms in Glasgow, attempted to design an instrument which when once in tune would remain so constantly and function reliably in all climates. He explained his new instrument in 1885 in a paper read to the Philosophical Society of Glasgow. The strings were replaced by steel bars bent to the shape of tuning-forks, the larger forks producing the deeper notes. The action was simplified and metal replaced various wood and cloth parts in the effort to produce reliability. The hammer, arranged below the key with its head pointing downwards, struck the steel bar and its vibrations were passed to the wooden bridge through a piece of spring steel, bent to the form of a semicircle and of the kind, its inventor stated, used in actuating timepieces. The vibrations were amplified by a double soundboard similar in form to that of a harp. Machell's instruments, compact and easily transportable, were used for entertainment in the trenches during the First World War, but the instrument had many limitations and so was little made after the war. Known or unknown to Machell, the idea of the tuning-fork had been tried by Müller of Ditanak-lassis fame in 1827 when he replaced the third unison string by a fork tuned to the pitch of the other two strings and which vibrated sympathetically with them. It was claimed that the tone became richer and more bell-like. The tuning-fork experiments are typical of the countless others which their inventors hoped would bring them fame, but which, after the patent had been applied for, failed to rouse any interest and so fell rapidly into oblivion or at best won limited acceptance for several decades. They are remembered now merely as further evidence of the mechanical competence and diversity of the age which bred them.

Other experimenters were more fortunate, at least winning some recognition during their lifetime with their ideas remembered by posterity, although they did not achieve widespread application. Some far-sighted designers believed that the piano would be forced to alter in order to meet new requirements after romantic values lost their appeal, and so they attempted to predict these inevitable changes. Several designs suggest that they grasped the belief that the conventional backcloth of tonality with major and minor keys would fall apart and that intervals smaller than a semitone might become appropriate. Then a re-design of the conventional keyboard with seven white and five raised black notes to the octave would be necessary. The traditional ordering of notes appeared capricious anyway and a restructuring making the keys more accessible to the fingers might be possible. Several revolutionary designs resulted.

The brainchild of a Hungarian nobleman, Paul von Jankó, proved of lasting fascination to musicologists. He presented the notes in novel fashion by allocating to his first tier C, D, E, F sharp, G sharp and A sharp, while the second higher tier took C sharp, D sharp, F, G, A and B. All keys were equal in width so that the twelve major scales could be played with only two different fingerings. Because his octave took up the space of only six conventional white keys to stretch Tenths and Twelfths became simple. Each key was provided with three striking places each higher than the last, Jankó aiming to provide greater flexibility for the hand in its movements forward and back, so that in total six different levels were provided on his essentially two rank keyboard.

In 1886 Jankó gave a recital on his new instrument which had been taken up by a small Viennese piano-maker. In the 1890s Decker, a well-known New York piano company, decided to produce on a commercial basis pianos with the Jankó keyboard and the Paul de Jankó Conservatory of Music was established. Although the more logical arrangement of the notes made many figures easier to execute and despite the promotional and educational work (a special class for the Jankó had been established at the Scharwenka Conservatory in Berlin), the Jankó keyboard never really got off the ground, even after Paul Perzina of Schwerin in 1910 improved the slightly sluggish touch and then devised a method so that a conventional and a Jankó keyboard could be interchanged on the same instrument.

In the 1840s the idea of coupling octaves appealed to the Berlin piano maker Schönemann who fitted both a pedal providing the octave of each note and a diminutive additional keyboard helping the hand to span two octaves. Mendelssohn amused himself by performing on it octave passages doubled eight times. Liszt had constructed by the Parisian organ builder Alexandre according to his own directions a 'giant grand piano' with three keyboards, pedals and sixteen registers, receiving 'my monster instrument' in 1854. In the present century Hungarian-born Emanuel Moór re-explored the possibilities of the second keyboard in his duplex coupler piano, a number of which were made by the Aeolian Company in London, for the American firm established a factory in England to take advantage of its strong player-piano position. Only one action with conventional stringing was provided, but the second raised keyboard supplied notes an octave higher than the lower keyboard while an additional pedal coupled the upper keyboard at an octave higher to the lower one. The ponderous system of coupling necessarily affected the touch, limiting the tonal variety which skilled touch produces and so Moór's idea, although it found a few proponents, proved short-lived.

Quarter-tone pianos were produced experimentally. In the 1920s August Förster of Saxony made a grand with one set of strings and one soundboard, but with an upper keyboard tuned a quarter-tone higher than the lower one. A class to teach technique for this instrument was established at the Prague Conservatory under the Czech composer Haba. Grotrian-Steinweg made an instrument which really joined two grands together so that two actions and two soundboards were utilized, but only one keyboard with black, white and brown keys. The latter provided the quarter-tone notes and the octave contained twenty notes instead of the usual twelve.

Practical difficulties confronting a rearranged keyboard are immense, but an even greater obstacle to its headway is the educational system. For a redesigned keyboard to oust the existing arrangement hallowed by centuries of dominance, existing pianists would need to re-learn how to play their instrument. An equal deterrent is the standard repertoire provided by composers for the most part no longer living, and which could not be adapted successfully to a novel arrangement of the keys. Although the keyboard's redesign offers benefits, it produces also new defects. Conversely characteristics seen by reformers as faults of the conventional keyboard often are converted by composers to benefits producing distinctive qualities. It is difficult to envisage radical experiments having any real chance of acceptance in the foreseeable future. Therefore contemporary composers who have written quarter-tone music have recognized that mechanical keyboard instruments cannot serve them satisfactorily and have turned instead to electronic means. A forerunner of the modern electronic piano and of contemporary application of electronics to music was the neo-Bechstein grand built in 1930–32 in conjunction with Siemens. The strings relied not on a soundboard for amplification, but on microphones leading to electronic amplification of the sounds. The microphones were of special significance in the treble in an attempt to improve volume and sustaining capacity. A pedal produced a crescendo effect and some prolonging of the note (up to at least a minute), but the tone produced was other than that associated with the orthodox piano.

Several designers turned to the shape of the grand piano and produced small grand models in an attempt to adapt its winged-shape to smaller domestic spaces. Some were called semi-grands and quarter-grands while Gounod nicknamed a small instrument by Pleyel 'crapaud' or 'toad'. Kaps of Dresden was one of the first to pursue this novelty, his 1·64 metres (5 feet) grand of 1865 winning instant popularity. The reduced length was achieved by the customary means of shortening and thickening the strings and of over-stringing. Double over-stringing was attempted in a further effort to provide longer bass strings for the short grand, the strings passing over each other two (in the case of instruments made by Ibach and later by Challen), three or, on an instrument produced in 1880 by Schreiber, four times. In 1888 H. J. T. Broadwood patented a barless frame of cast steel (the change of material perhaps a reminder of the belief that iron was detrimental to tone), and in the 1920s Broadwoods introduced a semi-barless frame for a 1·32 metres (4 feet) grand. In the inter-war years Strohmenger & Sons, returning to an idea tried as early as 1804 by S. Hoffmann in Berlin and later by Gunther of Brussels and by others, produced a semicircular grand which discarded the recess in the treble side allowing, it was claimed, longer bass strings and a larger area of soundboard in the treble—the latter usually is claimed to be unnecessary.

A further idea of long-standing was that a concave keyboard would suit the extension of the arms in the treble and bass, the straight board causing some distortion of posture. Neuhaus of Vienna attempted such a keyboard as early as 1780. Haidinger and Staufer also of Vienna returned to this idea in 1824, the keyboard fitted to their 'hollow pianoforte' designed with the short arms of children especially in mind. In 1910 Clutsam designed a keyboard of this kind and as recently as 1974 Schimmel of Braunschweig exhibited a grand with concave keyboard constructed for a Parisian pianist.

XIV

The Percussive Piano and Mechanical Entertainment, 1900-1939

In the early twentieth century contemporary ideas relating to the musical nature of the piano were explored.

Busoni, a founder of modern pianism, pondered music using intellect rather than sentiment as a corner-stone of judgement and his ability to place the part in correct perspective to the whole helped create a new appreciation of form. He expressed a growing restlessness with traditions which no longer commanded the automatic allegiance of questioning minds. The chromaticism of Wagner already had started to loosen the ties of the diatonic key system by introducing elements which blurred the unconditional acceptance of the traditional scale. By 1910 Busoni was departing from accepted ideas of consonance and dissonance, anticipating in several ways those who followed him. His later music often surrendered its sense of a stabilizing key as he experimented with different sequences of notes to form fresh scales. He explored also the division of a tone into three constituent parts rather than into two semitones, but this theory really only became capable of satisfactory realization with the development of electronic music.

Busoni was no lover of the recording studio in which it was notoriously difficult to capture piano tone successfully. In a 1919 letter he complained bitterly to his wife :

They wanted the Faust Waltz (which lasts a good ten minutes) *but it was only to take four minutes!* That meant quickly cutting, patching and improvising, so that there should still be some sense left in it; watching the pedal (because it sounds bad); thinking of certain notes which had to be stronger or weaker to please this devilish machine; not letting oneself go for fear of inaccuracies and being conscious the whole time that every note was going to be there for eternity; how can there be any question of inspiration, freedom, swing or poetry? Enough that yesterday for 9 pieces all of 4 minutes each (half an hour in all) I worked for three and a half hours![51]

Josef Hofmann and Serge Rachmaninoff reflected Busoni's novel stress on the composer's intentions and as this consideration gained wider recognition, remaining liberties with the printed note gradually disappeared. Great beauty of tone was valued and was combined with adequate technique. Rachmaninoff, the crew-cut Russian, grew to hate his famous Prelude in C sharp minor, which appeared in England as *The Day of Judgment* and even *The Moscow Waltz*!

Claude Debussy won greater acceptance than Busoni and the novelty of his effects reinforced the growing conviction that conventional melody and harmony were exhausted. The absence of semitones in the whole tone scale (C, D, E, F sharp, G sharp, A sharp, C) establishes the equal distance between all intervals and imparts a vagueness, losing all sense of attraction towards a home key. Debussy's frequent use of this scale combined with revolutionary pedalling led to the attainment of misty evocative sounds and to an aesthetic rooted in the French literary Symbolist movement. A reaction against the Romantics' full-blooded emotion, Symbolism sought to hint at meaning rather than to state it, and although lesser known it exercised as much influence on Debussy as did the Impressionists.

Debussy found an ideal vehicle in the piano, which he regarded as an instrument without hammers. He gave specific pedalling instructions in only a few of his pieces, but nonetheless the pedal is central to his achievement. Wide-spaced pianissimo chords and gentle dissonances were magnified by overtones brought into play by the pedal, creating harmonic combinations then novel, for few composers had explored in any depth scope offered by the sustaining pedal for adding resonance to discord. On occasion Debussy used both pedals simultaneously, adding resonance to softness. He introduced further haziness by employing parallel Thirds, Fourths, Fifths and Ninths while the Études and his other mature piano works explored the instrument's tone-colour by means of his various harmonic devices.

It was the 'percussive pianists' stressing aspects at the other extreme from Debussy, who made the avenues pursued by him and Ravel appear complete in themselves and incapable of further significant development, though they provided signposts to the twentieth century. Both Debussy and Bartók in their different ways reclassified the piano's scope as a solo instrument, their contributions proving valuable in enabling the piano to hold its own in the present century. Serge Prokofieff was the anti-romantic revolutionary. With Bartók, Stravinsky* and Hindemith he stressed the percussive nature of piano hammers and exhorted followers to treat the piano as they would a percussion instrument. Romantic warmth was cast aside for ferocious and complex rhythms. Using virtually no pedal, the austerity of his precise steel-like sound took a decade to achieve recognition.

In the early twentieth century Vienna, capital of the crumbling Hapsburg Empire, became the home of many progressive thinkers, among them Freud, Kokoschka and Wittgenstein. Then in 1922–23 Arnold Schoenberg's Twelve-note, or serial, technique appeared. It marked one of the century's incontrovertible turning-points. Lapsing of the disciplines associated with conventional key systems meant that individual notes no longer retained the old direct harmonic relationships to chords, and each chord relinquished its kinship with adjacent chords. Schoenberg hoped that the disciplines of his new theory would provide fresh forms to unite patterns which otherwise would disintegrate into a casual contrasting of ideas with little cohesion. The reader who does not wish to submit to a brief outline of serialism may turn to the bottom paragraph on page 170. Schoenberg's new theme was a 'series' or 'row' comprising the twelve notes contained in the chromatic scale. The twelve notes could be arranged in any order, but each was to appear once before any one was repeated. In this way there would be no Tonic and no feeling of tonality as the notes would be related only to each other. They could be sounded in succession forming a melody or simultaneously as a chord, but the chords would produce no feeling of harmonic advance as there would be neither major nor minor scales. Variety

---

* "The piano is an instrument of percussion and nothing else," he (Stravinsky) said. Karol (Szymanowski) argued: "I don't agree with you. The greatest composers have written for the piano masterpieces which demand a singing tone."
"They were all wrong," said the Russian composer.'[52]

was offered by three further versions of the original series. Firstly, its inversion in which the second note is lowered an octave to *below* the first note (whereas previously it appeared *above* it), to form a new interval with the first note. Likewise a note originally lower in pitch than the first is raised an octave to appear above it. Secondly, its mirror image with the notes played in reverse sequence the final note now coming first, and finally the inversion of this mirror image. These versions could commence on any of the twelve semitones in the row, meaning that each version could be transposed eleven times and provide a new equivalent of modulation. Further variations were developed. The arithmetical complexities available are obvious and it is also clear that to follow the system in its entirety a keen mathematical appreciation is necessary, for the average ear never would follow all the permutations of the original Twelve-notes unaided, nor would it have the sheet-anchor of the traditional system to guide it. Although in the hands of lesser composers the Twelve-note system rapidly may lose all interest, Schoenberg was seeking fresh expressive means to solve the crisis in tonality; for him serial technique was not merely a mathematical puzzle, for he wished the music's quality to take precedence over the principles of its construction.

Webern, Schoenberg's pupil, was less compromising. He abandoned all pretence of tonality in his later Twelve-note works and so his brand of serialism has proved a more important influence on contemporary compositions than his master's. The higher overtones contain dissonant intervals which Webern therefore maintained were as natural as consonant ones, their discovery delayed because they are found higher up in the range of overtones. As these higher notes are equally part of the natural law, Twelve-note series were completely natural and could provide a necessary unity and sense of form. Webern began to vary, more radically than Schoenberg, rhythm, note duration, rests, methods of attack and other factors, his growing serialization pointing towards greater advance determination of the elements employed in composition, using mathematical yardsticks and towards diminishing scope for the composer to vary his treatment by traditional tonal methods.

By the turn of the century some composers were dissatisfied with merely seeing their music distributed to more shopkeepers' daughters than ever before and stressed the originality of their compositions, although the results were appreciated only by a minority. The self-assertion of their individuality, the compositions of Stravinsky and others and the serialism of Schoenberg and Webern led to contemporary *avant-garde* experiment, while Prokofieff's anti-romantic tonal preference helped to popularize the bright shrill piano tone which is usual on today's concert platforms.

The pianist Artur Schnabel thought that tonal variations between the best piano makes were attributable to the wishes of the locally most influential pianist of an earlier generation. As the pace of technical development slowed, less tonal variation between different makes was evident than a century previously, but nonetheless varied tastes for mellow and brilliant timbres survived. The American preference for hard shrill tone was formed; German tone was characterized as possessing a heroic quality with reserves to fall back on when played fortissimo; German and English makers strove for fulness and roundness while French pianos were said to possess charming delicacy, translucent but sometimes thin.

Music of short light character was demanded and Cécile Chaminade, one of the earliest woman composers, was one of a number of talents who supplied pieces tastefully conceived and rich in melody while aspiring to no intricacy of form or emotion.

Interest in folk and negro music resulted in acceptance of a fresh medium, jazz, at first called 'ragtime', which fulfilled the yearnings of a dance craze in the 1920s noticeably more violent than the earlier waltz and polka. Restaurants provided background jazz and a medical authority soon suggested that the din be taken out of dinner. Trombone and saxophone supplied novel effects punctuated by chords at the piano. Constant Lambert remarked that jazz had 'suddenly achieved the status of a "school"' and suggested that it was the 'first dance music to bridge the gap between highbrow and lowbrow successfully',[53] a development aided by Gershwin's compositions, which were instrumental in the popularization of operas, symphonic and chamber music in jazz forms.

As the owners of many of several million pianos in American and European dwellings could not play them well, it was only a matter of time before the ingenuity of man adapted the customary keyboard instrument so that the keys either played without human prompting or were dispensed with altogether. Mechanical pianos of two kinds, the Street Piano often erroneously called 'Barrel Organ', and the Player-Piano enjoyed their spell of popularity. The barrel organ proper with pipes was highly developed as early as the late sixteenth century and later Handel, Haydn and Mozart wrote for it. Brass wire pins projected from a wooden barrel which was turned by either a handle or a clockwork spring.

The Street Piano (Pls. 51, 52) worked on the same principle, the teeth causing the action to throw hard leather hammers suitable for outdoors at the strings, each treble note often reinforced by a fourth string. Variations in volume seem sometimes to have been obtained by setting the teeth at different heights. There was neither keyboard nor dampers—hence the familiar blurred resonance. An Englishman early in the nineteenth century may have made the earliest street piano, but its real protagonists proved to be Italians, who specialized in making the cylinders in England and who pulled street pianos through the towns of the world. Mussolini, after his advent to power in 1922, recalled all Italians engaged in playing street pianos, believing their occupation to be beneath the dignity of his countrymen.

The cylinder and pin principle was applied to the spinet and harpsichord and in the early nineteenth century to the piano with keyboard (Pl. 36), for which numerous patents were registered. In 1842 Peytre of Lyons devised the pierced paper music roll, an idea perhaps adopted from the perforated cardboard which selected needles in Jacquard's improved loom. These and similar contraptions attracted little attention until in the 1880s and 1890s new pneumatic piano-playing devices appeared in North America, England and Germany. By 1900 the public was ready to surrender to the player-piano's enticement, bringing beloved melodies and favourite pianists to the humble drawing-room.

The early player-piano was a separate cabinet positioned in front of the keyboard of any piano (Pl. 54); after improvement the mechanism soon was built into the piano (Pl. 53). The roll was mounted behind the music desk, where air under suction or pressure revolved and unwound it at a regulated speed over a tracker-bar. The latter contained a row of holes rather like a mouth organ, one for each note of the piano, each hole connected to a pneumatic mechanism which gave impetus to the hammer. One of the best-known and earliest systems was the Aeolian company's 'Pianola', an inspired name, patented in 1900. Electricity soon replaced the harmonium-type foot-operated bellows and enabled the German Welte concern to introduce in 1904 a new mechanism, the 'Mignon'. Welte's novelty concerned the method of recording and enabled the roll to be cut not from the printed music, but by the pianist as he played. The artist completed an electric circuit with the aid of contacts located beneath each key, thereby activating lead pencils to produce longer or shorter traces on the moving paper roll. The length and spacing of the pencil marks corresponded to the player's rhythm and phrasing. Expression, noted by a musician on to a score during performance, was synthesized on the finished roll by cutting perforations near its edges to regulate the suction and thus vary the dynamics of the playing. The original playing could be reproduced with surprising accuracy, making instructions for the operator to adjust speed and dynamics (Pl. 55) no longer necessary.

American makers adapted Welte's principle and in 1913 Aeolian came out with the 'Duo-Art', which was built into Steinway grands and many other instruments. In 1916 the American Piano Co. introduced its 'Ampico' to Knabe, Chickering and other pianos. By 1919 over 53 per cent of American output consisted of player-pianos and a peak was reached in 1923 when 197,000 were sold. In the early 1920s, although the player-piano never carried all before it in England, over fifty makes were on sale and all prominent artists made rolls on the reproducing piano. Bad passages could be remade and wrong notes corrected on the roll! Aeolian arranged orchestral concerts with concertos to be played not by a soloist but by the Duo-Art. Another familiar trick allowed the pianist to take over from the roll in the middle of a passage where the paper was not perforated and then for the roll to relieve the pianist.

The player and reproducing pianos sounded slightly too mechanical (the Duo-Art had sixteen degrees of dynamic intensity), as if almost over-faithful to the printed note. The argument about authenticity of performances prescribed to paper rolls still rages, but for pianists of the time it was the only practicable way to leave to posterity a remembrance of their playing.

The 1920s marked a boom period for piano sales in the United Kingdom. Played and unplayed pianos enjoyed their swan song as status symbols. Their popularity was marked especially with the working class and some Welsh miners boasted a second piano in their parlour! Prior to the Great War many retailers in London and the larger towns made pianos for sale in their show-rooms, although this custom already was on the wane. The war over, many decided not to recommence production and the practice grew of larger manufacturers supplying retailers under their own names. In addition numerous small makers who had operated on a shoe-string did not reopen their doors.

Once the habit of sitting before a machine for relaxation was accepted, the piano was vulnerable to rivals. In 1928 the first 'talkies' from Hollywood arrived in London. By 1930 gramophone and radio, relatively cheap and offering greater flexibility, rapidly had killed the player-piano fashion and with the Great Depression threatened the industry's life-blood. The player-piano reduced the instrument to the level of a machine which like most machines could be used by all, leaving no distinguishing virtue in feminine 'accomplishments'. Ladies at last were allowed to earn their living, while servant problems and car ownership pointed to a partial devaluation of the home, a car becoming a more sought-after wedding present than the traditional piano.

Many makers were obliterated by the depression. In the United States output slumped in 1931 to a mere 51,750. Fresh impetus, necessary if the piano was to be resuscitated, was provided by the small upright. Progressive makers in the United States and England found salvation by introducing miniature uprights, under 0·92 metres (3 feet) high with a simple functional case. Over-stringing from corner to corner offered a longer string than the vertically-strung upright afforded and partially alleviated poor bass tone resulting from reduced height, which was considered aesthetically desirable and which often necessitated the installation of the action below the level of the keyboard. All manner of distortion was encountered in the attempt to minimize the piano's size. The smallest 'Minipiano' introduced by Eavestaff was only 0·84 metres (33 inches) high and brought the soundboard to the front of the piano so that it formed the bottom door (Pl. 20), necessitating radical repositioning of the tuning pins and strings.

Smaller homes emphasized the trend to the miniature piano. The high ceilings, drapes and over-stuffed upholstery of the Victorian era absorbed sound and so required enormous tonal power. Twentieth-century design favoured low ceilings and swept away excess draperies, providing rooms which were of sufficient acoustic brightness for the smaller piano to be capable of satisfying tonal requirements. For a few years it even seemed that the very short grand, 1·15 metres (42 inches) being the shortest, might rival the upright. Challen and Strohmenger were two English firms especially associated with the construction of 'baby grands', as they were called.

Output recovered in the 1930s. In England it crept back to sixty thousand in 1936 and in the United States to 107,000, mostly miniatures, in the following year produced by a mere three dozen makers.

XV

The Present and Future, from 1945

For the second time in the twentieth century war damaged the piano trade. As the tuning of the nation's pianos became neglected, local examinations sometimes were conducted at teachers' homes which during the Second World War often housed the best available piano. Piano production by the two central protagonists, England and Germany, largely ceased. After the ending of hostilities it quickly was resumed in England, while in Germany the 1950s was the decade of reconstruction. A number of firms, mostly old-established but with strictly local reputations before 1939, rose to prominence and a number of makers previously located in the new eastern zone of Germany re-established their businesses in West Germany.

In the last twenty years the fortunes of the piano have revived. Deposed from its pinnacle the future appears secure, although more modest and scarcely so sparkling as a century ago. Recent unspectacular but steady growth in sales, however, indicates that the future will be less subject to violent fluctuations.

Over three-quarters of a million pianos are made annually in the world today—more than ever before. New markets have been opened up. Japan was virtually a virgin market at the end of the Second World War, the rate at which western culture was absorbed having been restricted by low living standards. In the 1960s on the strength of a strong home market Japan became the world's largest piano-making country, producing 284,000 in 1972 of which 233,000 were sold on the domestic market and the remainder exported. Japan possessed a small piano industry at the end of the last century. In 1882 the first pianos were imported from Europe. In 1885 the first Japanese pianos were made and shortly afterwards Torakusu Yamaha made his first instrument—a harmonium. His first piano followed in 1900, by which time the Japanese piano had developed. Thirty years later Yamaha had increased production to 2,750 annually and in 1930 an employee, K. Kawai, left Yamaha to found his own company. By 1935 Japanese output had reached 4,370, but the war reduced this figure to 385 in 1945 and in 1947 Yamaha managed a mere seventy pianos. The 1960s saw rapid growth from 48,557 pianos in 1960 to 257,159 in 1969 and the predominance of Yamaha and Kawai was established. Towards 1972 output Yamaha, the largest maker in the world, contributed 187,600, Kawai about 73,800 and the remaining two dozen makers of whom the largest is comparable to many European producers, about 22,600 pianos.

United States output remains at a high level of about 180,000 produced by fifteen makers of which the four largest, the Aeolian American Corporation (incorporating the Chickering, J. & C. Fischer, Knabe, Mason & Hamlin and Weber companies), Baldwin, Kimball and Wurlitzer account for nearly 70 per cent. Russia produces an annual 170,000. Earlier German influence reflects in three of the names under which Russian pianos now are exported, Bechner, Irmbach and Rich. Weber, but the remaining three, Cherny, Estonia and Tchaika, are distinctly Russian-sounding, for Russia is the sole European communist country to distribute a significant proportion of its piano production among its own populace. Of the Western European 1973 output of approximately 60,000, West Germany accounted for about 26,000 made by some twenty-one manufacturers using approximately twenty-seven principal names, and England for over 20,300 produced by ten companies using nineteen principal brand names. By contrast only a few hundred pianos are produced now in each of two traditional centres, Paris and Vienna. Erard, Gaveau and Pleyel, the three leading French manufacturers, for some years combined production in one Parisian factory, but in 1971 the production of these historic makes was transferred to the Braunschweig factory of the largest German producer, Schimmel. This blow to French pride has been alleviated since by the establishment of a new piano producer, Rameau, which recently has opened a factory in Provence. In Vienna two manufacturers remain, the world-renowned Bösendorfer and Ehrbar, who in 1857 acquired the Seuffert business, established in 1801. Today the Ehrbar firm produces Ehrbar, Baumbach and Stelzhammer pianos. The Eastern European countries produce some 40,000 annually. East Germany, where in common with most eastern-bloc countries all the piano manufacturers are now state-owned and almost the complete output is exported, is the largest producer, its best-known and old-established names being Blüthner, Förster, Geyer, Niendorf, Rönisch and Zimmermann. Czechoslovakia with the makes Petrof, Rösler, Scholze and Weinbach, and Poland under the names Calisia and Legnica, also have sizeable outputs, while a few pianos are made in Hungary and Rumania. China numbers among the piano-producing nations, for in the mid-nineteenth century a Scotsman, Moutrie, commenced production in Hong Kong and afterwards Shanghai. Pianos are made also in countries as far apart as Australia, Brazil, Canada, Holland, Hong Kong, Italy, Korea, Mexico, the Philippines, the Scandinavian countries, South Africa, Switzerland, Taiwan and Thailand, the instrument possessing a world-wide heritage.

Several countries contributed to the piano's development, in which the English piano played an honourable role. Today British pianos again are esteemed all over the world and the willingness of Britain's piano-makers to assist each other, manifested at overseas exhibitions (the Frankfurt Fair has replaced the international exhibitions of the previous century) and in other ways, is the envy of piano producers overseas and demonstrates that ideals of mutual respect can be upheld in the modern competitive world. Nearly half of the annual production of British pianos is exported to over sixty countries including Germany; prior to 1939 only a small percentage was exported. In 1945 due to penal levels of purchase tax pianos scarcely could be sold on the home market and all were exported as overseas markets were obtained and developed with success. In the immediate post-war period the largest markets were found in South America and in the Commonwealth countries of Australia, New Zealand and South Africa. In the 1950s the Commonwealth markets predominated, although they receded in the 1960s, European countries coming to the fore. Thus the piano industry was one of many to find that traditional Commonwealth markets had to be replaced largely by continental ones, a trend firmly established several years prior to joining the Common Market.

Britain possesses also one of the most flourishing industries supplying specialized components with four action, key and hammer makers, two hammer felt makers, two ivory cutters and three iron frame foundries. The best piano wire, however, is German-made, the excellence of Röslau, Giese and Pöhlmann universally acknowledged, but West Germany sports only one action maker, Renner of Stuttgart, having lost the other best-known pre-war action producers. Fleming is today the leading East German action maker and Langer did not survive the war.

Factories of diverse size flourish, but the number of small piano producers is tending to decline as the predominance of medium-sized and large factories, each with a rational limited range of models, becomes more marked. In the early 1950s eighteen English factories produced pianos; twenty-five years later the number has shrunk to ten, while in West Germany some six factories have ceased in the last fifteen years. In many instances the name has been taken over and continued by another manu-facturer. A piano factory should be preferably at least a moder-ate size to be truly viable (a thousand pianos annually is a figure often suggested), a consideration elevating capital to a critical factor in its establishment. Consequently fewer firms commence in business as manufacturers than sixty years previously and existing makers commonly have long-established reputations.

Although mechanization has reduced the 'craft' content of a number of skills, the piano-maker seeks to combine the best from tradition with modern progressive elements. He is in an unusual position to succeed as his specialized machinery cannot be bought ready-made, but has to be designed and constructed under his guidance to meet his specific needs, and as unusual design skills are required to construct a complex musical instrument. Due to the diversity of crafts involved in the piano's construction and to the impossibility in many instances of replacing human skill by machines (the assembly and regulation of the piano action, for example, still are best done by eagle-eye and dexterous fingers), the piano industry is labour intensive compared with most manu-facturing industries of comparable size. When labour can be attracted and trained to a requisite level of skill, a more critical attitude towards mechanization and investment in plant can be adopted so that only machinery which either improves quality or reduces unit cost by shortening the job time is purchased. Overseas a different attitude sometimes is encountered, introduc-ing equipment which does the job no quicker than the skilled craftsman and which simply enables the job to be carried out by labour possessing a lower level of skill. This course often fails to reduçe cost especially after the experse of financing the capital equipment has been taken into account, and if handled by a person lacking experience in making pianos it may prove detrimental to quality.

The writer's grandfather remembered making soundboards in 1892 using a hand-saw, the only saw available to him. Early in the present century electricity was applied as a source of power to machines and in the 1970s numerical control methods are being introduced in an experimental manner to woodworking machinery with Britain among the leaders in this new application of advanced technology. Numerical control methods have been used to guide the cutting heads of milling machinery in the engineering industry for some years. Its late application to the dimensioning and drilling of wood is said to be due to the variety of timber sizes regularly encountered and to the handling time positioning planks before and after machining forming a high percentage of the total job time, compared with the processing of metal which takes a long time due to the material's hardness. There are often comparable valid reasons why some industries do not appear so technologically advanced as others, but despite its large number of varying techniques the application of machinery to piano production has improved productivity beyond all recognition. In the mid-nineteenth century the typical piano maker produced annually up to four pianos per employee. Today the Bentley factory, representative in method of medium-sized European producers (exceptional however in producing on its own premises all components except metal ones), completes twenty-five pianos per employee per annum—a tribute to modern production methods.

Nonetheless it is necessary to strike a happy medium. Undue stress on mass production methods and speed risk disastrous effects on quality as many American makers are only too well aware. Much may be done by rationalizing the range of models. The number of strung backs used by Bentley, for example, was reduced in the early 1960s from eight to three with consequent easing in production stresses, but nonetheless retaining the ability to offer as many varieties of casework as previously. Yamaha produces annually sixty thousand of one model. Production on this scale clearly offers economies and this manufacturer has pursued production policies which have upheld quality and resulted in cleanly presented instruments.

With output expanding most firms in Europe and beyond find difficulty in obtaining sufficient craftsmen as the pre-war generation approaches retirement. In many instances man cannot be replaced by machine except at enormous expense and reduction in quality, and consequently it is difficult to raise output of a craft product rapidly. Particularly in England a number of makers have kept production of grands at a low level in order to increase output of uprights. Lack of craftsmen for regulation of grand actions has proved a limiting factor. Furthermore because grands require much space and different methods ideally a separate factory is required for their production, it proving difficult to produce uprights and grands side by side efficiently.

The shortage of craftsmen applies particularly to tuner-technicians and repairers caring for over two million pianos in British homes alone and assures attractive career prospects for youngsters entering the piano trade, especially as the public at last is beginning to recognize the worth of the tuner-technician whose career places strenuous demands on his ear which first must undergo lengthy training. The formal training given in Germany is the best in the world. Tuners, owners of retail shops and leading factory personnel frequently bear the prefix to their names 'Master Piano Maker'. A master's training includes designing a piano starting with a blank piece of paper and building a piano in a factory—both strenuous tests of competence. Piano tuners traditionally were trained in piano factories and shops on leaving school. The five-year apprenticeship was rigorous and on its completion the majority of young tuners left the factories to join the staff of retail shops. This pattern was broken in England during the dark days of the 1930s when most piano producers could not afford the luxury of training tuners surplus to their factory requirements and demand for tuning shrank with the piano's decline. Half a century later the young men of the late '20s are either retired or nearing retirement and the shortage of tuners is growing more acute because only in the last decade have young people been attracted as tuning charges have risen. The tuner's down-at-heel image is fading as gradually it is recognized that he must earn as much as the electrician who services the television set if by the turn of the century pianos are to be tuned, toned or regulated at all. This change in attitude combined with careers publicity has helped to improve recently the quantity and quality of recruits to the manufacturing and servicing branches of the trade. Also helpful has been renewed recognition of the role of craft and small industries as the reaction against impersonal over-large companies has stressed the occupational satisfaction which interesting jobs in smaller firms offer.

Nonetheless strong pressures act against mastery of a craft by modern school-leavers. The urge to earn high wages from the outset of employment makes learners unwilling to spend long periods acquiring skills at lower earnings' levels. To attract labour therefore, and to achieve competitive production rates, many employers divide the craft into its smaller components and teach to each employee only a limited number. He is left short of mastery of the whole craft and with a knowledge incomplete compared with that acquired fifty years ago. These shortcomings are compensated for by a few men who have good all-round knowledge and can supervise quality in the various sections.

The quality of contemporary pianos is immensely superior to that of pre-war commercial instruments compared with which no inferior pianos are made today. The average piano has a life of several decades and as an investment retains its value to an extent equalled by few other 'consumer durables'. The small upright of about 0·97 metres (38 inches) height continues most popular in England, although recently there have been signs of a move towards taller instruments (already most sought-after in many continental countries), permitting a fuller tone above all from longer bass-string lengths. There is a frequent misconception that the miniature upright, low in height but otherwise virtually the same size as competing taller pianos, by its lowness conserves floor space. In furnishing a room the use made of floor area rather than wall space usually is decisive and so length and width of selected articles become more critical than their height. Indeed the low upright may require slightly more floor area than taller instruments as its length may be increased to permit maximum attainable bass-string lengths—an adjustment unnecessary when height is not a cramping factor.

Some design changes have won acceptance since 1945. Greater experience has produced tonal improvements in the miniature upright to win maximum tone from the limited area available (the smallest Knight and Monington & Weston models are exemplary), although height still is reduced occasionally with cheapness as the paramount consideration, thereby sacrificing quality and reinforcing the experience of countless designers who have found that there are few short cuts and that the quest for a satisfactory revolutionary cheap piano is incapable of fulfilment.

The 'backless' model, replacing wooden stress-carrying bracings by the use of more metal in the iron frame (Pl. 16), is popular although the back with bracings still is preferred by many. When the 'backless' was introduced it was feared that the absence of support from the wooden braced back would cause it to lack stability and therefore to go out of tune more rapidly, but several decades (and in assessing the value of innovation on an instrument with a life spread over several generations, decades sometimes are necessary!) have proved these fears to be groundless. The absence of bracings reduces the depth of the instrument, but carries the disadvantage that the weight of the iron frame is redistributed towards the back of the piano which becomes back-heavy and therefore must be handled with due care. Pianos with light metal frames of tubular steel and aluminium, introduced in the 1960s in an attempt to reduce weight, have been viewed sceptically, cast iron remaining the cheapest satisfactory material.

All pianos employ over-stringing and, unlike the majority of pre-war pianos, the dampers are placed below the hammers and not above them, assisting reduction in height. Plastics sometimes are used for those action parts where they appear advantageous, for example flanges, jacks, levers and damper drums (Pl. 18). Aluminium beams (Pl. 18) promising immense stability have been introduced by several action-makers, but synthetic materials often are more costly than natural. This fact is untrue, however, of ivory and ebony, traditionally used to cover the lower and raised notes respectively of the keyboard. A shortage of elephants and the preservation of wild life has caused dramatic increases in ivory prices. The desire of African states to process their raw materials has resulted in restrictions imposed on ivory exports, in the increased production of ivory trinkets and in much badly converted timber. Nineteenth-century experiments to find a key covering cheaper than ivory involved glass, porcelain and enamel. Before the Second World War celluloid was a common substitute.

183

Cut to comparable thickness, its yellow surface gave an impression of the characteristic graining of ivory. Since the war an acrylic perspex has replaced ivory on all but the most costly uprights. Thicker than ivory coverings, it is white in colour without a grain pattern and offers the advantage over ivory that it does not discolour with the years. A black plastic has won acceptance for the raised sharp notes. Ivory continues to be used for many grand piano keyboards and for all concert grands. Expert pianists maintain that ivory feels better to the touch, largely, because as a natural material it 'breathes' and finger perspiration does not 'cling' to it as the finger's heat is carried away from the key's surface. This property of natural materials to exist in harmony with their environment is one which synthetic materials can never imitate. Recently it has become possible to cover a key from one piece of ivory, so that the joint between two pieces of ivory where the raised note comes (Fig. 8) no longer is present. Cutting key ivory and laying ivories on the keys are highly skilled tasks.

Post-war glues give modern pianos a considerable advantage over their predecessors not built to endure modern conditions. Piano makers made the acquaintance of synthetic resin glues during the war when they were applied widely especially in aircraft manufacture (the body of the de Havilland 'Mosquito' for example was wooden and the glued joints were subjected to extreme demands). These glues provided the answer after the war when exports to humid tropical climates and to extremely dry areas in Australia, South Africa and Sweden were increasing. If the soundboard dried out, the tongue and groove joint made with animal glue might form a gap causing clicking noises. On the other hand synthetic resin glues enabled flat joints to withstand the strain of the strings. The term 'tropicalization' continues to apply to hammer and key coverings, although as confidence in resin glues was established many makers by the 1960s ceased producing solid cases, for which the matching of timber and jointing require more care to prevent later warping, and sent standard veneered pianos to the tropics fully assured that the veneer would not lift. Many also ceased to screw soundboard bars and bridges, confident that the glues were reliable and that should a glueline loosen, the jarring tone caused by a faulty joint would be unbearable. The introduction of multi-laminated tuning planks was hastened by severe climatic conditions. Formed of four to sixteen wood strips glued together, the grain runs in opposite directions minimizing possible shrinkage. They replaced solid tuning planks, usually of beech less likely to ensure that the piano stood in tune.

The benefits of modern glues were not bestowed without disadvantages, however, which often were learnt the hard way. Many synthetic resin glues are brittle and insufficiently elastic after setting. Consequently if veneer and the timber on which it is laid shrink and the glue is unable to stretch to accommodate the shrinkage, either the glue joint breaks or the veneer splits. Such difficulties were experienced on pianos sent to dry areas, for problems are identified and solutions found largely through experience spread over a number of years, generating caution which often causes craft industries to appear unduly conservative.

The care which purchasers devote to choice of wood finish indicates that a new piano remains a valued item of furniture. Modern polyester provides a more durable and translucent gloss finish than earlier french polish. Few factories in an age of mass-produced standardization are willing to finish woodwork to a customer's colour pattern matching other furniture in the home—piano manufacturers willingly provide this service. Mahogany, walnut, teak and oak veneers are popular. Elm, palisander, cherry and sycamore often are available. Fashions in finishing sometimes are set by the furniture trade and followed by the piano trade—an excellent example was the dominance of teak in the 1960s. England appears to be the only country to have continued this preference into the 1970s, when home designers introduced coloured (principally white) finishes which have won greater recognition on the continent than in England. Choice of veneer and finish varies, however, although the absence of protective trading barriers leads to regular exchange of information and goods, making the distinctive characteristics of one country more likely to be introduced to other countries, as the exporting lands adapt to meet individual market taste and then sometimes introduce the overseas styling to their own home market. Walnut on English pianos used to be figured and horizontally veneered (Pl. 25), a preference which can be traced back at least to the time of Kirkman and Shudi. Walnut with this appearance is preferred still, but as English makers have adopted a figureless straight vertically veneered walnut when exporting to the German-speaking countries where most pianos are sold in this uniform and even monotonous finish, this 'quiet' walnut is now acceptable in England. In France mahogany still is preferred, while in the United States a native timber unknown in Europe, pecan, is used and techniques have been developed to give to this and other veneers an impression of age and woodworm attack.

There are still, however, many variations in casework style throughout the world. The pianos made in Japan to be sold there are tall, bulky in appearance and in styling resemble those sold in Europe fifty years ago. The most popular American pianos on the other hand, are small 'spinets' (a term not to be confused with the plectra instrument) some 0·92–0·97 metres (36–38 inches) high, which commonly employ a 'drop action' located below the level of the keys. The elaborately shaped legs and fretwork desks (Pl. 57) are both often interchangeable with others so that the instrument's appearance can be rapidly changed prior to or even after sale. Exotic veneers retain their pull, but while great care is devoted to the fine casework, the tonal properties are often, to European and many American ears, poor. Production of the mass-produced American piano is geared to speed and in the choice of materials cost is often a paramount factor. For example the weight of the iron frame is often held at or even below the absolute minimum necessary for long-term tonal and even pitch stability, although the braced back and maple tuning plank (in preference to beech which is softer than maple) are expected on American pianos and clearly are factors promoting stability. Consequently the bright shrill tone preferred in the United States often sounds tinny and lacks the blending qualities (partly controlled by the harmonicity and relative strength of the overtones present) sought by European makers of bright-toned pianos. American pianos 0·97–1·09 metres (approximately 38–43 inches) high, usually with the action positioned above the keys, are called 'consoles' and retain the decorated casework styling of the spinet. The tallest (1·09 metres and up = 43 inches and up) instruments are designated 'studio' uprights. Simple in styling they are intended primarily for educational use.

German pianos are expensive, the majority being of a height sufficient to obtain good tone quality, for the German public has always valued musical qualities. English firms making pianos in the lower price bracket, on the other hand, have continued to build models economical in size because until recently the more keenly priced sector of the English market preferred the smaller upright.

National differences in weight of touch also exist. It has tended to be heavier on pianos made in Germany, where a firmer touch is preferred, than on English instruments. 52 grammes ($1\frac{7}{8}$ ounces) placed slightly inwards from the front edge of the white key after the damper is raised from the string, should be sufficient to sink the key with adequate impact for the strings of most English pianos to sound. National preferences soon are incorporated in the design—for instance the point of balance at which the key divides into front and back lengths affects the touch weight and so its determination is influenced by the preferred weight. Both division and weight in turn affect depth of touch, usually between 9 and 10·5 millimetres (7/20 and 4/10 inch) although English touch occasionally has been deeper. Reduced space makes the maintenance on the small upright of the distance the hammer travels (the 'blow'—Pl. 18) without increasing touch depth a problem, although not an insurmountable one. A solution frequently adopted maintains the correct touch depth, but reduces the blow and therefore the energy which the hammer imparts to the string—another compromise brought about by the fashion for reduced size. The measurements for the raised sharps differ from those for the lower naturals—the touch of the former is often heavier as the front length is shorter and the depth shallower.

Preference for various touch characteristics in different parts of the world causes problems for piano builders. In Britain a light, easy touch is demanded, making it easier for youthful beginners to press the keys, and teachers regularly recommend that a piano with light touch is preferable for their pupils' practice. In certain continental and South American countries piano teachers often recommend the opposite, a heavier firm touch, arguing that firmness helps to strengthen the wrists early on and thereby assists the achievement later of satisfactory technique. To adjust the weight of touch after the instrument has been designed makes compromise inevitable.

Clearly national preferences, often formed before modern ease of trade and communication acquired their influence in the formation of taste, are retained through decades and in some respects centuries. Consequently they continue to influence piano-makers in each country so that the piano-making traditions of the older countries continue to be significant in the modern world.

Nonetheless many influences are tending towards greater world-wide uniformity in piano taste and reduction in national variety. Some components are purchased from abroad rather than in the country where the piano into which they are fitted is made. The adaptability of the exporting countries to meet individual market taste has tended to diminish national variations. Recently two American makers introduced casework designs following European stylings, as they attempt to enter European markets. The only two Japanese firms which export have developed models similar in styling to American pianos for export to the United States, their largest export market, and also models with a contemporary European case design for sale in Europe. Japanese pianos, which when they first appeared on world markets in the 1960s were considered cheap, have become medium and even high priced as Japan ceased to be a low-cost producer. Other pianos have appeared to replace them at the lower end of the price bracket. In the 1970s Russia and China have started to export pianos in small quantities at low prices. A low cost producer just starting to export pianos is Taiwan (formerly Formosa).

Frequently pianos originating in countries not associated normally with piano construction have an awkward and even gauche appearance, lacking finesse. On occasion, however, experienced firms have either assisted less experienced makers or established assembly plants in areas where labour is cheap (for example in Korea and the Philippines). A leading Japanese manufacturer has named on sales literature the world-renowned German piano-maker with which it was associated prior to the Second World War, stating that at the time the leaflet was issued in the 1960s much of current design was an outgrowth of that co-operation. In the 1960s an acknowledged German designer was retained for a period by Japanese piano producers. Today the Japanese upright is regarded as an acceptable commercial instrument while Japanese grands are respected everywhere, although experts declare that they lack the tonal resonance of the best European instruments. Two of the most famous European manufacturers are owned by American firms. In the United States itself piano factories have been moved towards the Deep South in quest of cheaper labour. One American company has action parts shipped from Europe, then assembled by cheap labour in Mexico and finally forwarded to its own factory. Another American producer has had grands made under a different name in Japan.

Obviously in the last quarter of the twentieth century trends which make the world appear smaller and industry more interlinked than ever before have not passed by the piano industry. While the piano still was being developed, it was to be expected that there would be greater variety in instrumental types than after it reached maturity, when most makers adopted a much smaller range of variation from a broadly accepted norm. As with most craft products progress was empiric following observed experiment, rather than made by theoretical research developing a theory. As the piano reached a high level of development by such means, it is even today seldom thought worthwhile to undertake expensive fundamental research which would be unlikely to yield substantial benefits in design alterations. Tonal differences still exist, but there is a marked preference for a bright, brilliant tone, which most manufacturers have moved towards. The developed countries have become more interdependent with commerce in pianos becoming two-way—export and import. It is suggested sometimes that only the shipping companies carrying the goods stand to benefit! Modern management skills have produced a growing swiftness and willingness to adapt. Nonetheless differences between nations remain and tradition has survived these trends towards uniformity, although variety has become more muted and less striking than a generation ago. This experience is borne out by musical preference. In the West the interest in recent years in Indian and oriental music has been striking while in the East children grow up with the western classics and Chairman Mao's wife, Chiang Ching, introduced the pianoforte to Chinese opera as an accompanying instrument.

XVI

The Enduring Appeal of the Piano

Experimenters have endeavoured to adapt the piano to contemporary attitudes. The 'Prepared Piano' produces novel sounds
at the whim of its 'preparer'. Drawing pins may be thrust into
the felt hammers, or the strings loaded with pieces of wood and
rubber, or various foreign objects attached to any selected part.
The percussive nature of piano chords is readily adaptable to
experiments in electronic composition and piano sounds have been
isolated and combined with unrelated noises on tape recorders.

Avant-garde composers have developed the principles of
serialism inherited from Webern. The resulting preoccupation
with the nature of musical sound led directly to electronic composition, for the versatility of electronics made the control of
music's component parts possible to a degree hitherto only dreamt
of. Electronic methods of sound production overcome the limitations of conventional instruments, pitch, intensity, timbre and
other components being manipulated with greater accuracy at
the control panel—it is no longer necessary to write 'mf' or 'pp'
and leave the rest to the performer. A mathematical logic is
imparted which has caused the shifting of emphasis from the
relationship of notes to each other to an exploration of their
inherent construction.

Electronic sound generation and the tape recorder came into
their own in the 1950s. In 1954 the first concert of electronic
music was heard in the studios of the Westdeutscher Rundfunk
in Cologne. Stockhausen, Boulez and the Italian Berio became
leading names associated with electronic composition. They also
continued composing in serial style for conventional instruments,
for the composer of electronic music sees his work as providing
certain types of sound patterns more successfully than conventional instruments do, but not as replacing time-honoured instruments or attempting to rival them in generating sounds which
they produce superbly. Serialism taken to its logical conclusions

indicates rejection of all features, rhythmic, dynamic and structural, inherited from previous conventions, and ends in predetermination. A set of numbers or proportions may be substituted for the Twelve-note series and preoccupation with static arrangement replaces Schoenberg's thematic treatment. Some have followed this logic and given *avant-garde* composition its seeming arithmetical aridity with severely restricted emotional outlet—little room remains for the warm spontaneity of a waltz! As total predetermination curtails all freedom other composers already have reintroduced elements of chance and Stockhausen's *Klavierstück XI* comprises nineteen separate episodes, which may be played in any order selected by the performer. It is notable that serial composers, when composing for conventional instruments have often selected the piano without seeking to modify it, but treating differently the tone it produces. Several works central to the development of serialism have been for the piano. Schoenberg's first purely Twelve-note work was his *Piano Suite, Op. 25.* Messiaen's *Modes de valeurs et d'intensités*, first performed in 1951 at the seminal Darmstadt Summer School for New Music, in its serial treatment provided a link between pre- and post-war generations; significantly Stockhausen and Boulez, who both have composed important piano works, studied with him.

Many startling notions have been dreamt up. Henry Cowell introduced 'tone-clusters' to be played by fists, elbows and forearms, and required the artist to pluck the strings. Ben Johnston's *Knocking Piece* instructed two performers to tap the inside of the piano case with mallets in no set pattern for eleven minutes. The Italian composer Bussotti has gone further requiring 'the pianist to dismantle the piano during the work'! Advanced notation (Fig. 34) often is indecipherable and the composer's instructions may take hours to understand. By contrast the American John Cage's *4 Minutes and 33 Seconds* provides for the performer (he needs no musical skills) to look at the keyboard without playing a note, the only sound to emanate from the opening and closing of the lid three times to mark three movements.

A sympathetic interpretation claims that modern composers are protesting that everything worthy of expression in conventional idioms has been voiced already. Modern media make culture of all kinds readily available for mass consumption and musicians (Stravinsky included, for his several 'periods', experi-

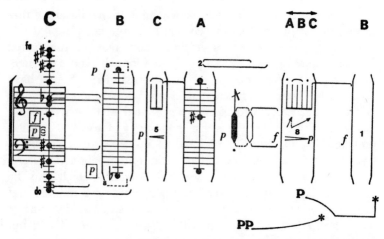

Fig. 34. Extract from 'Metapiece (Mimetics) für Klavier 1961' by Mauricio Kagel. The composer's 'Explanation' remarks that 'stones of different sizes can be put on the strings and/or on the keyboard' and that 'obsessive-sounding repetitions of short fragments can be included, even when there are no repeat signs. Rapid mechanical rhythms (like those of a cracked record) with slight aperiodic alterations could be attempted'. The 'signs' indicate, for example, that the key is to be released slowly enough for the sound of the dampers springing back to be heard; or clapping : as a key is pressed with one hand the palm is struck *simultaneously* by the free hand.

menting with different techniques and examining styles of composition from the past, symbolize the unparalleled diversity of styles followed by contemporary musicians) have confessed to difficulty in clearing the mind of undue interference from past artistic influences. This view offers an obvious interpretation of Cage's silent piece—to persuade 'listeners' that present-day composition should be approached with a mind as free as possible of preconceived judgements. In previous centuries the living composer was prized above his dead predecessors—the reverse of today's situation.

Cage's startling notions mirror the contradiction of an unsettled age. He attempts to banish the idea of any relationship between the parts of his compositions maintaining that even mistakes are not out of place, 'for once anything happens it authentically is'. By elevating chance he opposes the serialists' predetermination. In wishing to destroy meaningful convention, to exalt the correctness of wrongness, he is seeking meaning when the traditional paths of western music appear exhausted. As man cannot help perceiving relationships between sounds, by making random elements determining factors he demonstrates that there must after all be principles. His piano piece 'Music of Changes' has been explained even by reference to freedom of choice in a capitalist society and has been related to Maoism, counter-revolution and imperialism!

The twentieth century is anti-romantic and the reaction against musical sensuousness has led to the loss of that beauty of touch and tone which characterized the romantic school. 'Scholar pianists' hold the field and grasp of structure combined with faithful interpretation of the composer's intentions are regarded as paramount. In about 1888 Erard and Pleyel constructed the first harpsichords to be made since the piano killed interest in plucked instruments, their modern versions aiding Wanda Landowska's demonstration on the harpsichord of the clarity of Bach's music. This remarkable lady won gradual recognition that Bach arrangements by Liszt and Tausig sounded too thick and today a number of pianists have dropped baroque music from their programmes, leaving it for the harpsichord to which it belongs. Paradoxically interest in romantic composers is less pre-ponderant than earlier and a programme omitting Chopin no longer arouses horror.

Landowska's work led to renewed study of the instruments for which music of different periods originally was intended so that today a number of workshops make harpsichords and clavi-chords, elegant testimony to the twentieth-century revival. Con-ditions in these workshops are far closer to those of harpsichord workshops centuries ago than is possible in the piano industry where mechanized batch production has prevailed. Volume production of harpsichords is not required because playing the instrument is a minority interest of the professional and sophisti-cated amateur musician; the market is too restricted to attract capital investment on the scale of the piano industry. Many harpsichord workshops turn out only a handful of instruments in the year, largely by hand methods. The nature of the instrument, its dependence on human skill and the low level of output make it ill-suited to mechanization. There are few recognized suppliers of major components and while keyboards may be purchased, the action, varying from instrument to instrument and very personal to the harpsichord craftsman, normally is made by the craftsman himself. The number of employees is small and the predominance of human skill with lack of substantial capital investment leads to the frequent appearance of new and disappearance of existing harpsichord builders. Well-known makers include in England, de Blaise, Dolmetsch, Goble and Morley, and in Germany Neupert, Sassmann, Sperrhake and Wittmayer.

Many adherents of an 'improvement' school of thought have enlarged and strengthened the body of the instrument (although the characteristics of the piano age introduced at the turn of the century during the early years of the revival, for example the covered bass strings, iron frame and diagonally barred soundboard of Pleyel's harpsichords, are regarded unfavourably today) in attempts to impart greater stability unavailable to their forbears. For a time a 16-foot register became a regular feature in the belief, later found to be erroneous, that J. S. Bach's harpsichord incorporated a 16-foot. Based on investigations by German scholars in the early part of the century, this belief became a major feature in the German revival of harpsichord making. In the 1950s two American makers, Hubbard and Dowd, recognizing the validity of claims by English makers and musicians that original antique instruments rather than modern continental harpsichords were the possessors of true harpsichord tone as known by the ancient masters, initiated a movement back to the original sources of eighteenth-century English, French and Flemish harpsichords. More recently attempts have been made by European experts to upstage the American contribution by placing greater emphasis on early Italian models built when the harpsichord was developing, rather than on the finest later examples of the maker's art from England and France. Currently there is renewed stress on reproducing faithfully the simplicity of historical models without attempting to incorporate modern alterations, which are often regarded by their opponents as retrogressive rather than as improvements, giving rise to much disputation, a facility in which harpsichord and organ builders are well-versed!

Parts of the action have been improved. For example plectra of delrin, a plastic, were introduced in the 1960s, championed by musicians who found delrin an ideal substitute for quills. Morley has replaced leather with moulded delrin plectra which require minimal voicing, enjoy a long life, are easier to produce and, it is claimed, bear greater tonal resemblance than leather to plectra of quill. A major cause, however, why comparatively small-seeming changes readily arouse controversy among harpsichord specialists is that, unlike the heavier piano, all the case components of the lightly built harpsichord may be thought to influence the tonal character.

The problem of the validity of playing music on instruments other than those which the composer intended, gives rise to prolonged altercation among scholars. Sometimes it is uncertain which instrument compositions were written for—did Bach intend a piece for the clavichord or harpsichord or both? If a work is performed on another instrument are the tonal characteristics of that instrument matched to the character of the piece or do they distort it? How did the harpsichord sound when first built? Even the answer to this question is by no means as certain as might be thought. The stringing and the balance between the strings, bridge and soundboard of surviving historical specimens inevitably have altered down the centuries. The elasticity of the wood shows fatigue which, combined with twisting of wooden parts, lessens the vibrational response. To reproduce historical models faithfully in every detail and to learn by this means how they sounded when new, is fraught with complications. The composition of historical materials may have altered and the manner in which they are worked today may yield different results. Pitch has risen since the age of Ruckers meaning that the scaling should be adjusted if the intentions of the original designer are to be honoured. To raise the existing scaling to a higher pitch would court disaster and at the very least would yield a timbre at variance with the original. Furthermore hand craftsmanship inevitably varied measurements from one instrument to seemingly identical ones. It soon becomes no facile matter to decide which harpsichord is most fitted for a particular piece of harpsichord music, let alone to offer a verdict on the validity of performing the keyboard music of Bach and his contemporaries on the modern pianoforte.

To consider the latter problem, in the home there is frequently no alternative, for a piano is more likely to be found than a harpsichord or clavichord. Our Victorian forbears never dreamt of any alternative to the piano and would have regarded it as incongruous if a harpsichord had been fetched forward. They preferred to play Bach in arrangements by Liszt and Tausig which forfeited the clear-cut sparkle of the eighteenth century and elevated above Bach Victorian tonal concepts. Today those, and they are numerous, who still mount the concert platform to perform Bach on the piano, think differently. They regard it as paramount that his precise polyphonic textures should be retained and that pedalling and gradual building up and fading away of volume should be strictly controlled—in other words that the composer's intentions should not be swamped by the wide variety of treatment facilitated by the piano. The presumption, at its best doubtful, that Bach approved of Silbermann's early piano-fortes and therefore if he had lived longer he would have composed for the piano (the great doctor, missionary and Bach scholar, Albert Schweitzer, maintained that Bach would have applauded the perfection of the piano action), is dubious justification for performing Bach's keyboard music on the piano. If Bach had been a piano composer his music would have acquired a different character better suited to the piano, for he took the strengths and limitations of contemporary instruments into account. Bach represented the summit of the polyphonic style, a style best suited to the clarity of the harpsichord. Both the style and its instrument passed simultaneously, replaced by the piano.

Mozart and Beethoven composed for pianos vastly different from those we know today, and in tonal character about half-way between the harpsichord and mature piano. Recently interest in listening to their music on the original instruments has grown, but the modern piano continues to be selected for the large majority of performances. The supposition often is put forward that if Beethoven had known the mature piano he would have lauded it and composed for it. Doubtless it is true—he suffered from the poor sustaining capacity of his pianos, while the power and pedalling effects he required often are attainable only on later pianos. Without the shrill clipped tone of the early piano his music requires different treatment, and it should not be overlooked that if he had possessed a modern piano, in some way he would have adapted his style towards it. Nonetheless the nature of the modern piano, of its immature forerunners and of the singing melodic music composed for them is essentially the same, responsiveness to finger touch lying at the core of the new style which proceeded from Mozart.

It appears logical to play music written for the early piano on its modern successor. On the other hand to pay due regard to the musical thought of periods preceding the piano, it seems more apposite to perform harpsichord and clavichord music on those instruments. Great circumspection, skilled arrangement and responsible performance are required if the piano should be utilized. Modern preference for small instrumental forces and for return to historical models rejects the Victorian philosophy of inevitable progress, which underlay most aspects of life and which assumed that Bach's music must be 'improved' by rearrangement for the piano. Today we think of catholicity, diversity of taste and of the pendulum's swing.

The harpsichord revival has assisted the piano by focusing attention on the necessity of matching the instrument to the music, thereby highlighting its essential role in the creation of that music. Recent research has focused on baroque music and increasingly on the medieval and nineteenth-century periods, compositions by Hummel, Dussek and Paderewski being performed on the radio.

Contemporary pianists offer punctilious musicianship and often a certain severity. Technique serves musical goals and planning replaces verve. The showman has been supplanted by pianists who dare not be over-eccentric or over-demanding for fear that with intense competition, concert agents would look askance at avoidable difficulties. Few venture further than the Canadian pianist who asked for the air-conditioning to be turned down so that he could hear himself hum. The pianist who travels with his own piano is seldom encountered now. Arturo Michelangeli, whose piano and tuner have accompanied him on tour, maintains that the expense is justified as it provides him with an instrument which is regulated precisely to his wish, essential if he is to produce the tonal shading he seeks.

Exquisitely balanced formal relationships and magnificent tone are both acknowledged. When the inevitable reaction against current values comes, it could take the form of renewed appreciation of romantic excellence. Already pointers can be seen in the adoption by some of freer tempos and renewed acceptance of improvisation. Some critics, however, maintain that the twentieth century, seeking new timbres as a way out from romanticism,

197

tends to ignore the standard solo instruments and searches for novelty by writing instead for little-tried instrumental groups. In an age of specialization the composer who is also a virtuoso performer has become the exception rather than the rule, a trend leading to a reduction in the amount of music devised for the piano by individual composers. In addition some composers, continuing in traditions of mild tonality, have shown little feeling for the piano and lacked adequate skill in writing for it.

The piano continues to attract gimmicks. The 'honky-tonk' effect is achieved by deliberately placing the strings slightly out of tune, producing a cracked sound. Pre-occupation with records may be thought of as a modern pastime, although the Victorians established a record for continuous piano playing when in 1894 Napoleon Bird, a Stockport barber, created a world record by publicly playing for forty-four hours without repeating any piece. This achievement has been surpassed on numerous occasions in recent years, most recently in 1974 by Michael George, coincidently also from Stockport, who played continuously for two hundred hours and thirty-five minutes establishing a new British record.

An attempt was made in the early 1960s to reintroduce an old enticement, the player-piano. Sales in the United States reached eight thousand in 1964 with Aeolian at the forefront. This brief stimulus then died away. A handful of American player-pianos were exported to Europe, but there appeared to be little response. The instrument was expensive, its player mechanism increased the depth of the piano at a time when emphasis was placed on slimness and perhaps its complicated mechanism was out of sympathy with the plastic age, which readily accepts 'hi-fi' and other sources of reproduced music.

The burning of over-age pianos on public bonfires has drawn attention to the harm that poor instruments do to the playing of the young. The most bizarre advertisement, however, was conceived several years ago in Jordan:

By marrying a lovely piano you will be able to banish gloom and forebodings coupled with loneliness and moroseness for you will be able to acquire the art of piano playing and trumpet to the world that the acquisition of a piano in the miracle making country has climaxed in a miracle. . . . Dear friends, I am here right in the heart of the desert waiting for your call and praying for your patronage and support and beseeching the Almighty to harden your hearts and souls to come to my aid and rescue by hiring or buying a piano. . . .[54]

Electronic pianos, attempting to reproduce piano sound by electronic means, cease to be pianos in the accepted sense, but nonetheless have achieved some popularity, offering advantages of ready portability and silent playing through headphones—a useful benefit for modern housing blocks in which thin partitions with little sound insulation are all that separate the occupants of one flat from those adjacent. Court cases have been fought on the freedom to play a musical instrument, although constituting a nuisance to neighbours. The electronic piano has a restricted compass of five or exceptionally six octaves. When there is no action to rest on the end of the key, piano touch is extremely difficult to simulate by artificial means. Consequently the sense of touch is other than that of a conventional piano and its responsiveness is not truly reproduced, the decay of the tone often sounding unnatural. In theory it is possible to reproduce exactly true piano tone on an electronic piano, but it would be unacceptably expensive. The overtone pattern of a normal piano varies from note to note and with the volume of that note, which in turn depends on the strength used to strike it. The pattern varies again during the life of each note as the relative rapidity with which the different overtones die, depends largely upon their relative strength shortly after the hammer's impact. A further complication is the sympathetic vibrations of other strings which mingle with the note sounded when the sustaining pedal raises the dampers. All these factors, so variable, inconstant and seemingly irrational, are ill-suited to reproduction by electronic means, for modern electronics, to capacitate large scale production at competitive cost, prefers constant patterns so that selected electronic components can serve a number of notes. An electronic piano which reproduced faithfully the tone of a normal piano with hammers striking strings would be more costly than that piano. Consequently the electronic instrument usually offered is a compromise and will never replace the customary upright or grand piano.

Following an increasing number of experiments on both sides of the Atlantic in the 1920s, which grew from the development of wireless and gramophone, Laurens Hammond in 1935 made the electronic organ a commercial proposition in the United States. 1947 marked the new instrument's first significant year, sales in the United States reaching eight thousand. In 1958 they reached 100,000 for the first time and in the 1960s were continuously around 120,000, a figure considerably below that for piano sales in the United States. In the '60s the electronic organ's popularity grew rapidly in Europe, although in England earlier than in its continental neighbours whose primary loyalties to the piano were longer retained. In a normal year some 27,000 organs are sold in the United Kingdom—twice the number of pianos sold.

In the instrument's early years American manufacturers established their names throughout the world, followed in the 1960s by Japanese, Italian and Benelux manufacturers. England and West Germany have never succeeded in establishing a significant electronic organ industry, although numerous attempts have been made. English and West German firms have met with greater success, however, in establishing themselves as makers of electronic church organs, for which there is a need as they offer fewer short-term maintenance problems than pipe organs and are less expensive to purchase. Many authorities, however, will not countenance them for ecclesiastical purposes and their musical suitability is hotly disputed.

The majority of electronic organs find their way into domestic use. In the 1960s the organ had the advantage over its more staid counterpart, the piano, of novelty. Problems of touch responsiveness happily are absent, a note continuing to sound until the key is released, and easy-play techniques convinced would-be performers. Such techniques are successful in imparting rapidly a limited knowledge, but to acquire lasting skill in performance applied practice is required as with any other instrument. There being few private electronic organ teachers, many shops selling organs provide group tuition facilities and as a further means of promoting sales mount free demonstration-concerts by celebrity organists.

When an instrument's novelty palls, new attractions must be found. Electronic organs dispense with the craft skills necessary for piano manufacture and so perpetual changes of specification and the introduction of 'gimmicks' assist their sale, emphasizing that they are not built to last for up to half a century, the life span of the average piano. Many owners commenced with a small organ, later exchanging it for a more ambitious instrument, repeating the process several times. A 'cassette' (small tape recorder) fitted to an organ is useful for self-tuition. Automatic rhythm instruments, providing as many as sixteen dance rhythms (beguine, rumba, etc.) as a backing to the organ sound, appear an almost compulsory mounting. Further features, often of limited long-term value but of importance while novel, include the provision of complete chords and figures when the left hand presses a mere single note and of electronic memories repeating accompaniment chords on lower manual and pedals until countermanded.

Most pianos are bought not merely to decorate the drawing-room, but to be played either by adults who play already or by children learning. When the pianos of previous generations are rejected from modern homes, the days of the unplayed piano will be largely over, although it is to be feared that the untuned piano will remain. Now that piano playing is neither a social convention nor the only means of leisure and of hearing music, for switching on the gramophone or television is an easier option, it is clear that other motives prompt people to turn to the piano. Television, once regarded as the enemy of activities requiring effort and self-discipline, now is believed to encourage piano playing and other leisure activities as strenuous as mountaineering. Piano lessons for beginners have been given on television by Sidney Harrison and master classes by famed concert artists also demonstrate the positive role television can play. It is to be hoped that increasing leisure will assist the reaction away from pre-packaged entertainment towards constructive hobbies. Already two million people in the United Kingdom find pleasure and relaxation playing the piano.

Schools play an essential role in piano teaching and learning to play usually is regarded as a pleasurable pursuit and no longer an inflicted torture. Music lenient in its demands on finger dexterity is composed especially for teaching purposes by prominent composers, Bartók's *For Children* inspired by the hunger of young pianists for satisfying music, providing a shining example. Some parents are placing their children's names soon after birth on piano teachers' waiting lists as their services are in heavy demand. Lengthy lists are causing a growing number of forward-looking teachers to adopt the group concept, which has proved that it has a number of successful and legitimate uses. Should a serious shortage of teachers develop, group methods of teaching the piano are certain to be applied more widely.

Overseas, particularly in the United States, Japan and latterly Germany, various applications of the group concept have won greater recognition than in England. The Piano Class Movement originated in the United States in the years following the First World War and met with an initial success restricted by the inadequate musical and psychological grounding of the methods employed. In England pioneer work was done by J. T. Bavin, but interest collapsed when the main object of the piano group protagonists, to secure a place for the piano group in primary school regular timetables, was not achieved. Some teachers persisted, however, and one, Miss Florence Axtens, secured a degree of co-operation from Tobias Matthay and persuaded the London County Council to introduce her method at a number of evening institutes. Widespread introduction of the piano group idea was limited by the popularity of the Musical Appreciation Movement, at its height in the 1920s, and which stressed listening to the detriment of music-making; it was succeeded by the growth of recorder, percussion band and school orchestra playing, often to the detriment of the piano. The spread of the piano group was hampered also by scepticism concerning the practicability of teaching music, normally audible, on dummy and later silent keyboards and by the difficulty of uniting the skills of school teachers versed in class teaching but not in music, with those of private music teachers lacking class teaching experience.

Since 1945 the group concept has been applied with growing intensity to keyboard instruments and the application in the 1950s of electronics to the piano group has opened up a new range of possibilities, as instruments bearing closer resemblance to the requirements of the group situation can be designed.

In 1954 Yamaha, the Japanese musical instrument manufacturer, commenced experiments in group instruction which led to the establishment of its Junior Music Course. Kawai also started to establish music schools and by the mid-1960s Yamaha and Kawai had established several thousand schools. A range of instruments is taught, each pupil receiving a weekly lesson of up to thirty minutes' duration and it is hoped that the schools locate and encourage the pianists of the future. The Yamaha method uses conventional pianos and also four-octave electronically blown reed instruments, for it is thought that children of pre-school age can grasp more easily a continuing tone than a note which sustains inadequately. The underlying belief is that a two-year grounding in the musical ingredients of rhythm, harmony, melody and later notation, is most likely to be successful with young children between the ages of four and six when group instruction proves more attractive than individual lessons. Serious study of the instrument chosen should wait until the child is aged seven, when he is ready to commence lessons with a private teacher. Run in conjunction with local music shops, the Yamaha course was introduced in the United States in 1965, in Canada and Thailand in 1966, and in Australia, Iran, Mexico, Singapore and West Germany in 1967.

Parallel with the Japanese, Wurlitzer, the large American piano and electronic organ manufacturer, was investigating the potential of group teaching. In 1955 the company introduced its electronic piano dispensing with strings and soundboard. Special hammers strike steel reeds and the sound is then picked up and amplified electronically. The introduction of electronics brought new concepts to group teaching. By the use of earphones the student can play so that only he himself hears the sound he produces—consequently several pupils, each at a separate instrument, can play 'silently' simultaneously without the tones produced mingling in discord. This facility was impossible using conventional pianos. With the new arrangement each pupil can play for the larger part of each lesson and no longer is obliged to listen to other pupils and impatiently wait his turn. The electronic piano is supplemented by the 'Electronic Communication Centre', the teacher's master instrument, enabling him to converse with each pupil, listen to his playing, speak and demonstrate to him while the other students continue their practice undisturbed. Up to twenty-four pupils can be connected.

In 1968 Baldwin introduced the Electropiano Instruction Laboratory, also with a master instrument for the teacher. The individual seven-and-a-quarter-octave pianos, however, possess action, hammers and strings, the sound then being fed to an electronic system rather than passed to a soundboard.

There are now over four hundred 'Youth Music Schools' (*Jugendmusikschulen*) in West Germany and one thousand are planned by 1980. In 1968 the German musical profession expressed concern at the number of foreign singers (one in every four) it was proving necessary to engage for the nation's numerous opera houses, and at the problems of training an adequate number of future orchestral players. Musical education had failed to win the acceptance within normal school curricula which it had in other countries (including Britain). It was decided therefore to expand the music schools, standing outside the school system and catering for all ages, through a programme teaching musical rudiments to four- to six-year-olds. Previously musical training had commenced at the age of seven. It was hoped that a musical grounding prior to this age would make it possible to start a proper instrument at age six or seven and that as the notes would be familiar already, the technique of the chosen instrument could be concentrated upon. By these means an adequate technical standard could be reached and acute conflict with the pressures of general examinations during adolescence be avoided. Furthermore a reduction in the serious loss in all countries of teenage piano pupils might be achieved.

The new programme gave each pupil seventy-five minutes' instruction weekly with twelve children per class. It incorporated a new instrument, the '*Tastenspiel*' ('key play'), developed especially to meet the requirements of early education and made by the piano-builder Schimmel, for the combined West German piano industry was instrumental in the establishment of the programme. The '*Tastenspiel*' incorporates a two-and-a-half-octave glockenspiel which is struck with drumsticks or sounded by pressing down the notes of the keyboard.

These developments overseas aim not to leave the abilities already present in children undeveloped any longer in the preschool phase, but to take advantage of the early years when learning ability is high. In addition the positive benefits of musical education to intellectual development are stressed.

Some instruments employing electronics suffer drawbacks. The tone may bear poor resemblance to conventional piano sound. When the normal piano action is not employed, touch sensitivity often is inadequate (although touch resistance may be capable of partial regulation) and the touch approaches that of an organ, making it impossible to achieve adequate gradation of tone. The best electronic instruments designed for group teaching, however, provide a piano tone adequate for their purpose and demand mastery of a different kind of touch response. Using them teaching laboratories overcome some of the obstacles confronting previous group teaching methods and make a valuable contribution.

In North America many private teachers are adopting piano group methods for all their instruction and the piano group has met with growing recent success. In many States all children of primary school age are now given the opportunity to join a piano group at school and after primary school the piano group remains influential. In England, however, instruments designed as aids to piano group instruction have made little headway. There has been renewed interest in recent years in the group and a number of successful practitioners, for example Miss Meriel Jefferson, Miss Yvonne Enoch and some education authorities, have shown what the piano group can achieve. For a number of years in Inner London Education Authority primary, grammar and comprehensive schools Miss Jefferson taught at conventional pianos, often supplemented by silent keyboards with movable keys, over 150 children weekly with a minimum of four and maximum of six per lesson. Currently at the Guildhall School of Music she applies the Baldwin Electropiano system, arranged for six pupils simultaneously (Pl. 56), to the teaching of advanced sight reading and of students learning the piano as a second instrument. She has shown that the piano group can be developed along lines which had been unexplored previously in the United States, where its application normally is confined to beginners, and that pioneer work in establishing higher piano group standards than are current in North America can be accomplished on this side of the Atlantic.

Usually Grade Six of the Associated Board is considered the highest level that can be aspired to through group instruction, although several pianists have passed diploma examinations without resort to individual tuition. The group, however, normally leads to the conventional individual lesson. The group system offers the teacher greater scope for general musicianship and when, as at present, the supply of teachers perhaps is inadequate, also the chance to concentrate individual lessons on more advanced students. To the aspiring pianist it offers cheaper lessons and also the opportunity of learning alongside others. Progress can be compared and the sense of isolation which is felt by immature pianists can be conquered. The group develops the critical faculty, it is fun and youngsters join because others do, but each individual still can feel important. Group methods also provide adequately for the needs of those who wish to relax by playing for their own amusement and help to remove the old persistent image that every pianist should practise for hours, the only justifiable goal being solo performance to an assembled audience.

'Easy' methods to increase learning speeds for pianists without lofty ambitions have been devised for almost as long as the piano has existed, but with little lasting success. Either they are founded on a gimmick, or good habits in technique are violated, or only one of many necessary skills is covered—frequently all three criticisms are levelled at once and many systems have suffered the same fate as Logier's 'Chiroplast'. Problems encountered in mastering touch and expression have raised insuperable obstacles to the satisfactory application to the piano of easy-play techniques. In order to progress beyond a rudimentary ability there is no doubt that regular practice and more orthodox tuition are necessary. The prospect of continuing practice deters many would-be pianists and inroads made by other instruments could give rise to future concern. The resurgence of the guitar in the 1960s produced the suggestion by a few distinguished musicians that the guitar should supplant the piano as the indispensable instrument in musical education. It must not be forgotten, however, that only a keyboard instrument can offer acquaintanceship with music's complete repertoire.

The piano has been under attack. It was said to be an antisocial instrument at the time a new ideal won acceptance for musical activity to be in groups. Singing and the recorder lend themselves to group participation, but the piano's indispensability was reasserted once it was understood that melody-note instruments, on which the beginner creates the notes and their pitch, are superior for ear and scale training, but are insufficient for a complete musical education.

The piano suffers from the disadvantage that, since its individuality rests in responsiveness to finger touch and in the comparatively short duration of its notes, it is not an easy instrument to learn to a standard of moderate proficiency compared with the guitar and electronic organ. The popularity of the latter in the 1960s, however, contrary to some fears has not harmed the piano.

It is a brave person who dares to predict the future. The trend towards the survival of fewer but larger piano manufacturers probably will continue. In England and West Germany, the two principal piano-producing countries in Western Europe, the piano-building firms are family businesses, but the modern environment is sometimes hostile to the long-term survival of the family business. A number of larger corporations are involved in piano manufacture, some producing other musical instruments in addition. A musical instrument, a craft product, is likely to ensure that firms engaged in its design and production retain a larger element of distinctiveness in an age showing marked tendencies towards drab uniformity. The realization in the late 1960s that the size of giant firms does not guarantee greater efficiency coalesced with renewed appreciation that humanizing influences are required to produce employee satisfaction. Together they created a climate more sympathetic to the small specialist firm. What is certain is that the piano is likely to remain the indispensable instrument. Much incomparable music certain to remain at the centre of musical appreciation was composed for it. Complete in itself it provides harmony throughout the musical compass and its expressive powers flow directly from finger touch, unlike its rivals resorting to mechanical aids. The pianoforte will continue to be highly prized.

Some Important Dates in the Piano's Development

c. 1709   Cristofori built first piano in Florence.

c. 1730   Silbermann built first pianos known to be made in Germany.

1732   First published work specifically for the piano, Giustini's *12 Sonate da cembalo di piano e forte detto volgaramente dei martellati*, appeared in Florence.

1739   Domenico del Mela built a vertical 'pyramid' piano.

1742   Socher in Upper Bavaria built earliest known square.

1750   Death of J. S. Bach, the greatest contrapuntalist.

1753   First part of C. P. E. Bach's 'Essay on the True Art of Playing Keyboard Instruments' published.

1760   First piano makers arrived in England.

1764   Earliest known work for four hands at one piano composed by Mozart.

1767   Earliest known public performance on a piano given by Mr Dibdin.

1768   Earliest known piano solos at a concert given by Henry Walsh in Dublin and J. C. Bach in London.

c. 1770   Stein added Escapement to 'Viennese' Action.

1773   Clementi published his sonatas often regarded as earliest compositions showing full understanding of the piano.

1775   Behrent made probably the earliest American piano.

1777   Mozart started to compose for the piano, endorsing Stein's instrument.

1777   Robert Stodart patented the 'English' Action.

1783   Broadwood introduced the sustaining pedal.

1784   Earliest known public two piano performance given by Clementi and Cramer.

1794   Broadwood extended the compass to six octaves.

1795   William Stodart patented his 'Upright Grand'.

c. 1798   First 'Giraffe' upright made in Vienna.

1799   Beethoven composed his Sonatas Op. 14, his first specifically for the piano.

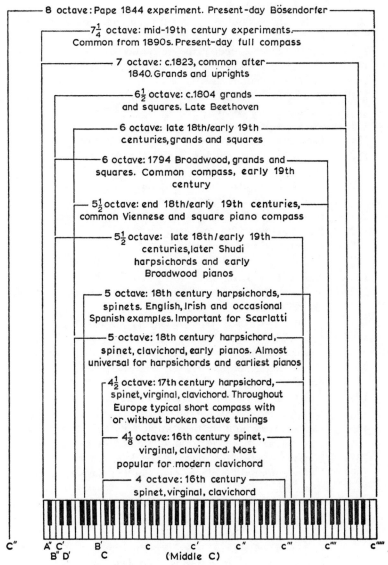

Fig. 35. The extension of the keyboard

1800   Müller's 'Ditanaklassis' and Hawkins' 'Portable Grand Pianoforte' extended upright piano's strings below keyboard to floor level.

1804   J. B. Cramer published his first studies, earliest of their kind.

1807   Southwell's 'Cabinet Piano' introduced.

1808   Broadwood began experiments with iron tension bars.

1808   S. Erard invented Agraffe.

1810   Brooks founded in London first specialist action-making business in the world.

1811   Wornum produced small upright.

1817   Clementi completed his *Gradus ad Parnassum.*

1821   S. Erard completed his 'Repetition Action' with double escapement.

c. 1823   Multi-piano performances popular.

1824   Liszt gave his first Paris concert.

1825   Babcock cast first complete one-piece iron frame.

1826   Pape patented felt hammers.

1828   Pape introduced over-stringing.

1833   Chopin's first set of *12 Études*, Op. 10 published.

1836   Kirk patented complete iron frame for upright.

1839   First concert for piano alone, without supporting artists, given by Liszt.

1842   Wornum patented 'tape-check' upright action.

1842   Isermann's action factory in Hamburg one of earliest German specialist component factories.

1843   Chickering patented first one-piece cast-iron frame for a grand.

1845   de Meyer first leading pianist to tour in U.S.A.

1859   Steinway produced first over-strung grand.

1861   Hallé played publicly the complete Beethoven Sonatas.

1863   First pneumatic player-piano patented by Fourneaux.

1874   Steinway perfected 'sostenuto' pedal.

1897   Votey patented his player-piano system, basis of Aeolian's 'Pianola'.

1904   Welte patented 'Mignon' reproducing piano.

1918   Prokofieff arrived in U.S.A.

1923   Schoenberg's *Five Piano Pieces*, Op. 23, first work to employ Twelve-note, or serial, technique.

1932   Construction of miniature upright, leading to its renewed popularity.

1936   World's largest grand, 3·55 metres (11 feet 8 inches) long, weighing over 1 ton, built by Challen of London.

Bibliography and References

The quotations in the text are listed below and permission to quote granted by the publishers is acknowledged with gratitude.

Ref. no.

1   Ottomarus Luscinius, *Musurgia seu praxis Musicae* (Strasbourg, 1536).

2, 4   Charles Burney, *The Present State of Music in Germany, the Netherlands, and United Provinces* (London, Second Edition, 1775).

3   Andreas Werckmeister, *Orgelprobe* (Frankfurt and Leipzig, 1698).

5   *Original Unpublished Papers Illustrative of the Life of Sir Peter Paul Rubens,* ed. W. N. Sainsbury (London, 1859).

6   *The Diary of Samuel Pepys,* ed. H. B. Wheatley (Bell, London, 1962).

C. P. E. Bach, 'Essay on the True Art of Playing Keyboard Instruments', 1753 and 1762, translated by W. J. Mitchell (Cassell, London, 1949).

7   Part 1, Embellishments.

10   Part 1, Introduction.

11, 12   Part 1, Fingering.

13   Part 2, Foreword.

8   Francesco Scipione Maffei, 'Giornale de' Letterati d'Italia', vol. 5, article 9 (Venice, 1711).

The Letters of Beethoven, collected, translated and edited by Emily Anderson, 1961 (by permission of Macmillan, London and Basingstoke).

9   Letter to Tobias Haslinger, 1817.

19   Letter to Eleonore von Breuning, 1794.

25   Letter to Frau Nanette Streicher, 1817.

28   Letter to J. A. Streicher, 1796.

29   Letter to J. A. Streicher, 1810.

30   Letter to Frau Nanette Streicher, 1817.

31   Letter to Frau Nanette Streicher, 1817.

32   Letter to Nikolaus Zmeskall von Domanovecz, 1802.

14, 23   John Russell, 'A Tour in Germany and some of the

BIBLIOGRAPHY AND REFERENCES

Ref. no.

Southern Provinces of the Austrian Empire in 1820, 1821, 1822' (Edinburgh, 1828).

Mozart's Letters, translated by Emily Anderson, edited by Eric Blom, 1956 edition (by permission of Macmillan, London and Basingstoke).

15, 16   Letters to his father, 1777.

17   Letter to his father, 1782.

18   *The Chappell Story, 1811–1961* (Chappell, London, 1961).

20   *A Short History of a Great House* (Collard & Collard, London).

21, 22, 33, 34, 35, 36, 37,44   Charlotte Moscheles' 'Life of Moscheles, with selections from his Diaries and Correspondence', adapted from the original German by A. D. Coleridge (Hurst and Blackett, London, 1873).

Michael Hamburger, *Beethoven: Letters, Journals & Conversations* (Cape, London, 1951).

24   From the Autobiography of Louis Spohr.

26   From the *Biographical Notes* of Ferdinand Ries.

27   From an account by Johann Andreas Stumpff.

38, 39   Franz Liszt, *Frederic Chopin*, translated by Edward N. Waters (Free Press of Glencoe, Macmillan, New York, 1963).

Letters of Franz Liszt, collected by La Mara, translated by Constance Bache (London, 1894).

40   Letter to Monsieur Pierre Wolff (Junior), 1832.

43   Letter to the Princess Belgiojoso, 1839.

41, 42   Julius Kapp, *Liszt, eine Biographie* (Berlin, 1911).

45   Oscar Paul, *Geschichte des Klaviers* (Leipzig, 1868).

46, 47   Louis Moreau Gottschalk, *Notes of a Pianist*, ed. Jeanne Behrend (Alfred A. Knopf, Inc., New York, 1964).

48   Tobias Matthay, *The Act of Touch* (London, 1903).

Busoni—Letters to his Wife, translated by Rosamond Ley (Arnold, London, 1938).

49   Letter of 1913.

51   Letter of 1919.

50   *The New Era of the Pianoforte* (Brinsmead, London, c. 1885).

52   Arthur Rubinstein, *My Young Years* (Cape, London, 1973).

53   Constant Lambert, *Music Ho! A Study of Music in Decline* (Faber, London, 1934).

54   T. S. Boutagy & Sons, Amman, 1964.

Index

213

66, 70–1, 76, 81, 85, 87, 112,
114, 117, 121, 136, 162, 168,
184, 187
Hammond, Laurens, 200
Handel, 25, 48, 50, 80, 95, 172
Hanover Square Rooms, 127–8
Hansing, 146
Harmonica, 124
Harmonic bar, 115–16
Harmonie Universelle, 22
Harmonium, 176
Harp, 39, 45, 82–3, 103–4, 157–8,
162
Harp family, 15
'Harp' stop (harpsichord), 48
Harpsichord, 19, 31, 35–6, 38, 39–
51, 63, 70, 72, 74, 76–7, 81,
88–92, 103, 105, 110, 130,
152, 160, 172, 193–7
Harpsichord family, 36, 39–51
Harpsichord-piano, 89, 134
'Harpsichord with hammers', 72
Harrison, Sidney, 201
Hass family, Pl. 6
Hass, Hieronymus, 46
Haward family, 46
Haward, Charles, 47
Hawkins, Isaac, 110, 132–3, 135,
Pls. 26, 27
Haydn, Hans, 70
——, J., 50, 77, 84, 87, 95, 98–100,
106, 128, 130, 172
Head rail (harpsichord), 45
Heath, Edward, 151
Hebenstreit, Pantaleon, 19, 74–5
Heilmann, Pl. 22
Helmholtz, 142–3
Henry VIII, King of England, 46
Hero and Leander, 129
Hervé, Samuel, 107
Herz, Henri, 108, 114, 120–1, 126–
8, 156, Pl. 39
Hewitt, Daniel, 140
Hiller, 123, 126
Hindemith, 169
Hitchcocks, 47, Pl. 10
Hitch pin, 116–17, 141
Hitch pin table, 107, 110
Hoffmann, S., 166
Hofmann, Josef, 143, 168
Holland, 178
Hollywood, 174
Holst, Gustav, 22

Hong Kong, 178
'Honky-tonk', 198
Hopkinson, John, 160
Hubbard, 194
Hummel, 87, 94, 197
Hungary, 20, 178
Hurdy-gurdy, 24, 70

Ibach, Rud., Sohn, 145–6, 158, 166,
Pl. 49
Idiochord zither, 17
Improvizations, 93–4, 126, 197
India, 139
Industrial Revolution, 90, 105
Inner London Education Authority,
205
International Exhibition (1862), 111
Intervals (musical), 21–6, 31
Iran, 203
Irmbach, 177
Iron frame, 54, 110–11, 118, 121,
138–9, 141–2, 145–6, 158,
183, 186
'Iron Grand Concert Pianofortes',
111, 145, 156, 159
Isermann, L., 122
Italy, 29, 36, 43, 74, 121, 161, 178

Jacquard, 172
Jahn, Frederikus, Pl. 31
Jankó, Paul von, 163–4
Japan, 18, 176, 186, 188–9, 202
Jazz, 171
Jefferson, Miss Meriel, 205, Pl. 56
John Bull, 127
John II, King of France, 69
Johnson, Dr, 81
Johnston, Ben, 191
Jordan, 198
Joseph II, Emperor, 91
Jugendmusikschulen — see YOUTH
MUSIC SCHOOLS
Just intonation, 30

Kagel, Mauricio, 192
Kalkbrenner, 91, 94–5, 97, 119–20,
128
Kapp, Julius, 125
Kaps, 165
Kawai, K., 177
—— (firm of), 202
Keene, Stephen, 47, Pl. 9
Kemble, 161